Behold, My Mother and My Brethren!

Behold, My Mother and My Brethren!

The Beginning of the Gospel and Becoming a Christian in (Post) Christendom, Volume 1—Mark 1:1 to 4:41

A KIERKEGAARDIAN READING OF THE GOSPEL OF MARK

BRYAN M. CHRISTMAN

RESOURCE *Publications* • Eugene, Oregon

BEHOLD, MY MOTHER AND MY BRETHREN!
The Beginning of the Gospel and Becoming a Christian in (Post) Christendom,
Volume 1—Mark 1:1 to 4:41

A Kierkegaardian Reading of Mark

Copyright © 2022 Bryan M. Christman. All rights reserved. Except for brief quotations in critical publications or reviews, no part of this book may be reproduced in any manner without prior written permission from the publisher. Write: Permissions, Wipf and Stock Publishers, 199 W. 8th Ave., Suite 3, Eugene, OR 97401.

Resource Publications
An Imprint of Wipf and Stock Publishers
199 W. 8th Ave., Suite 3
Eugene, OR 97401

www.wipfandstock.com

PAPERBACK ISBN: 978-1-6667-3879-7
HARDCOVER ISBN: 978-1-6667-9990-3
EBOOK ISBN: 978-1-6667-9991-0

08/15/22

Scripture quotations marked ESV are taken from The ESV® Bible (The Holy Bible, English Standard Version®), copyright © 2001 by Crossway, a publishing ministry of Good News Publishers. Used by permission. All rights reserved.

Scripture quotations marked KJV are from the King James Version, Public Domain

Scripture quotations marked NASB are taken from the New American Standard Bible®, Copyright © 1960, 1971, 1977, 1995, 2020 by The Lockman Foundation. All rights reserved.

Scripture quotations marked NIV are taken from the Holy Bible, New International Version®, NIV® Copyright ©1973, 1978, 1984, 2011 by Biblica Inc.® Used by permission. All rights reserved.

Scripture quotations marked NKJV are taken from the New King James Version®. Copyright © 1982 by Thomas Nelson. Used by permission. All rights reserved.

Scripture quotations marked NLT are taken from the Holy Bible, New Living Translation, copyright © 1996, 2004, 2015 by Tyndale House Foundation. Used by permission of Tyndale House Publishers, Inc., Carol Stream, Illinois 60188. All rights reserved.

For Debbi—my first and only love. . .
For countless walks under the trees,
in dappled light and conifer breeze.
In rain, in snow, falling at ease,
in love—always, with thee.
Thank you for the time to spend, most every waking hour,
Reading, writing, wrestling, with Mark and Kierkegaard.
I should have fixed the plaster cracked and falling on our heads,
. . . and we lived with the words—God be praised.

Contents

Series Preface		ix
Abbreviations		xiii
Introduction to Volume 1		xv
1	"The Beginning" of Mark's Sacred History and Kierkegaard's "Mirror" of Existence-Communication	1
2	Two Voices Crying in the Wilderness . . . of Despair	11
3	God's Earnestness: "And Everyone Shall Have an Opinion About It"	17
4	Temptation as Our Problem and Christ as Our Prototype	26
5	"The Moment" in the Fullness of Time: The Coming of Heaven and Earth	36
6	The Call to Contemporaneity with Jesus through the Middle Term of Death and the Dynamic of "Spirit"	43
7	"The First Day" in the Sacred History of the Contradiction: Foreshadows of Resistance and Faith, Fame and Infamy, Treason and Redemption	55
8	Concluding Preface to "The First Day": Glory in Solitude and the Glory Made Manifest	63
9	Mark's Leper and "A Leper's Self-Contemplation": Jesus leprosus and the Gospel's Inversion of the Fortunate and the Unfortunate	74

10	"Your Sins are Forgiven!": "The Happy Passion" and Unhappy Revolutions at the First-Century Crossroad and the 1840s Fork	98
11	Jesus and Kierkegaard on Gaining the World: "It is not the Healthy but the Sick . . . there is no Bliss except in Despair, Hurry Up and Despair"	113
12	"Thy Disciples Fast Not?": Fasting Disciples and Feasting Christendom: Either/Or?	126
13	The Sabbath Dialectic: God Made the Sabbath for Man—On the Sabbath Man Plotted Death for the Son of Man	134
14	Truth, Boredom, and Crushing Publicity: Popular, Demonic, and Regarding Kierkegaard's Uneven Trousers	147
15	Plundering the "Goods" of the Strong Man: Mark and Kierkegaard as Exorcists in "The Present Age" . . . of Anxiety	157
16	The Sower of Human Freedom, Responsibility, and Fruitfulness, and "The Parable of the Sower in Christendom"	171
17	"If Anyone Has Ears to Hear . . . for Disciples the Road is How"	183
18	The "Fine Species" of Seed that Sows Purity of Heart: God's Unity and Man's Disunity	191
19	The Lowly Mustard-Plant Growing in "The Present Age" . . . of Loftiness	196
20	The Situation for Coming to Faith: "Out on 70,000 Fathoms of Water"	204
Epilogue: Jesus and Jonah, and the Ordeal of Sin and Death		210
Conclusion to Volume 1		217
Bibliography		221
Index		231

Series Preface

What would Kierkegaard think of a "Kierkegaardian Reading," a sort of commentary, on the Gospel of Mark? His view of the "commentaries" of commentators in general is anything but a glowing recommendation of their trustworthiness: "Following the path of the commentators is often like traveling to London; true, the road leads to London, but if one wants to get there, he has to turn around."[1]

Thus, a commentary of sorts, purporting to be a Kierkegaardian reading of Mark, might be *anathema* to him. This would be especially so if it could serve what Pascal called *diversion,* which in relation to God's word was held by Kierkegaard to consist in "reflecting" upon "the mirror" of God's word rather than looking *in* it to see oneself and be changed accordingly. We hope therefore, that our readings derive from what we have found in Kierkegaard's writings that in some manner is relatable to Mark in a way that leads to *seeing oneself* and *response.*

Some readers of this preface may intuit that we take as a given a primarily *biblically* informed and concerned Kierkegaard. This is because scholars since at least the latter 1900s have increasingly recognized the *biblical* Kierkegaard, and that correct recognition is the basis for the very possibility of "Kierkegaardian" readings of Mark in this series.[2] This also means that Kierkegaard has been largely "rehabilitated" from the notoriety he had previously received, both negative—from Evangelicals on the one hand, and positive—from Existentialists on the other, regarding his supposed "existentialist" and "irrational" thought.[3]

---

1. Kierkegaard, JP, I:83, #203.
2. For a brief narration of this progress see: Pyper, *The Joy of Kierkegaard,* viii.
3. On the misattribution of modern existentialism to Kierkegaard, and his biblical

Mark's gospel reveals that its author also had no use for passive "reflection" on the fervent personality and confrontative redemptive actions of Jesus the Christ. To that end Mark created a "moving" new literary genre fitted to the fiery love Jesus lived in the outworking of God's "violent" redemption of humanity. His new genre encapsulated the Genesis-like beginning of God's apocalyptic socio-religious movement called "the kingdom of God" fulfilling, albeit in wholly unforeseen ways, the expectations of God's covenant people, Israel. For these reasons and more, the Gospel of Mark is considered the most influential book ever written:

> Mark has proved the most influential of human books. All other books from four thousand years of epics, plays, lyrics, and biographies have touched human life less potently.[4]

This "potency" is certainly due to the fact that, humanly speaking, this "Gospel" helped facilitate a revolutionary life-change for portions of humanity that believed in and to some extent followed Jesus: an itinerant Israelite sage, preacher, exorcist, and miracle worker who "suffered under Pontius Pilate, was crucified, died, and was buried . . . and was resurrected from the dead."[5] After several centuries, following waves of persecutions of Christians by the Romans, the emperor Constantine became a Christian, opening the door for Christianity to eventually became "Christendom." Ironically, Kierkegaard is perhaps best known for his "Attack on Christendom."

Who then was Kierkegaard? He is no longer the household name he was in his native Denmark where he was widely known for things as disparate as his slight hunchback, uneven trouser legs, or that he "had carried on a one-man theological revolution . . . calling the pastors cannibals, monkeys, nincompoops, and other crazy epithets."[6] On the other hand he is widely known and esteemed as one of the greatest minds of the nineteenth century for his "prophetic" psychological and sociological insights regarding the era of modernity in relation to Christendom and the great challenges that "synthesis" presented to the individual and to society at large.

Therefore, to consider Kierkegaard's milieu is to turn from the beginnings of the gospel "revolution" to the time over 1800 years later when the Christian movement not only survived the Roman Empire but fully replaced it as *the earthly power* of the West. But it was now giving way to the "death of God" in the secular order. Most *insider* "Christians" of Kierkegaard's time

---

non-existential emphasis on human *character* see Roberts, *Recovering Christian Character,* 5, 44–61.

4. Price, *Three Gospels,* 38.
5. From "The Apostle's Creed."
6. See Kirmmse, *Encounters With Kierkegaard,* 97; Garff, *Soren Kierkegaard,* xvii.

did not recognize what he and others, like Friedrich Nietzsche, were seeing, namely that Christendom was dying or dead. But the religious *outsider* Soren Kierkegaard, the oft melancholic, ever poetical, and biblically joyous genius thought that the social and political form that Christianity eventually "achieved" tragically mirrored the "earthly glory" of its Roman predecessor, and thus had already "spiritually" died.[7] In short, he thought that Christendom had essentially become pagan again, and in some respects was fallen below paganism, leaving the positive vestiges of primitive Christianity behind in the process.[8] Kierkegaard therefore waged a "one-man theological revolution" against Christendom, seeking to reintroduce Christianity to it.[9]

Mark thus represented the beginning of a world revolution, and Soren Kierkegaard the restoration of that same revolution of "primitive Christianity" nearly two millennia later. Mark and Kierkegaard had the same concerns, to "move" those hearing "the gospel" to receive its new form of human existence, living as true followers of Christ—*the God-man*—who showed the new way of *human* life that he *lived* for all. This series therefore explores the writings of Mark and Kierkegaard, looking for the ways that their "gospel" concerns are related to our present concerns. Their writings represented collisions between their respective "established orders" and the "social revolution" known as "the city of God," which *promises* to collide with and eventually overcome the "city of man."

For all these reasons, and more that will become evident, I believe that a "Kierkegaardian Reading of Mark" is warranted by the world-revolution begun in Christ. But we must clarify, because "revolution" is a word that often conjures up disturbing memories of past holocausts. But this revolution is "good news"—the meaning of the word "gospel." It is pre-eminently the revolution of God's love for all humanity which ultimately brings the salvation of the world already won by Christ. Therefore, this reading brings into proximity the writings of an *apostle* of the gospel, and those of one of its poetic *geniuses*, both of whom swam "out over 70,000 fathoms" of its life-giving waters.[10]

---

7. The case for Kierkegaard as "religious outsider" is presented by Allen, *Three Outsiders*, 53–95.

8. Though it was pagan in relation to Christianity, it had fallen *below* paganism in vital human ways of existence. See Christman, "Lewis and Kierkegaard."

9. Garff, *Soren Kierkegaard*, xvii. For a book length treatment under this framing see Tietjen, *Kierkegaard, Christian Missionary*.

10. One of the favorite phrases of one of Kierkegaard's pseudonyms, Johannes Climacus. Kierkegaard, CUP:1, 232.

Abbreviations

BIBLE VERSIONS

ESV	English Standard Version
KJV	King James Version
NASB	New American Standard Bible
NIV	New International Version
NKJV	New King James Version
NLT	New Living Translation

KIERKEGAARD'S WRITINGS

ALSC	A Leper's Self-Contemplation
AC	Attack Upon Christendom
CA	The Concept of Anxiety
CD	Christian Discourses
CUP:1	Concluding Unscientific Postscript Vol. 1
EO:1	Either/Or Vol. 1
EO:2	Either/Or Vol. 2
EUD	Eighteen Upbuilding Discourses
FSE/JFY	For Self-Examination/Judge For Yourself
FT	Fear and Trembling
GNG	"Guilty?"/ "Not Guilty?"
LTK	The Living Thoughts of Kierkegaard (Auden)
JP	Journals and Papers
PC	Practice in Christianity
PH	Purity of Heart is to Will One Thing

PF	Philosophical Fragments
PSW	Provocations: Spiritual Writings of Kierkegaard (Moore)
SLW	Stages on Life's Way
SUD	The Sickness Unto Death
SWK	Spiritual Writings: Gift, Creation, Love (Pattison)
TA	Two Ages
TDIO	Three Discourses on Imagined Occasions
UDVS	Upbuilding Discourses in Various Spirits
WOL	Works of Love

SCRIPTURE

Col	Colossians
Cor	Corinthians
Eccl	Ecclesiastes
Eph	Ephesians
Exod	Exodus
Ezek	Ezekiel
Gal	Galatians
Gen	Genesis
Hag	Haggai
Heb	Hebrews
Isa	Isaiah
Jas	James
Jer	Jeremiah
Lev	Leviticus
LXX	The Septuagint
Matt	Matthew
Mic	Micah
Nah	Nahum
NT	New Testament
OT	Old Testament
Pet	Peter
Phil	Philippians
Rev	Revelation
Rom	Romans
Thess	Thessalonians
Tim	Timothy

Introduction to Volume 1

And his mother and his brothers came, and standing outside they sent to him and called him. And a crowd was sitting around him, and they said to him, "Your mother and your brothers are outside, seeking you." And he answered them, "Who are my mother and my brothers?" And looking about at those who sat around him, he said, "Here are my mother and my brothers! For whoever does the will of God, he is my brother and sister and mother." (Mark 3:31–35 ESV)

"Here are my mother and my brothers!" So declares Jesus of those individuals that were doing God's will by following him as "disciples." The declaration informs the title of this first volume of our Kierkegaardian reading and is supplemented with the subtitle, "The Beginning of the Gospel and Becoming a Christian in (Post) Christendom." The question of "becoming a Christian in Christendom" was perhaps the main concern of Kierkegaard which he desired for himself and his fellow countrymen in his native Denmark. It is fitting that the statement of Jesus from Mark's "beginning of the Gospel" places the emphasis on individuals responding to the person of Jesus instead of "objective" doctrines or human characteristics about him. For the Kingdom of God that was being "birthed" consisted of normally incongruous persons becoming "family" through relation to Jesus rather than the "normal" way of human "association" where "like attracts like," whether in Mark's Jewish, Kierkegaard's "Christian," or our (Post) Christendom culture.

BECOMING A CHRISTIAN IN CHRISTENDOM

Mark's prioritizing of "faith seeking understanding," rather than the reverse, reveals a priority and order that Kierkegaard thought essential. And that priority also implies that understanding is *not* essential or *must* follow. Kierkegaard also believed that a passionate response of decisive action was integrally related to becoming a true self, and without that, people, including "Christians" would remain *without* true selves, without "spirit."

Mark and Kierkegaard agreed that Jesus sought "followers," not "admirers"—often called "believers"—to mitigate the shortfall.[1] In Mark's day, and before the onset of "the age of reason" which bore fruit in "the age of anxiety," the gospel meant to communicate a new way of non-anxious existence, not merely a set of doctrines for "believers" to hold to "objectively" apart from *subjective* change. That disciples became "mothers" and "brothers" (and sisters), and not mere "believers," points to significant subjective change, akin to becoming "born again" in a new family (John 3:3–6).

Another order of activity, additional to "faith seeking understanding" and subjective response, needs to be recognized, namely the prior activity of "Jesus seeking faith." In other words, the *gospel* emphasis is on what *Jesus* was seeking, not firstly on what humans were seeking. For we generally want God to deliver *according* to our prior desires. But Jesus who seeks our faith cultivates our proper desires, ones fitting to his newborn "family relatives."[2]

Jesus' genuine "mother and brothers," in contrast to his actual mother and brothers who sought to "control" his "unorthodox" behavior, reveals that the latter were playing the part of his opponents in his conflict with the Jewish socio-religious order, the "Christendom" if you will, of his own day! Mark's Gospel demonstrates how naturally humans desire what is *against* God's will and kingdom. Mary and Jesus' brothers, wanting Jesus to *follow them* "home," were thereby against Jesus doing God's will. Later, Peter the chief disciple becomes a mouthpiece of Satan by also speaking against God's will for Jesus. To Jesus, Mark and Kierkegaard, discipleship is following God's terms thereof, not "following" those of our own.

---

1. See Kierkegaard, PC, 233.

2. Murray Rae writes "Reading the New Testament, Kierkegaard discovers that Jesus cannot be accommodated within prior categories of thought and that the condition for recognizing the truth of Christ is a gift given by God rather than some innate human capacity." Rae, *Kierkegaard and Theology*, 170.

BECOMING A CHRISTIAN IN (POST) CHRISTENDOM

That Mark and Kierkegaard both largely frame their gospels in collision with the first century Jewish and nineteenth century Christian establishments raises the question of the applicability of those to the establishments outside their immediate purviews. The answer is simply that there is commonality in any and all forms of societal establishments. Therefore, the specific religious establishments Mark and Kierkegaard aimed at thereby also "hit" any human establishments. The most important commonality is that societal establishments are always meaning-giving "sacred canopies" that provide "religious" unity for the society, even if they are not viewed as religious.[3]

Of course, there is also religious commonality between Christendom and post-Christendom, since much of the sacred canopy of the former remains, though the now worn and tattered fabric contains many holes "repaired" with numerous ill-fitted "secular" patches. In other words, post-Christendom still contains powerful sub-currents of Christianity. And because of this, Kierkegaard's challenge of becoming a Christian in Christendom still applies to today's gospel collision with post-Christian existence in the West.

To serve as an example, we will consider the term that perhaps most exemplifies the ideals of the West, namely "humanism." But humanism arose because of the gospel and Christianity, and therefore "Christian humanism" has been appropriately presented by scholars such as Jacques Maritain and Jens Zimmermann.[4] Because of this prior Christian inoculation, G. K. Chesterton said that the modern humanistic world is where the old Christian virtues "wander wildly . . . gone mad because they have been isolated from each other and are wandering alone" and thus also bring "terrible damage."[5]

To summarize this point, Mark's gospel and Kierkegaard's writings were applicable not only to becoming a Christian in relation to their times, but also to today's (Post) Christendom.

BECOMING A CHRISTIAN IN "KIERKEGAARDIANDOM"

We have coined this odd phrase to demonstrate another pervasive influence of Christendom which seems to have come into cultural prominence

---

3. See Berger, *The Sacred Canopy*, vi, loc. 31.

4. See Maritain, *Social and Political*, 155–170; Zimmermann, *Incarnational Humanism*, 21–162.

5. Chesterton, *Orthodoxy*, 191–192.

because of Kierkegaard himself. Charles Williams wrote the following of Kierkegaard:

> He was the type of a new state of things in which Christendom had to exist, and of the new mind in which Christendom knew them . . . his sayings will be so moderated in our minds that they will soon become not his sayings but ours.[6]

Though Williams lamented that this "moderation" of Kierkegaard would be due to his becoming "fashionable" so that there would be an unfortunate and inaccurate "trafficking" in Kierkegaard, his above statements nonetheless demonstrates that Kierkegaard represented, or perhaps instigated an existential/spiritual/psychological "sea-change" in Christendom and the psyche of the modern West. Similarly, Harvie Ferguson writes that, "sociologists, and anyone else interested in the character of modern life, should read Kierkegaard."[7]

If Williams and Ferguson were correct, it seems probable that Kierkegaard contributed to today's individualism and obsession with "identity." It is likely that Kierkegaardian concerns loom beneath today's "selfie" culture, such as the irrepressible longing for "becoming a self," even if—through our favored "isms" of secularism, materialism, and consumerism—falling short of conscious recognition of the ontological end calling it to the pursuit, namely, God's call to self-hood.[8] The point is that most post-Kierkegaardian people do, to some extent, think Kierkegaardian. And as Williams notes, this new "Christian" psyche in relation to Christendom, its "type" and "mind," was exemplified in Kierkegaard.

It may well be that Kierkegaard would be appalled at the notion of Kierkegaardiandom, just as Mark would be at a notion of "Markdom." For they were both presumably like John the Baptist who said, "he must increase, but I must decrease" (John 3:30 KJV), and even like Jesus (see John 12:25–28).

In sum, our Kierkegaardian reading of the first four chapters of Mark will seek to juxtapose these ancient and modern writers and their times, to behold the new family of Jesus and reveal the manner of becoming a Christian in post-Christendom.

---

6. Williams, *Descent of the Dove*, 213.

7. Ferguson, *Melancholy and the Critique*, ix.

8. See Kierkegaard, SUD, 14. God's ontological call is to become a self by "resting transparently in the power that established it."

1

"The Beginning" of Mark's Sacred History and Kierkegaard's "Mirror" of Existence-Communication

Mark 1:1 (ESV) The beginning of the gospel of Jesus Christ, the Son of God.

God's Word is the mirror—in reading it or hearing it, I am supposed to see myself in the mirror. —*Soren Kierkegaard*[1]

Some commentators on the Gospel of Mark might point out that the first verse in our translations may not have been the first verse in Mark's original Gospel.[2] Also, many modern translations of Mark's Gospel, such as the *English Standard Version* cited above, provide a footnote indicating that the words "Son of God" are omitted in some of the ancient manuscripts. These are merely two examples of "Bible difficulties" which can cause doubt and uncertainty for modern readers regarding the Bible being the word of God. The collision of these two factors, the Bible as God's word, and the Bible as seemingly incomplete or fallibly constructed, *can* bring our looking to the Bible for guiding light and truth to a halt.

---

1. Kierkegaard, FSE/JFY, 25.
2. Wright, *New Testament*, 390n67.

So where might this leave us at the beginning of a "Kierkegaardian Reading of the Gospel of Mark?" Does it leave us stalled at the gate? No, for it actually leads us to the "working method" of Kierkegaard for reading the Bible.[3] He believed that the Bible was meant to serve as a mirror for the reader, and therefore he said, ". . .you must not look at the mirror, observe the mirror, but must see oneself in the mirror."[4] Though Kierkegaard saw some legitimacy of "biblical criticism," he also saw it as a dangerous *distraction* for the Christian who might expend more energy looking *at* the mirror than looking into it and thereby missing its call to obey as the means by which we should gain true "existence." Even worse was the fact that seeking "better understanding" through "commentators" oftentimes was an evasion of it's plain call for immediate decisiveness. He writes,

> It is a very simple matter. Pick up the New Testament: read it. Can you deny, do you dare deny, that what you read there about forsaking everything, about giving up the world, being mocked and spit upon as your Lord and master was—can you deny, do you dare deny, that this is very easy to understand, indescribably easy, that you do not need a dictionary or commentary or a single other person in order to understand it? But you say, "Before I do this, however, before I risk such a decisive step, I must consult with others." Insolent, disobedient one, you are cheeky! You know very well that it is nothing but blasphemy, for you, you cheat, you are looking for a way out, an excuse, since you know very well that every human being will recommend whatever indulges you and advise you to follow what best pleases flesh and blood, and will say: For God's sake, spare yourself.[5]

Of course, his method presupposes two things. First, that there was "a mirror" given by God through the twin phenomena of *inspiration* and *revelation*, and second, that God's purpose of revelation was to provide a mirror in which I "see myself" as responsible before God's *immediate* call therein.[6] Of course, that does not mean to see *only* oneself, as though the

---

3. Timothy Houston Polk writes that Kierkegaard's method was "the ancient church's Rule of Faith." Polk, *The Biblical Kierkegaard*, 2.

4. Kierkegaard, FSE/JFY, 25.

5. Kierkegaard, JP, III:267–268, #2865.

6. We will not try to exhaustively discuss Kierkegaard's view of inspiration. But in passing we note that against a *rationalistic proof* view of a *humanly* perfect scriptural product he somewhat satirically though quite seriously wrote of "A New Proof for the Divinity of the Bible." This "proof" was its "carefully contrived discrepancies" which were *superintended* "precisely because God wants Holy Scripture to be the object of faith." And that faith would be circumvented if one could "*directly* sense that it is God's

mirror is meant to create narcissists. The point is to see oneself in relation to the will of God and to live accordingly. We will therefore consider this opening text of Mark, to see the gospel's "beginning" and what that means for how *our* life fits into *God's* story of the world's redemption.

"THE BEGINNING" OF MARK'S SACRED HISTORY

We will see that Mark, perhaps because of his sparse style, embeds deep meanings meant to starkly collide with the status-quo understandings of human life. Thus, "the beginning of the gospel" does not merely indicate that Mark's story of the gospel begins here, though it does. For it more deeply signifies that the gospel is a new beginning for the world. Via writes "It can hardly be doubted that the *arche* of Mark 1:1 has a paradigmatic or metaphorical relationship to the *arche* (LXX) of Gen. 1:1, especially since Mark speaks of the *arche* of creation in 10:6."[7] Via adds that,

> The very beginning of the story, even before Jesus actually appears in his public ministry, is the advent of the newness of creation which is also eschatological time. There is another first time despite the fatigue of world history.[8]

Given the new-cosmos significance of the gospel it is significant that Jesus, the agent of this new creation will inevitably collide with "the powers that be." We will see that part of Mark's style, perhaps again augmented by sparse but precise repetitions, presents cohesive themes with foreshadowing, development, and eventual culmination. Thus, the very first words of his story are pregnant with the foreshadowing of conflict in the apocalypse of "the beginning of the gospel." As we move on to consider Kierkegaard's understanding of "the mirror" we must not leave behind the cosmic apocalyptic context, provided by Mark's mirror. For that determines why the apocalyptic gospel of Christ, and those responding to it in "microcosmic apocalyptic," invariably collide with the present word.[9] This collision is inevitable because the *eschaton* is "*not the* extension, the result, the consequence, the next step in following out what has gone before, *but* on the contrary, it is

---

word" based on its internal and comprehensive "perfect harmony." Kierkegaard, JP, III: 275–276, #2877. For further helpful discussion see Roberts, *Emerging Prophet*, 12–34.

7. Via, *Mark's Gospel*, 45.

8. Via, *Mark's Gospel*, 45.

9. Ziegler, *Militant Grace*, 7. Speaking of Gerhard Forde, Ziegler writes, "In essence, Forde gives an account of justification that republishes the "microcosmic apocalyptic" discerned by Luther to be the heart of personal salvation."

the radical break with all that has gone before, but also precisely as such its original significance and motive power."[10]

KIERKEGAARD'S "MIRROR" OF EXISTENCE-COMMUNICATION

God has given his word so that we can see ourselves in it, just as we see ourselves in a mirror. The mirror has no other purpose. If we merely look at the frame of the mirror, how it is standing, attached to the wall, or wonder how it was manufactured or who officially interprets its meaning for us, we will miss its purpose. God has not provided his word for us to merely look at it in any of these ways. It was given for seeing ourselves therein. Kierkegaard thoroughly discussed this manner of "communication" and the temptation to "complications" in *For Self-Examination*, the first part of which was based on not merely hearing, but doing God's word, as narrated in James 1:22–27. Kierkegaard asks his "listener" to consider how apt the words of James are, as though "coined for our times and our situation and in general for the later ages of Christendom."[11] He then illustrates the present difficulties in reading God's word:

> "God's Word" is indeed the mirror—but, but—oh, how enormously complicated—strictly speaking, how much belongs to "God's Word"? Which books are authentic? Are they really by the apostles, and are the apostles really trustworthy? Have they personally seen everything, or have they perhaps only heard about various things from others? As for ways of reading, there are thirty thousand different ways. And then this crowd or crush of scholars and opinions, and learned opinions and unlearned opinions about how the particular passage is to be understood . . . is it not true that all this seems to be rather complicated! God's Word is the mirror—in reading it or hearing it, I am supposed to see myself in the mirror—but look, this business of the mirror is so confusing that I very likely never come to see myself reflected—at least not if I go this way.[12]

---

10. Karl Barth, as cited by Ziegler, *Militant Grace*, 8. This statement also reveals the basis of Kierkegaard's view of the essential epistemological difference between Socratic maieutic *self-knowledge* and Christian self-transcending *revelation*, which difference nevertheless provides an overall redemptive dialectic, which is the ultimate purpose of PF (on transcendent revelation) and CUP:1 (on Socratic knowledge) when taken together. On this relation of PF and CUP:1, see Connell, *Kierkegaard and the Paradox*, 130–151.

11. Kierkegaard, FSE/JFY, 25

12. Kierkegaard, FSE/JFY, 25–26.

Kierkegaard mentions, but does not at this point fully explore, the "temptation" to assume that "the full force of human craftiness has a hand" in this complication and the reality that "we really do not want to see ourselves in the mirror and therefore have concocted all this that threatens to make the mirror impossible."[13] So does Kierkegaard simply present an impasse that can only be overcome by a blind "leap of faith" in which the one leaping simply hopes that the Bible is actually God's word? To Kierkegaard, this was not an insurmountable impasse, if one is willing to go another way. The other way is not to pretend that "higher criticism" of the Bible does not exist, which Kierkegaard obviously did not. Nor is it to construct the "theological proof-texting and system building of those who attempted to offer an apologetic for the Christian message."[14] For Kierkegaard the only sufficient "apologetic" was that "the message of the Bible and its existential fit are the only 'proofs' of its authority."[15] In other words, when the Bible is approached properly, according to its *design* as a mirror, the seeing of oneself therein resonates truthfully to *that* observer, and the "existential fit" of correlation between God's eternal word and finite human experience provides the "proof" sufficient for discovering the truth of God *in relation to* the human self.[16] Timothy Keller relates the story of Emile Cailliet as one who found this "existential fit" and declared, "Lo and behold, as I looked through them [the Gospels] the One who spoke and acted in them became alive to me . . . This is the book that would understand me."[17]

Mark composed his Gospel to be a sort of sacred space wherein the first hearers and subsequent readers could observe themselves in relation to the kingdom of God begun in Christ. Thus, we might even consider the gospel the presentation of a "thought experiment." But the point is that we can only "experiment" *within that frame*, not by remaining outside it.[18] Most of us willingly participate in thought experiments, whether novels, movies,

13. Kierkegaard, FSE/JFY, 26

14. Rosas, *Scripture in the Thought*, 144

15. Rosas, *Scripture in the Thought*, 148.

16. To Kierkegaard, "objective truth" of God as an object of human knowledge was more invalid than unattainable.

17. Keller, *King's Cross*, xv-xvi.

18. "Because the Gospel of Mark is a coherent narrative with a powerful impact, it is important to experience the narrative as a whole. Those who first experienced the Gospel of Mark would have heard the whole Gospel proclaimed to them in groups on single occasions. They undoubtedly were engaged by the drama of the story, experienced the tension of the conflicts, identified with the characters, and felt suspense about the outcome. Emerging from the experience of Mark's story world, they were perhaps able to see the world round them in a new way and to have new possibilities awakened in them." Rhoads et. al., *Mark As Story*, 4.

or even philosophical treatises, so we ought to realize the necessity of going along with the narrator. This is especially important if the narrator just might be our creator and the point of the narration consists in how our life fits into the whole of existence. Eugene Peterson writes,

> What we must never be encouraged to do, although all of us are guilty of it over and over, is to force Scripture to fit our experience. Our experience is too small; it's like trying to put the ocean into a thimble. What we want is to fit into the world revealed by Scripture, to swim in this vast ocean.[19]

Therefore, Kierkegaard says one must "see oneself in the mirror." We are not to observe the mirror, nor as Peterson explains, to shrink the mirror to only be about our self. For it is a mirror that, looked deeply enough into, reflects God's word on the scope of human reality. Kierkegaard's Copenhagen, situated in the coast of Denmark, certainly provided him with an immediate knowledge of the ever-present depths of the sea, and the inspiration for his description of faith as both terrifying and exhilarating, "out upon the deep, over seventy thousand fathoms of water."[20]

BECOMING NEW SELVES THROUGH MARK'S GOSPEL

Kierkegaard would say that God's "mirror" is ultimately provided for the purpose of "existence-communication." Narcissists notwithstanding, most of us know that the purpose of a mirror is not to merely see oneself, or to be sure we still exist. Normally the mirror is a practical aid for the general maintenance of our bodies. Shaving or applying mascara without a mirror might be somewhat dangerous to those accustomed to using one. On a less dangerous level, although perhaps more important to many, is the assurance that we can go out in public as relatively presentable. But the purpose of the mirror of the word of God goes beyond such things, as important as they may seem at the moment. For, the moment before the mirror is the point at which we as finite time-bound creatures meet the eternal, there encountering the criterion of God's will. The purpose of the mirror of God is not for self-reflection, or mere self-maintenance, but for self-transformation through God. Many, or perhaps most of us wish that our home mirrors might be "magic mirrors" with transformative powers. Kierkegaard seemed to think God's mirror is so imbued and exclaimed how the mirror in which we see God as our criterion does change everything.

19. Peterson, *Eat This Book*, 68.
20. As cited in Kierkegaard, PSW, xxix.

> And what infinite reality the self gains by being conscious of existing before God, by becoming a human self whose criterion is God! . . .The child who previously has had only his parents as a criterion becomes a self as an adult by getting the state as a criterion, but what an infinite accent falls on the self by having God as the criterion![21]

Having God as one's criterion has become a rarity in the age after Kierkegaard. For he recognized that the loss of God as the ultimate criterion, was a crisis that would threaten all lesser criterions. This was the civilizational crisis that Friedrich Nietzsche saw as the immediate consequence of what he called the "death of God." Kierkegaard also saw this erosion as in progress and intuited what it meant for the individual: "Our age . . . has lost all the substantial attributes of family, state, race and must entirely leave the individual to himself, so that, in the strictest sense, he becomes his own creator."[22]

The "death of God" would produce all sorts of problems as Nietzsche and Kierkegaard correctly foresaw. Many experts diagnose these problems, but in general the masses only feel the general malaise of "the age of anxiety." This is only exacerbated by the cognitive dissonance resulting from the fact of our technological and economic advances that ought to be making us all "happy." Joakim Garff comments,

> Precisely because modernity has lost its most fundamental determinants, including the religious foundation that had previously been conceived as given, we are *condemned* to be our own creators.[23]

This "condemnation" is accurately if not chillingly described in a timely analysis of our apocalyptic dystopian times by showing some compassion for those perhaps bearing the brunt of the situation, the young faced with the terrible responsibility and uncertain outcome of self-authorship:

> We can decide to make no choices at all about our futures, extending adolescence for a long time, as some have been in the habit of doing. But that is also a kind of choice, one that usually ends in our parent's basements. And this is maybe why today's Millennials and Generation Z deserve more understanding than they get. They are doing a kind of metaphysical heavy lifting at an incredibly young age that was not only *not required* by earlier generations but also nearly unthinkable. Small children are now expected to be able to competently identify their own genders.

---

21. Kierkegaard, *SUD*, 79.
22. Kierkegaard, as cited by Garff, "Formation," 259.
23. Garff, "Formation," 259.

> Young generations are expected to discover themselves with almost no education, and with almost no life experience, and they are hyper-aware of their lack of both.[24]

Some may claim that contains overstatement, but give it a few more years, since we all see the writing on the wall (or perhaps more accurately the lack of any *authoritative* writing at all).

Finding self through finding God as one's criterion ought to be manifestly "good news" (gospel) to people in this present age, burdened to create themselves *ex-nihilo* by the fanatical pseudo-religious demands of "liberating authorities" that "crush people with unbearable religious demands and never lift a finger to ease the burden" (Matt 23:4 NLT). For Jesus says, "my yoke is easy and my burden light" (Matt 11:30 ESV). Of course, discovering God as one's criterion is only the potential of a beginning through "the beginning of the gospel"—observing oneself in it, seeing what God promises, changing one's way of thinking, and becoming transformed. Kierkegaard called this "existence communication" saying "Christianity is not a doctrine but an existence-communication."[25]

What Kierkegaard means by that seemingly *philosophical* statement is that Christianity is *not* a "philosophical doctrine" that relates primarily to the intellect, as though knowledge of "objective truth" or mere acceptance of "paradoxes" is what Christianity is essentially about. James 2:19 shows that believing the objective truths of God is what "the demons believe." But they do so *apart* from "faith" and damningly so. Christianity is not merely, or mostly about believing "doctrine." Even less is it about *understanding* its paradox, which is an impossibility—hence the word *paradox*. Rather, Christianity is subjectively living by faith in the passionate embrace of the gospel that was revealed for us in Christ.[26] Kierkegaard's definition, "existence-communication," may sound austere. But it means that "the gospel" is the best news we have ever heard. It *communicates* or transmits to us a new form of *existence*. We become selves not by self-creation out of nothing, but through the new creation of Christ.

It does seem odd to juxtapose Kierkegaard's grammar of "existence-communication" with Mark's of "good news." But this grammar does not signify real difference. Humans have perennially asked the question who they are or should be in relation to God, others, and the world. Of course, this question is always closely related to the fact of death.[27] This is evident

---

24. Joustra, et al., *How To Survive*, 186.
25. Kierkegaard, CUP:1, 570.
26. Walsh, "Kierkegaard's Theology," 293.
27. In a chapter "The Existential Meaning of Death," Westphal writes, "When death

in the pre-Christian times of the Greeks like Socrates and Plato, and of OT writers including Qoheleth, the writer of Ecclesiastes. Humans have asked "the big question of personhood" for thousands of years, and it is "perhaps *the* driving question of the Secular age" of today.[28]

As this "Kierkegaardian Reading" continues we hope to demonstrate that Mark's Gospel does have the same essential, and Kierkegaardian-style *existential* concerns.[29] For Mark exhibits the crowd as a backdrop against which to reveal *individuals* in various *existential* situations, through whom even his original audience could see themselves in God's mirror and receive the new existence provided in the *life-giving* gospel. Mark of course was giving what became the *"given"* of Christianity, the objective "beginning of the gospel of Jesus Christ, the Son of God" which calls for what Kierkegaard so strongly emphasized as the complimentary *"given"*—a *subjective* life-response and life-reception by those who heard. But the given of subjective response had for the most part become so lost in Christendom that it became the objective fact that to be born and baptized in Denmark, for all practical purposes, *meant* to be born a Christian. Therefore, Kierkegaard's life-task became to re-introduce Mark's objective gospel, *and* the *given* of subjective response, reception, and reduplication of the life of Christ, to Christendom.[30]

Of course, to call the gospel "objective" is in Kierkegaardian *and Marcan* parlance a dangerously reductive misnomer. For the truth is that the apocalyptic, cosmos-shaking, re-creating, gospel of Jesus Christ the Son of God is the height of the all-surpassing earnestness of the "subjectivity"

---

is looked squarely in the face, what is the meaning of this life, and how should it be lived? . . . Freedom is an awesome gift, or perhaps a dreadful responsibility, for it is ours to choose who we will be. But it is not ours to choose whether we will be." Westphal, *God, Guilt, and Death*, 95.

28. Joustra et al., *How to Survive*, 182.

29. The "existentialism" Kierkegaard is considered to be "the father of" is a misnomer since the thinkers who are identified as "existential" were largely atheistic and saw the existential task as a wholly autonomous affair. Sponheim sees the appropriation of Kierkegaard by the most noted existentialists of the twentieth century as "an explicitly atheistic (mis)appropriation." Sponheim, *Existing Before God*, 101. Nevertheless, a Kierkegaardian-style "existentialism" does seem useful, since Kierkegaard did use the term existence-communication and may have coined the term "existential." Therefore, we will use the term, but when connected to Kierkegaard it always signifies his existentialism, not that of Sartre, Camus, Heidegger, or others of the twentieth century, or even that of Nietzsche or Dostoevsky in the nineteenth century. For an informative overview of the basic existential *commonalities* of all those just mentioned plus several others, with Kierkegaard, see Marino, *Existentialist's Survival Guide*, 1–18.

30. The reduplication of the life of Christ simply means following the life of Christ as one's pattern or prototype for living.

of God. As we continue, Mark's gospel-mirror, and Kierkegaard's method of seeing ourselves therein, will enable us to further see God's passionate subjectivity and the passionate subjective response it calls forth from each of us.

2

Two Voices Crying in the Wilderness . . . of Despair

Mark 1:2–8 (ESV)

2 As it is written in Isaiah the prophet,

"Behold, I send my messenger before your face,

who will prepare your way,

3 the voice of one crying in the wilderness:

'Prepare the way of the Lord,

make his paths straight,'"

4 John appeared, baptizing in the wilderness and proclaiming a baptism of repentance for the forgiveness of sins. 5 And all the country of Judea and all Jerusalem were going out to him and were being baptized by him in the river Jordan, confessing their sins. 6 Now John was clothed with camel's hair and wore a leather belt around his waist and ate locusts and wild honey. 7 And he preached, saying, "After me comes he who is mightier than I, the strap of whose sandals I am not worthy to stoop down and untie. 8 I have baptized you with water, but he will baptize you with the Holy Spirit."

Christianity is certainly not melancholy, it is, on the contrary, glad tidings—for the melancholy; to the frivolous it is certainly not glad tidings, for it wishes first of all to make them serious. —Soren Kierkegaard[1]

SOREN KIERKEGAARD'S VOICE IN THE WILDERNESS

In 1836 at the age of about 23, Soren Kierkegaard wrote in his journal that "the present age is the age of despair."[2] Almost a decade and a half later, one of his pseudonymous authors named "Anti-Climacus"[3] elaborated on this declaration in Kierkegaard's *The Sickness Unto Death*:

> "In any case, no human being ever lived and no one lives outside of Christendom who has not despaired, and no one in Christendom if he is not a true Christian, and insofar as he is not wholly that, he still is to some extent in despair."[4]

If the reader is familiar with the Apostle Paul, this may seem reminiscent of his statement in Romans 2:9 that "all, both Jews and Greeks, are under sin." In Kierkegaard's statement Jews would be like those within Christendom, while Greeks would be like those outside. Thus, Kierkegaard is close to Paul, and in fact does equate "despair" to "sin." But Kierkegaard places more emphasis on sin and despair as only being known as such on a spectrum of consciousness before God. Thus, to Kierkegaard, pagans, whether ancient ones or those in Christendom who are "practical pagans," are often not only unconscious of despair, but also not conscious of sin *as sin*. For sin is only known as sin when God is the criterion of the self. "Sin is: before God in despair."[5] This seems to be confirmed by Paul when he writes that apart from the law there is no knowledge of sin, although there is certainly the fact of sin. (Rom 3:20, 7:7).

But despair is not to be equated with common "depression." Stephen Backhouse explains,

---

1. As cited in Dru, *Soul of Kierkegaard*, 129
2. Kierkegaard, SUD, ix.
3. The prefix "Anti" gives a false connotation to modern readers and does not signify "against" but "before." Kierkegaard used it to say that the viewpoint in this book was from someone at a higher level of Christian ideality than Kierkegaard felt himself to be. See Kierkegaard, SUD, xxii.
4. Soren Kierkegaard, SUD, 22.
5. Kierkegaard, SUD, 81

> Despair is to be differentiated from depression ... One can be depressed without being in despair, and alternatively, one can live in full comfort but be despairing. Despair has to do with living a life without finding one's true meaning, or in Kierkegaardian language, without finding one's authentic self.[6]

So, in Kierkegaard's view, despair is a universal phenomenon of self-meaninglessness which is only "known" through God as the criterion of human meaning. Sin is also universal, to "fall short of the glory of God," of the meaning or purpose of life (Rom 3:23, ESV). The fact that everyone does not "feel" their despair or sin does not nullify their reality. In the excerpt from Kierkegaard at the head of this chapter, the frivolous would be those who do not "feel" that they are in despair. As Stephen Backhouse noted, despair is to live without finding "one's true meaning," even if one does it "*in full comfort.*" Kierkegaard presented his "formula" for this type of despair with this heading: "The Despair That Is Ignorant of Being Despair, or the Despairing Ignorance of Having a Self and an Eternal Self."[7]

Kierkegaard regarded this as the "lowest" form of despair because it consisted in the lowest level of consciousness. This could also be stated as being the lowest because it was the lowest level of "spirit." Human spirit in Kierkegaard's thought was very close to what most of us think of as "will." Persons that live at the *lowest* level thus live in a state void of choice, decision, passion, will. This may become clearer by noting that Kierkegaard considered the *highest* level of spirit and despair to be that exhibited by the devil. The devil is "sheer spirit," not so much in contrast to a bodily existence, but rather regarding his "will" that is potently expressed in "absolute defiance."[8] Therefore the devil's conscious despair is also the most absolute. By contrast, the one that exists in unconscious despair is almost "too spiritless to be called sin."[9] But "almost" is only almost. It is *still* sin and despair and does consists in a *degree* of "obstinacy." Kierkegaard explains,

> For example, if a man is presumably happy, imagines himself to be happy, although considered in the light of truth he is unhappy, he is usually far from wanting to be wrenched out of his

---

6. Backhouse, *A Single Life*, 249–50.

7. Kierkegaard, SUD, 42. It is important to note Kierkegaard's own disclaimer regarding the application of formulaic "doctrines" to human lives: "Actual life is too complex merely to point out abstract contrasts such as that between a despair that is completely unaware of being so and a despair that is completely aware of being so. Very often the person in despair has a dim idea of his own state, although here again the nuances are myriad." (48.)

8. Kierkegaard, SUD, 42.

9. Kierkegaard, SUD, 104.

error. On the contrary, he becomes indignant, he regards anyone who does so as his worst enemy, he regards it as an assault bordering on murder in the sense that, as is said, it murders his happiness ... Imagine a house with a basement, first floor, and a second floor planned so that there is or is supposed to be a social distinction between the occupants according to floor. Now, if what it means to be a human being is compared to such a house, then all too regrettably the sad and ludicrous truth about the majority of people is that in their own house they prefer to live in the basement. Every human being is a psychical-physical synthesis intended to be spirit; this is the building, but he prefers to live in the basement, that is, in the sensate categories. Moreover, he not only prefers to live in the basement—no, he loves it so much that he is indignant if anyone suggests that he move to the superb upper floor that stands vacant and at his disposal, for he is, after all, living in his own house.[10]

The question for our reading is this: can we relate the call of Kierkegaard to his generation to realize they are living in their spiritual "basements" to John the Baptist's call to the spiritually impoverished of his generation? Was John's call in any way *existentially* like Kierkegaard's? We think yes.

JOHN THE BAPTIST'S VOICE IN THE WILDERNESS

To try to demonstrate similarity between Kierkegaard and John, it may be necessary to mix some metaphors. For there seems to be similarity between the spiritless "basements" occupied by those of Christendom and the "waste place" wilderness where Israel lazily languished and fell short of entering the promised land. For it also must be noted that John the Baptist was calling his generation of Israel *to the wilderness*. In essence calling the crowds of Israel *back* to the wilderness is meant to reveal that, spiritually speaking, they still lived there, and not in "the promised land."[11] And therefore, John's call is to truly leave the wilderness, cross the "river Jordan" in a "baptism of repentance for the forgiveness of sins" while looking toward the coming "Lord" who will baptize, not with water, "but with the Holy Spirit." John's call to that generation of Israel to pass *through* the waters of the Jordan was a deeply significant reenactment of Israel's history necessary for *a present*

---

10. Kierkegaard, SUD, 43.

11. "Mark tells us that for whatever reason they come to John in droves—'the whole Judean countryside and all the people of Jerusalem'—to get this cleansing in the desert. They are in effect, backtracking to the place where Israel had so many beginnings." Garland, *Mark*, 45.

relationship with God. Mark Horne elaborates saying, "passing through water means moving closer to where God is and typically involves repentance and abandonment of or deliverance from the old order to attain the new."[12] Thus, it seems proper to say that John called the crowds to earnestly leave their waste-place "basement" dwellings, eagerly confess their despair and sin, and become more "spirit," in the expectation of faith for the coming one with the greater baptism of the Holy Spirit. And today God calls each person to become conscious of having a self, an eternal self, and through faith *become* spirit through the Holy Spirit. In and of ourselves, apart from God, we are without possibility to become spirit. Kierkegaard explains that, "Spirit is restlessness . . . spirit is sheer wakefulness and actuosity, and man is more or less drowsiness."[13]

Therefore, Kierkegaard's emphasis on human "spirit" does not present a "works-based" relationship with God. To Kierkegaard, faith is the opposite of sin, not virtue. God's call to repentance and confession is thus not a call to virtue, but essentially a call to faith expressed in repentance and confession. Kierkegaard's "working definition" of faith, where spirit as "restfulness, wakefulness and actuosity" comes home, so to speak, in faith, not in virtue, was this:

> Faith is: that the self in being itself and in willing to be itself rests transparently in God. Very often, however, it is overlooked that the opposite of sin is by no means virtue. In part, this is a pagan view, which is satisfied with a merely human criterion and simply does not know what sin is, that all sin is before God. No, *the opposite of sin is faith,* as it says in Romans 14:23: "whatever does not proceed from faith is sin." And this is one of the most decisive definitions for all Christianity—that the opposite of sin is not virtue but faith.[14]

TWO VOICES CRYING IN THE WILDERNESS OF DESPAIR

Ultimately, the two voices calling in quite different wildernesses, nevertheless represented God's call to the crowds of each generation to leave their indifference and hopeless despair. Kierkegaard writes, "Most men are characterized by a dialectic of indifference and live a life so far from the

---

12. Horne, *Victory According to Mark*, 25.
13. Kierkegaard, quoted in Andic, "The Mirror," 346.
14. Kierkegaard, SUD, 82.

good (faith) that it is almost too spiritless to be called sin—indeed almost too spiritless to be called despair."[15] God does not leave us in that wilderness. Rather he sends prophets to that wilderness to call us to the place of consciousness of despair and sin, and to challenge the hopelessness that otherwise becomes a fate of indifference, and to overcome it with the good news of the coming baptism with God's Spirit.

What do we see as we look in this part of the gospel-mirror of Mark? He reveals our solidarity with the generation's basement existence in the "wilderness of despair," whether experienced in "melancholy" or "frivolity." He calls us to fully enter that wilderness, become immersed in the *death* of our sin and despair—only to come out in *the hope* of *resurrection* on the other side—crossing God's river that *is* Christ to enter the promised land of "straight paths" of new human life in the Spirit of the "firstborn among many brethren" (Rom 8:29, KJV).

---

15. Kierkegaard, SUD, 101.

3

God's Earnestness

"And Everyone Shall Have an Opinion About It"

Mark 1:9–11 (ESV) 9 In those days Jesus came from Nazareth of Galilee and was baptized by John in the Jordan. 10 And when he came up out of the water, immediately he saw the heavens being torn open and the Spirit descending on him like a dove. 11 And a voice came from heaven, "You are my beloved Son; with you I am well pleased."

When God lets himself be born and become a man, this is not an idle caprice, some fancy he hits upon just to be doing something, perhaps to put an end to boredom that has brashly been said must be involved in being God—it is not in order to have an adventure. No, when God does this, then this fact is the earnestness of existence. And, in turn, the earnestness in this earnestness is this: that everyone shall have an opinion about it. —Anti-Climacus[1]

The sign of offense and object of faith has become the most fabulous of all fabulous characters, a divine Mr. Goodman. —Anti-Climacus[2]

---

1. Kierkegaard, SUD, 130
2. Kierkegaard, PC, 35–36

MARK'S NEW GENRE FOR A NEW CREATION

One of the first things readers of Mark's gospel notice is its abruptness and brevity. The striking scenes change rapidly, the characters constantly and dramatically move around.[3] Major characters simply appear as out of nowhere. Even Jesus, the obvious main character does so. One would think that Mark might make an exception for his "star character." But no. We are presented with no history, no background, nothing. The word "immediately" is also used frequently, probably to call attention to the implicit demand of his message. In a sense, Mark's style boldly "violates our personal space." Unless we believe that Mark suffered from a short attention span or simply had bad manners, we are probably warranted to understand these characteristics as intentional. If Mark were a movie director, he would be following the new school of "fast cutting" seen in the Jason Bourne films and dubbed as "chaos cinema" for basically transgressing the traditional rules of spatial and temporal continuity. Many NT scholars credit Mark with inventing the vastly influential "gospel" genre. Price writes, "Mark has proved the most influential of human books. All other books from four thousand years of epics, plays, lyrics, and biographies have touched human life less potently."[4]

Scholars have debated exactly what ancient genre Mark's gospel can be categorized as, whether history, biography, apocalyptic, or even what it is most like. It may be best to summarize that he was doing something *new*.[5] Wright pictorially describes Mark's "uncooperativeness," saying,

> "Mark, at first blush the easiest of the synoptics, retreats from the advancing interpreter like a rainbow's end... Mark is a book of secrets, of veils, of mysteries.[6]

New things, whether they are new literary "gospels" like Mark's, or new human beings *like Jesus*, resist placement in pre-existing categories. In Mark, Jesus declares that the new reality of God's kingdom cannot be "kept" in old vessels of practice or understanding:

> No one sews a piece of unshrunk cloth on an old garment. If he does, the patch tears away from it, the new from the old, and a

---

3. Ched Myers compares the opening scenes to "minimalist theater, collapsing a world of meaning into a few concentrated images, or a chiaroscuro painting, with vivid profiles etched in a dark, obscure backdrop. Punctuated by divine voices offstage and human cries at center stage, the prologue narrates the story of an invasion, throwing existence-as-usual into sharp relief." Myers, *Binding the Strong Man*, 91.

4. Price, *Three Gospels*, 38.

5. See Garland, *Theology of Mark*, 85–89.

6. Wright, *New Testament*, 390.

worse tear is made. And no one puts new wine into old wineskins. If he does, the wine will burst the skins—and the wine is destroyed, and so are the skins. But new wine is for fresh wineskins (Mark 2:21–22, ESV).

It seems that Mark's new literary style was a way to convey a modern idea, that "the medium is the message." A medium that was disruptive, deconstructive, and even evoked a sort of "chaos," was possibly Mark's way to present what new wine is to an old wineskin, *uncontainable*.

SOREN KIERKEGAARD'S "ATTACK ON CHRISTENDOM"

One of Kierkegaard's primary criticisms of "Christendom" was that it sought to domesticate Christ by trying to "shrink" the paradox, the "chaotic" aspects of his person and work to the human understanding. At that time, a few centuries short of two millennia of "Christian" history had culminated in a "Christ" who was all too easily accommodated to affirming the values and customs of the "Danish Golden-Age."[7] This meant that the person and work of Christ were "a matter of common sense" necessary for their "Christian" society in which the masses were simply "Christians" as a "given."[8] Kierkegaard saw the Christ of this social construct as amounting to a pseudo-Christ, and the Christians thereof as a pseudo-Christianity. Kierkegaard's voluminous writings were for the most part variations on a theme that sought to introduce *true Christianity* to a culture that for all practical purposes was without it. Kierkegaard's writings exhibit a progression of development, employing various literary tactics of indirect or direct communication. He moved from clandestine subtlety to cantankerous forwardness and ultimately sought to "sow discord in the coteries."[9] Kierkegaard's practical tactic in much of his mission was to disrupt the status quo's actual indifference to the true Christ, though the ultimate intention was

---

7. "The term 'Golden Age' designates a cultural phenomenon, namely a remarkable outpouring of artistic, scientific, literary, philosophical, and theological productivity within the compass of a relatively brief period of time, c. 1800–50, and largely within the confines of a single city, Copenhagen." Kirmmse, "Kierkegaard and the End," 28.

8. Backhouse, *A Single Life*, 253.

9. Kirmmse, "Kierkegaard and the End," 41. Kirmmse explains that "Kierkegaard began by searching for the 'idea' for which he was 'willing to live and die' and ended by attacking Mynster and the Established Church with an appeal over the heads of the Golden Age elite to 'the common man.' Between these two termini came Kierkegaard's 'education', his disillusionment with the 'coteries' who constituted the Danish Golden Age." (Kirmmse, 40.)

always for upbuilding, and especially for "the common man."[10] His overall method is clear in the following summary:

> When Christianity came into the world, it did not need to call attention (even though it did so) to the fact that it was contrary to human nature and human understanding, for the world discovered that easily enough. But now that we are on intimate terms with Christianity, we must awaken the collision. The possibility of offense must again be preached to life. Only the possibility of offense (the antidote to the apologists' sleeping potion) is able to waken those who have fallen asleep, is able to break the spell so that Christianity is itself again.[11]

Kierkegaard thought that the world's natural offense at the paradoxes of Christianity was what preserved its authenticity. The more that Christendom's "apologists" successfully made the paradoxes more comfortable and less offensive, the more they transformed the awakening gospel into a "sleeping potion" for the masses. Hence Kierkegaard's conclusion for his time was that "One best becomes a Christian—without "Christianity."[12] In sum, Christendom's attempt to contain the gospel's new wine in their old wineskin, resulted in the destruction of the wine (Mark 2:22).

MARK'S "ATTACK ON CHRISTENDOM"

This heading is obviously anachronistic, but purposefully so to consider whether Mark wrote with a purpose of challenging or critiquing his current sociopolitical situation. David Garland, commenting on something we noted in the previous section on God's calling Israel to the wilderness, says this: "Mark's account of the beginning starts in the wilderness, on the fringe of civilized existence that is alien to human habitation, *not* in the holy temple in Jerusalem, as in Luke."[13] This possibly indicates that Mark's Gospel was not as concerned with pointing out the gospel's continuity with Israel's expectations as with discontinuity. Hence, Mark's "chaos cinema" of disruption. Of course, Mark does begin his Gospel with Isaiah's prophecy of Messiah's coming as fulfilled in Jesus of Nazareth (Mark 1:2–3). Nevertheless, discontinuity was

---

10. Bukdahl writes of Kierkegaard's *attack,* "The only remaining task was to explode the church for the sake of the common man." Bukdahl, *Soren Kierkegaard,* 115.

11. As cited in Kierkegaard, PSW, 167. Note that the excerpt is from Kierkegaard's book called "Works of Love"—showing his ultimate purpose always being for upbuilding (edification).

12. Kierkegaard, PSW, 210.

13. Garland, *Theology of Mark,* 207.

perhaps Mark's major chord of the gospel because of Israel's expectations. Wright shows how Mark's "new-style apocalypse" was discontinuous with the then-current expectations and was thus subversive of those, *because* there was paradox in their manner of fulfillment.[14] He writes,

> Like Elisha at Dothan, Mark intends to draw back the veil for a moment, allowing the heavenly reality to be seen in the midst of the earthly. Mark has told the story of Jesus in such a way as to say: the glorious expectation of Israel, as expressed in just these Jewish writings and traditions, has been fulfilled, *paradoxically*, in the death and resurrection of Jesus, and is to be further fulfilled (or, perhaps, has recently been further fulfilled) in the destruction of Jerusalem. The gospel *subverts the normal* Jewish apocalyptic tellings of Israel's story, not by renouncing the ideas and literary modes of apocalyptic, but by redirecting its central thrust. Jerusalem is the great city that has opposed the true people of Israel's God; like Babylon, this city will fall as the sign of liberation of that true people. The suffering righteous ones who hold on to their God-given calling and are vindicated in the great reversal are not those who rely on the intensification of Torah, but are quite simply Jesus *and his people*.[15]

So, Mark's Gospel most likely supports the view that he wrote to support the paradoxical nature of the Gospel, which thus became an offense to those that did not accept this manner of fulfillment which to their traditional understandings amounted to non-fulfillment. But we must emphasize that the paradoxes of the gospel were not merely about doctrine, for they had very real-life consequences for believers and unbelievers, as Wright historically describes above. For Christ was the catalyst of a great apocalyptic conflagration, spelled out more fully by Wright:

> The coming of the Kingdom does not mean the great vindication of Jerusalem, the glorification of the Temple, the real return from exile envisaged by the prophets and their faithful readers. It means, rather, the destruction of Jerusalem, the destruction of the Temple, and *the vindication of Jesus and his people*.[16]

What must be remembered is that these "destructions" and the "vindication" that Wright is discussing were the disintegration of the major social structures of their world, and the real-life fallout that would accompany

---

14. Wright, *New Testament*, 393.
15. Wright, *New Testament*, 393, (emphasis mine).
16. Wright, *New Testament*, 395, (emphasis mine, to demonstrate the vindication of the "mother and brethren" that do God's will.)

these things because of the alternate *anti-Christian* meanings the Jews and Romans would ascribe to these cataclysms. In short, the *Christian* paradoxes would not only prove to be offensive to those that didn't accept them, but they would also bring persecution and suffering to those that did. In sum, the paradoxical fulfillments of God's kingdom coming in Christ meant that Mark's gospel was what can only be considered by the existing socio-religious powers as a sort of "attack on Christendom" as qualified above.

THE FALLING OF CHRISTENDOM: EVERYONE SHALL HAVE AN OPINION ABOUT IT

So, moving forward again to Kierkegaard's day, he simply asked what price paradox then cost the "Christians" of Christendom? The truth was, little or none. Because somewhere along the way, Christianity, despite its paradoxical claims, had prevailed historically. After even more time it culminated in "Golden Age Denmark." In that process the paradoxes became "old hat." "The eternal God became a man . . . of course he did!" "Jesus of Nazareth is the Son of God . . . of course he is!" "Jesus' death on the cross was not a scandal, but salvation . . . of course!" In response Kierkegaard thought that the only way Christianity could be recovered, was for the offense of the faith to return. But in the meantime,

> Everything became as simple as pulling on one's socks—naturally, for in that way Christianity has become paganism. There is in Christendom an everlasting Sunday babbling about Christianity's glorious and priceless truths, its gentle consolation, but, of course, one bears in mind that it is eighteen hundred years since Christ lived. The sign of offense and object of faith has become the most fabulous of all fabulous characters, a divine Mr. Goodman.[17]

What we must now recognize, as we move to the text of this chapter, is that Christendom fell from its lofty height. The paradoxes of the faith came back with a vengeance because of the growing "rationalism." But this only meant that the gospel could sound more primitively to the ears of its hearers. Given the events recorded in Mark 1:9–11, we should expect no less. For Jesus did not come from the unconventional Nazareth of Galilee, so that convention could prevail. Jesus did not pass through the deathly baptismal waters of the Jordan so that "gentle consolation" could be provided. The heavens were not ripped open—signaling God's divine penetration of the

---

17. Kierkegaard, PC, 35–36

human realm—so that worldly powers, whether social, political, religious, or philosophical could remain unchallenged. The Spirit didn't descend on Jesus so that humanity could remain unchanged. The voice from heaven didn't declare Jesus as "my beloved Son in whom I am well pleased" so that the alienation of all humankind, supported by its rationalism, could continue.

Kierkegaard summarized what these upheavals of the violent gospel meant: "everyone *shall* have an opinion about it."[18] We must note the strong emphasis of "shall." God was not merely presenting a survey for public opinion's sake. Rather, God intends to be the criterion of each person, and require either offense or faith. As the paradoxes are again recognized, and as the possibility of offense increases, *faith* becomes possible where it had been nearly impossible under Christendom and its "divine Mr. Goodman." Kierkegaard writes,

> And with this, Christianity begins, that is with making every man a single individual, an individual sinner; and here everything that heaven and earth can muster regarding the possibility of offense (God alone has control of that) is concentrated—and that is Christianity. Then Christianity says to each individual: You shall believe—that is, either you shall be offended or you shall believe. Not one word more; there is nothing more to add. "Now I have spoken," declares the God in heaven; "we shall discuss it again in eternity. In the meantime, you can do what you want to, but judgment is at hand."[19]

As the gospel is proclaimed, Christians will increasingly suffer the real-life fallout of the paradoxes of the apocalyptic cataclysm between humankind's "sacred canopies" and God's kingdom which collides with them. But Mark and Kierkegaard would proclaim the original gospel as heard in apostate Israel and wayward paganism, mingled with the possibility of offense:

> Woe to him, therefore, who preaches Christianity without the possibility of offense. Woe to the person who smoothly, flirtatiously, commandingly, convincingly preaches some soft, sweet something which is supposed to be Christianity! Woe to the person who makes miracles reasonable. Woe to the person who betrays and breaks the mystery of faith, distorts it into public wisdom, because he takes away the possibility of offense! Woe to the person who speaks of the mystery of the Atonement without detecting in it anything of the possibility of offense. Woe again to him who thinks God and Christianity are something for

---

18. Soren Kierkegaard, SUD, 130
19. Kierkegaard, SUD, 122.

study and discussion. Woe to every unfaithful steward who sits down and writes false proofs, winning friends for themselves and for Christianity by writing off the possibility of offense.[20]

Kierkegaard sets a very high standard, but it is one that must always be remembered. Christians may find it helpful in their witnessing efforts to proclaim that Christ was a great teacher. But learning "life lessons" from Christ does not remove the paradox of his person, though the desire to "understand" Jesus in that way is "natural" for all in our rationalistic age. It therefore becomes a temptation for believers to allow that "Divine Mr. Goodman" characterization to become too prominent in their witness of him. In *Mere Christianity* C.S. Lewis famously pointed out that many would love to see Jesus as perhaps the greatest of human teachers. But he pointed out that if Jesus were *only* human, his forgiving the sins of others as though he were in union with God would not be the characteristic of a great, wise, and humble teacher, but rather the declarations of a liar or lunatic.[21] In his book about Kierkegaard and other "societal outsiders," William Hubben reminds us that,

> Christ, claiming to be God and man, is the absolute paradox; he is eternal truth coming into being in time . . . he is a 'sign of contradiction' as are his parables and miracles, and, finally, he is as much an offense to our logic as he was unacceptable to his contemporaries. Belief alone can comprehend the paradox, an attitude that will risk an experiment in living.[22]

The paradox of Christ especially pervades Mark 1:9–11, although this is but the introduction of Jesus the Christ. His paradox will be further "fleshed" out and its sociopolitical "fallout" will become inescapable as Mark's narrative proceeds.

Part of the paradox is that Jesus was himself baptized, although Mark calls less attention to it than Matthew does (Matt. 3:14–15). It seems likely that this indicated the solidarity of Jesus with all the "baptized," through that only opens a further paradox in the fact that though only some consciously submit to God's call to baptism, all of humanity was baptized into the death of Christ (2 Cor 5:14).

Another paradox is that in the baptism of Jesus *the moment* had arrived, the point in time when God's eternity and human temporality intersect. This moment reenacted an earlier one, temporal Israel's passing

---

20. Cited in Kierkegaard, PSW, 167.
21. See Lewis, *Mere Christianity*, 40–41.
22. Hubben, *Dostoevsky, Kierkegaard, Nietzsche*, 21.

through the waters to inherit eternal God's promise. Mark's original hearers were undoubtedly encouraged through the baptismal accounts to be baptized themselves. Their own passing through the waters would signify that, left behind, on the far riverbank of the waste-place wilderness, remained the desolate "holy" temple and city of the Jews (Matt 23:38). Those ruins testified to the dashed expectations of worn-out wineskins that would not, and therefore could not, receive the new wine.[23] But Jesus, and those following him into his watery apocalyptic death, emerged unto the Father in heaven's declaration of filial love, the Holy Spirit's abiding descent, and to fulfilled human life that was previously "what no eye has seen, nor ear heard, nor the heart of man imagined" (1 Cor 2:9, ESV).

GOD'S EARNESTNESS: EVERYONE SHALL HAVE AN OPINION ABOUT IT

Hearers of Mark in Kierkegaard's day, and present-day hearers, are always meant to see themselves in the mirror of Christ's baptism. In essence, Jesus was baptized, so that we *shall* have an opinion about it. Of course, that begs the bigger question, how shall *we* respond since Kierkegaard says that we must:

> No, when God does this, then this fact is the earnestness of existence. And, in turn, the earnestness in this earnestness is this: that everyone shall have an opinion about it.[24]

But God's earnestness does not merely call for response, but for the answering earnestness of our existence. God's "*shall*" brings us before him as our criterion, bringing us to the moment, the present as the synthesis of eternity and time, and thus brings us to what is most essentially ours in this moment: choice. Kierkegaard further explicates the significance of this gift of choice, writing that,

> A decision joins us to the eternal. It brings what is eternal into time. A decision raises us with a shock from the slumber of monotony. A decision breaks the magic spell of custom. A decision breaks the long row of weary thoughts. A decision pronounces its blessing upon even the weakest beginning, as long as it is a real beginning. Decision is the awakening to the eternal.[25]

---

23. Whether Mark's first hearers would see the temple and city as *near* destruction or *now* destroyed of course depends on the date that Mark's Gospel was written, whether before or after "The Jewish War" of 66-70AD.

24. Kierkegaard, SUD, 130

25. Kierkegaard, PSW, 3.

4

Temptation as Our Problem and Christ as Our Prototype

Mark 1:12–13 (ESV) 12 The Spirit immediately drove him out into the wilderness. 13 And he was in the wilderness forty days, being tempted by Satan. And he was with the wild animals, and the angels were ministering to him.

"I am wondering," said the woman's voice, "whether all the people of your world have the habit of talking about the same thing more than once. I have said already that we are forbidden to dwell on the Fixed Land. Why do you not talk of something else or stop talking?"

Because this forbidding is such a strange one," said the man's voice.[1]

C.S. LEWIS AND SOREN KIERKEGAARD: TEMPTATION IN PERELANDRA AND EDEN

The short excerpt above narrates part of a lengthy conversation overheard by a man named Ransom, in the C. S. Lewis novel *Perelandra*. Perelandra

---

1. Lewis, *Perelandra*, 89.

(being Venus) is covered by the sea but has numerous bog-like "floating islands" and only one continent, called the "Fixed Land." The woman is "The Green Lady," a newly created "Eve" figure who is the Queen of Perelandra. The man is a scientist from Earth named Weston who traveled to Perelandra to further humankind's "inevitable" progress and perfection, which of course includes colonizing any inhabitable planets. The conversation is near the beginning stages of a sort of "forty-day temptation" of the woman, aimed at enticing her to transgress the command of "Maleldil" (God) to not stay overnight in the Fixed Land.

Unknowingly, Weston is serving as the serpent did in Eden, being the agent of Satan to tempt the Green Lady and then her husband (the King) to transgress the command of Maleldil. In the process of acting as Satan's agent, Weston had at this point become fully possessed and bestial, so that Ransom then calls him the "Un-man." Ransom, is the Christ-figure, brought to Perelandra from Earth through angelic transport to stop Weston and prevent this new humanoid race from sinning as the humans of Earth did. The husband/King is nowhere to be found during this period of temptation since the primeval couple had become separated due to the movements of the floating islands. What Lewis portrayed in this novel provides invaluable insight into the "psychology of anxiety, temptation, and sin." Several commentators discuss this scene, saying,

> Perelandra . . . has one inexorable law: no one is to remain overnight on the continent. The great temptation, then, is to seek an artificial permanence. How easy it would be to imagine that stability and security are found in life on the continent, rather than in Maleldil . . . In some ways, the Perelandrian temptation is one common to all—the desire to abandon God for a "false infinite" that can never fully satisfy. This temptation can be understood as making a permanent idol out of a temporary, merely present, understanding. No matter what one knows about anything, especially about God, it must be abandoned for a more robust understanding. The Un-man thinks his way is the ultimate way; to linger long on the continent is to make permanent what ought to be held loosely. Ransom's role on Perelandra is to fight for true permanence in God and against artificialities. He fights for triumph during temptation.[2]

So now, with those details filled in, we can focus on several things in the dialogue between the Green Lady and Weston:

---

2. Martindale et al., *Soul of C. S. Lewis*, 87–88

First, the "fixed land" is a wonderfully helpful metaphor for the permanence we seek but cannot attain as human beings. Lewis often spoke of humans as amphibians:

> Humans are amphibians . . . half spirit and half animal . . . as spirits they belong to the eternal world, but as animals they inhabit time. This means that while their spirit can be directed to an eternal object, their bodies, passions, and imaginations are in continual change, for to be in time, means to change. Their nearest approach to constancy, therefore, is undulation—the repeated return to a level from which they repeatedly fall back, a series of troughs and peaks.[3]

Kierkegaard had similar conceptions, and in major works on the subject presented humans as "an unfinished synthesis of the eternal and temporal, the infinite and the finite, soul and body."[4] Kierkegaard believed that the synthesis-existence of humans created anxiety, and that is the aspect of our being that Satan exploits toward sin. C. Stephen Evans clarifies this:

> Anxiety, for Kierkegaard is not the cause of sin, and it does not explain why human beings sin. However, it does explain why it is possible for human beings to sin. To understand this, we must focus on a special type of anxiety, which I shall call *fundamental anxiety* . . . Kierkegaard sees persons as fundamentally dependent on God, yet free to ground themselves in what is less than God. To turn from God is to turn away from being our true selves. Fundamental anxiety is awareness of the possibility of one's nothingness. It is an awareness that, though God has created me and endowed me with freedom, I can use this freedom to cut myself off from God and will my own destruction . . . I want to will my own independence and autonomy, even if it means my destruction.[5]

The Fixed Land is therefore an apt metaphor for humans' temptation to "ground themselves" in a "false infinite" rather than in the true God. And being faced with *possibility*, an unsecured "floating" existence causes "fundamental anxiety." The "fixed land" *temptation* versus the "floating islands" *reality* of finite creaturely life, of the ever-imaginative Lewis, helps provide an embedded "flesh and blood" context like the approaches of the pseudonymous "authors" Kierkegaard created to systematically deal with

---

3. Lewis, *The Screwtape Letters*, 45–46.
4. Evans, *Kierkegaard's Christian Psychology*, 69.
5. Evans, *Kierkegaard's Christian Psychology*, 61–62.

the anxiety of the human condition. Kierkegaard's psychologist/watchman "Vigilius Haufniensis" in *The Concept of Anxiety*, and the ethical/religious "Anti-Climacus" in *The Sickness Unto Death*" were two.[6] The literary similarities and indirect communications of C. S. Lewis make him an invaluable interlocutor for comparison with the same in Soren Kierkegaard.

Second, sin and temptation rely on *repetition* to break down the defenses against it. The Lady asks Weston why he keeps asking the same question. Of course, this explains the single-minded *relentlessness* of Weston on Perelandra, the serpent in Eden, and Satan in the wilderness. Mark emphasizes that Satan *continually* tempted Christ during these "forty days."

Third, the limitation of God's creatures to rationally comprehend the Creator's prohibitions makes them susceptible to temptation and sin. To accentuate this, Weston replies to the Lady that "this forbidding seems such a strange one." Mark decided not to present specific temptations as did Matthew and Luke, but those Gospels show that the idea of *reasonableness* played largely in Satan's barrage of questions. The implication throughout is the unreasonableness of the whole "wilderness" situation of apparent danger, impoverishment, unfreedom, and insecurity, and therefore the unreasonableness of God. And entertaining the suggestion of unreasonableness leads to suspicion and mistrust.

Fourth, temptation is something that all must go through, apparently because we are "unfinished creatures." Why didn't God "finish us" then? Probably that is the whole point of being humans endowed with freedom. We are given what Kierkegaard called "the dizziness of freedom."[7] But this is the possibility and opportunity for faith whereby through positive response to God's gracious provisions we become the selves we were created to become, *selves in relation to God,* which thus provide an alternative to a "Fixed Land."

The discussion so far has revealed four basic aspects of being tempted to disobey God, which may be summarized as: 1) how our fundamental human anxiety makes us susceptible to temptation; 2) how repetition serves to make it a continual part of our experience; 3) how Satan inflates our limited powers of reason to become a false standard that judges God and leads us to disobedience; and 4) our creaturely status as "unfinished" does not necessitate sin but rather is the opportunity for faith which unites us to our Creator who provides for our true needs.

---

6. See Watkin, *Historical Dictionary,* 401, 407.
7. Soren Kierkegaard, CA, 61.

TEMPTATION AS OUR PROBLEM AND CHRIST AS OUR PROTOTYPE

Now that we've considered some of the basic elements of the human experience of temptation, we can ask what can be gained by considering Christ's experience. Does his being tempted change anything about our being tempted?

First, we assume that Christ was fully human, and so it would not seem proper to believe that he was not tempted. The author of the Book of Hebrews confirms this assumption: *"For we do not have a high priest who is unable to sympathize with our weaknesses, but one who in every respect has been tempted as we are, yet without sin"* (4:15, ESV). That Christ suffered as a human *like us* means that the sympathy of our "high priest" toward our temptations is not merely due to God's sympathy, but to the actual human solidarity of Jesus with our human nature. Gregory Nazianzen wrote, "the unassumed is the unhealed," meaning that human nature had to be fully assumed by the incarnate Christ for us to be able to receive the help of God against temptation and sin.[8] In regard to the temptation of Jesus, all we can surmise from Mark's general, non-specific presentation, is that he was tempted "immediately," following Heaven's voice that he was the "beloved Son." This seems an affirmation that Jesus was God's *human* "Son," also confirmed as such in the mission immediately beginning in the wilderness, where he was tempted as, and because, he was fully *human*.

Second, Garland notes that the Spirit's descent on Jesus drives him into the desolate wilderness rather than bringing him to some place of sublime tranquility.[9] Henry Turlington points out that the Spirit's obvious "appointment" to this testing immediately following his baptism would provide encouragement to new Christians hearing Mark's gospel that may have been undergoing various trials and temptations.[10] This illustrates *human* solidarity between Christ and his followers in the very beginning of Christian experience. In baptism we are indeed baptized "into Christ" *because* Christ was "baptized" into 'Adam' (man).[11]

---

8. See Torrance, Incarnation, 62, 201. "The Christian church insisted that we must take very seriously the fact that in the incarnation, the holy Son of God assumed our fallen, enslaved human nature, our twisted, distorted, bent mind, *but* that in assuming it right from the very beginning our Lord converted it, healed it, and sanctified it in himself." Torrance, Atonement, 440.

9. Garland, Mark, 50.

10. Turlington, Mark, 270.

11. See Hebrews 2:14–18.

Third, Jesus being led into the wilderness obviously parallels the history of Israel as narrated in the Old Testament. The forty days may be an allusion to the forty years of wandering after the exodus of Israel from Egypt. This is another example of a correlation between the experience of Jesus and that of believers, seen beforehand in Israel's paradigmatic trials. Mark here parallels the use of the OT by Paul in 1 Cor 10:1–6, in which we should also note the emphasis on the temptation of Christ's followers in 10:11–13.

Fourth, all these points demonstrate that Christ is meant to be not merely the savior, but the "prototype" for Christians, a term that Kierkegaard used frequently in his explicitly Christian writings. Christopher Ben Simpson explains that Christ as our "Mediator of Truth in Existence" is manifested in two distinct portraits, one active and one passive, and provides this explanation:

> First, Christ is an active agent—the giver of Truth. As such, he is depicted as the teacher, the Gift or the savior. This portrait of Christ as the active Mediator of truth in Existence stresses divine activity in relation to the individual. Second, Christ is seen as a passive agent—as the model of Truth. As such, he is depicted as the Prototype, the Pattern, or the Exemplar. This portrait of Christ as the passive Mediator of Truth in Existence stresses the individual's activity in relation to Christ . . . These two portraits also show how the individual's response to Christ is both passive, insomuch as we receive and accept the gift of Christ, and active, insomuch as we respond to and imitate Christ.[12]

Fifth, Mark may well be depicting the temptation of Jesus in the wilderness as nearly continual since "he was in the wilderness forty days, *being tempted* by Satan." This would be another instance where Christ was tempted as we are, with a measure of repetition. Kierkegaard agrees with what Mark seems to imply, saying,

> His life from the very beginning is a story of temptation; it is not only one particular period in his life, the forty days, that is the story of temptation—no, his whole life is a story of temptation (just as it is also a story of suffering). Every moment of his life he is tempted—that is, he has this possibility in his power, to take his calling, his task, in vain. In the desert it is Satan who is the tempter; otherwise, it is the others who play the role of tempter, sometimes the people, sometimes the disciples; perhaps also at one time, especially at the beginning, the mighty tried to tempt him to secularize his calling, his task—and then, in one way

---

12. Simpson, *Truth is the Way*, 148.

or another, he would have become someone important in the world, king and ruler.[13]

The strong point that Kierkegaard makes here is perhaps shocking to many, but this begins to transform some of our ideas of how the temptation of Christ relates to our temptations. It seems that the commonly held view is just what Kierkegaard is critiquing, that Christ underwent a few episodes of temptation but overcame Satan such that temptation itself was halted for long periods of time. But most Christians that walk with some level of self-examination know that their experience with temptation is more continual than episodic. The recognition of the more continual nature of Christ's temptation will help Christians that feel as though they are not "overcoming" because they experience temptations.

Sixth, another factor is brought to our attention by Luke's closing comment to the wilderness episode, "And when the devil had ended every temptation, he departed from him until an opportune time (Luke 4:13, ESV). This would indicate two important things. First, that Satan seeks "opportune times," and, second, that as Lewis said, our "nearest approach to constancy" is "undulation" in repeated series of "troughs and peaks." These two observations seem to warrant the idea that Jesus also experienced "troughs and peaks" not only because of Satan, but because of circumstances in relation to his human nature, and even body chemistry that may play a part in human "undulations." This may not be the way we tend to think of Jesus, but perhaps we should ask ourselves why not. Jesus certainly experienced grief and sorrow as in Gethsemane and at the grave of his friend Lazarus, and if he could experience those strong emotions episodically why should we think it odd to think he did not also experience "undulation" as described by Lewis?

Seventh, partly returning to the first point, we must not overlook the positive purpose for which the Spirit drove Christ into the wilderness. God's purpose in allowing temptations is not to induce failure, but to produce what 1 Peter 1:7 calls the "genuineness of faith." We may not consider the occasions in the gospels when Jesus went off by himself for nights of prayer as akin to the wilderness experience, but they may well be "voluntary" examples of what are called spiritual "retreats" to which we are driven by the spirit of *earnestness*. Thus, "spiritual disciplines" are another human commonality between Christ and us that is important to realize as the basis for following him as our prototype. Kierkegaard also discussed the value of such experiences for anyone:

---

13. Kierkegaard, FSE/JFY, 58–59.

> When one or another extraordinary event occurs in life, when a world-historical hero gathers heroes about him and performs deeds of valor, when a crisis occurs and everything gains significance, then men want to have a part in it, because all of this is educative. But there is a simpler way in which one may become more thoroughly educated. Take the pupil of possibility, place him in the middle of the Jutland heath, where no event takes place or where the greatest event is a grouse flying up noisily, and he will experience everything more perfectly, more accurately, more thoroughly than the man who received the applause on the stage of world-history if that man was not educated by possibility.[14]

Kierkegaard's description of this "wilderness experience," and its potential for "upbuilding the solitary individual" seems to demonstrate the profitableness of Spirit-driven wilderness experiences such as those of Jesus, and that as our prototype this implies actual imitation of his *practice*.

Eighth, the Spirit driving Jesus into the wilderness as our prototype speaks strongly against the comfortable Christianity of Christendom, as discussed in chapter 3. Christ and his imitators are not driven to the wilderness in preparation for a return to leisurely and luxurious living, but in preparation for persevering in God's costly grace. What Dietrich Bonhoeffer, a well-known follower of our prototype wrote, holds true for disciples of every era: "Cheap grace is the mortal enemy of our church. Our struggle today is for costly grace."[15] And this "costly grace" is also pictured in the baptismal rite, which signifies the constant reality of Christian existence, that "all of us who have been baptized into Christ Jesus were baptized into his death?" (Romans 6:3, ESV.)

CHRISTIAN IDEALITY AND HONESTY: CHRIST AS OUR SAVIOR

To conclude this section on the problem of temptation and following Christ as prototype it is necessary to consider what Kierkegaard called Christian "ideality" or even "severity." This has to do with an important balance in Christian discipleship. Ideality is setting before one the "ideals" of following Christ. Naturally, Christ himself is the ideal, which is why he is the prototype. In fact, he is the only perfect prototype. But the question is, can we follow him perfectly? Kierkegaard often wrote in terms of ideality, and in

---

14. Kierkegaard, *CA*, 159.
15. Bonhoeffer, *Discipleship*, 43.

terms of what might be called "practicality," although it seems he preferred the term "honesty." He wrote "I am not Christian severity contrasted with Christian leniency. I am . . . mere human honesty."[16] It may be helpful to consider a few samples of ideality in Kierkegaard's writings, before then adding his comments on the relationship of ideality to imitation (of Christ the prototype):

> Each person must choose between God and the world . . . What immeasurable happiness is promised to the one who rightly chooses . . . If you can become absolutely obedient, then when you pray, "Lead us not into temptation" there will be no ambiguity in you, you will be undivided and single before God . . . But with the merest glimpse of wavering, Satan is strong and temptation is enticing, and keen-sighted is the evil one whose trap is called temptation and whose prey is called the human soul . . . But the person who surrenders absolutely to God, with no reservations, is absolutely safe . . . There is a tremendous danger in which we find ourselves by being human, a danger that consists in the fact that we are placed between two tremendous powers. The choice is left to us . . . Let us not forget this tremendous danger in which we exist. To forget is to have made your choice.[17]

If we consider all those statements and apply them to Christ, we can picture him as able to fulfill them. But when we look at ourselves, it seems if we are honest, we will come up short. Nevertheless, Kierkegaard believed it would be wrong to not proclaim ideality, for Christ is there as prototype so that we would strive to imitate him. But Kierkegaard also wrote to convey "honesty" so that the end result is a "dialectic" that holds two seemingly disparate things together in a tension. Most of us would simply call it a sort of balancing act. In his journal, Kierkegaard summarized:

> Yet it must be firmly maintained that Christ has not come to the world only to set an example [Exempel] for us. In that case we would have law and works-righteousness again. He comes to save us and to present the example. This example should humble us, teach us how infinitely far we are from resembling the ideal. When we humble ourselves, then Christ is pure compassion. And in our striving to approach the prototype [Forbilledet], the prototype itself is again our very help. It alternates; when you are striving, then he is the prototype; and when we stumble, lose courage, etc., then he is the love which helps us up, and then

---

16. Kierkegaard, LTK, 3.
17. Kierkegaard, PSW, 10–12.

he is the prototype again. It would be the most fearful anguish for a person if he understood Christ in such a way that he only became his prototype and now by his own efforts he would resemble the prototype.[18]

Temptation is indeed our problem, and Christ is our prototype, but lest we be tempted to despair, by ideality and honesty, Christ is simply our Savior.

---

18. Kierkegaard, JP, I:140, #334.

5

"The Moment" in the Fullness of Time

The Coming of Heaven and Earth

Mark 1:14–15

14 Now after John was arrested, Jesus came into Galilee, proclaiming the gospel of God, 15 and saying, "The time is fulfilled, and the kingdom of God is at hand; repent and believe in the gospel."

If . . . time and eternity touch each other, then it must be in time, and now we have come to the moment . . . Only with the moment does history begin.
—Vigilius Haufniensis[1]

A moment such as this must have a special name. Let us call it: "the fullness of time." —Johannes Climacus[2]

"GO TO HEAVEN" AND "DON'T LOOK DOWN"—"CRITIQUE OF HEAVEN" AND "CRITIQUE OF EARTH"

One of the chief characteristics of "the gospel" of American Evangelical Christianity, is its preoccupation with "going to heaven when you die." The

1. Kierkegaard, CA, 87, 89
2. Kierkegaard, PF, 18.

1980 album of the legendary American "psychedelic-rock" group, the Grateful Dead is titled "Go to Heaven." It depicts the group all smiles, cleaned-up and decked-out in white suits against a white background—presumably the clouds of heaven—as if to say they made it, now truly grateful dead. Guitarist Bob Weir appears to give some "knowing" sort of a thumbs up to the whole joke they all appear to be in on.

Perhaps "The Dead" had been previously inspired by the similar cover of The Ozark Mountain Daredevils' 1978 album "Don't Look Down" which portrays the eight-member "country-rock" group suspended in the "obscured by clouds" sky, precariously standing on a rope the outermost members are holding.[3] Something was definitely "in the air" in popular culture. It seemed that all time-honored beliefs were being challenged everywhere. Was "Go to Heaven" challenging the very idea of an afterlife, critiquing the televangelists capitalizing on "heaven," or viewing the evangelical preoccupation as irresponsible escapism?[4] Was "Don't Look Down" a questioning of the precarious epistemological thread that modern humans were standing upon? Were all meaning-giving meta-narratives, including those of heavenly or even earthly existence in danger of dropping out beneath us all? Were the Dead reading the Masters of Suspicion (Nietzsche, Marx, and Freud) or the Daredevils the French postmodernists?

For this chapter, we chose these album covers to illustrate a problem concerning popular conceptions of what domain of reality the gospel is concerned with. The Grateful Dead's cover seems to self-assuredly ooze a sentiment of skepticism, perhaps even of pessimism. I'm tempted to call it a "critique of heaven." The Daredevils' cover seems to also convey a skepticism, but with a more self-reflective pessimism. I'm tempted to call that a "critique of earth." I use this terminology for the following reason:

> "Heaven" has traditionally been held to be the main and, as has sometimes been falsely supposed, even the sole concern of theology. Conversely, many people have appeared to claim the earth for the non-theologians. My Lectures start from a different premise, namely that the "critique of heaven" is a central task for theology, and that a "critique of earth" is its necessary corollary. On both levels theology can and should accomplish its essentially critical task.[5]

---

3. I recommended that the reader find these album covers on the internet, because "a picture is worth a thousand words." The phrase "obscured by clouds" was the title of a 1972 album by Pink Floyd and may also signify epistemological obfuscation.

4. See on the "Gospel of Escapism" in Christman, *Gospel in the Dock*, 122–126, 244–251.

5. Van Leeuwen, *Critique of Heaven*, 6.

Therefore, my observations of these "slogans" are coming from that "critical" point of view. The Dead perhaps epitomizing the critique of heaven, with skepticism of its existence, or at least pessimism that its "spokespersons," especially the televangelists and religious/political leaders of the Right—with 1976 called "The Year of the Evangelical," knew as much about heaven and how to "get there" as they claimed. But it must also be said that their pessimism may have been of heaven as the "pie in the sky" that provides the oppressive ruling class with Marx's religious opiate that pacifies the lowly masses regarding their miserable lives in the here-and-now.

The Daredevils perhaps epitomized the critique of earth, with a slogan of blissful ignorance against looking down to see the reality that we stand upon an "epistemological rope"—providing the meaning of life—that we are holding up. The Dead's slogan may have critiqued the world-denying hopes of heaven that make it a false positive. The Daredevil's seems to critique the false positive of our earthly epistemological rope, our vain attempt to *autonomously* give meaning to our existential crisis—which is, as Kierkegaard liked to say, "out over 70,000 fathoms."

Thus, in both slogans, we could perhaps see either the *optimistic* struggle for opiate-less positive and meaningful life, or *pessimistically* see *nihilistic* surrender to the opiate-den humanity necessarily lives in. A compromise might be an *atheistic* existentialist decision to pull ourselves up by our bootstraps to "courageously" live against reality's meaningless face.

Or is it possible that the gospel of Christ, provides the true critique of false either/or "theologies"— *heaven or earth*—because it provides the true theology of *heaven and earth*? "Go to heaven" and "don't look down" are valid but limited critiques, because neither reveals the full problem, or the remedy of heaven *and* earth, to which we now turn.

"NOW AFTER JOHN WAS ARRESTED"— THE EARTHLY CONTEXT

"*Now after John was arrested . . .*" (Mark 1:14a) will begin to help us see that Mark's gospel is not primarily about "going to heaven." Some readers, knowing that John is eventually executed at a party by the spineless Herod might think it shows that "going to heaven" is what the gospel is about. But that is to allow Mark's gospel to be overridden by the reductive "theology" of "going to heaven." The simple remark of John's arrest points the way forward in the metaphysical scope of the narrative. For it is the first explicit reference to the nature of the actual sociopolitical situation in which the gospel arrived. John was arrested. No explanation is given, but Mark's economy of words speaks volumes. Was John saying or doing something wrong? Obviously, someone thinks so, but who? If this happened to John, might something similar happen to Jesus? Of course, the original hearers of Mark would already know what "the powers that be" did to John and Jesus and might do to them if they follow their lead. In any case, Mark is building the tension by hinting at the unspoken danger which reacts to Christ's own "violent" invasion of the present order of that particular space and time.

Kierkegaard considered the incarnation of Jesus—"the Word became flesh and dwelt among us" (John 1:14, ESV) —*as* the manifestation of God's earnestness, as seen in chapter 3 above. Mark portrayed such earnestness apocalyptically in 1:10 when the heavens were *"torn open"* (ESV) as the Spirit made his advance. The Spirit *descended* on Christ, *driving* him first to the *wilderness* to *battle* Satan, be "with the *wild* animals" and receive the *ministry* (service/ relief) of the Angels of heaven (see Acts 11:29—'*diakonia*'). The point is that God's "heavenly" earnestness was re-forming the earthly situation, moving into the earth through Christ and the Angels, even into the wilderness with the wild animals. Jesus battled Satan, the prince of the world, and John battled Herod, one of Satan's princes. Through such *invasion*, earth was becoming the dwelling place of God, through the incarnate God-man, Jesus.

"JESUS CAME INTO GALILEE"—THE EARTHLY DIVINE ACTION

The God-man Jesus was then driven to the "men from earth" by God's earnestness: *"Jesus came into Galilee, proclaiming the gospel of God, and saying, 'The time is fulfilled, and the kingdom of God is at hand'"* (Mark 1:14b-15).[6] We again see further movement from heaven to earth. Jesus comes into Galilee, proclaiming his message to the people, that what Isaiah foretold, recorded in Mark 1:2–3, was fulfilled. The kingdom of God was "at hand," at the very door. It should be obvious that the kingdom that was "at hand" *then and there* would not be fulfilled "in heaven." God's earnestness was heaven invading, fulfilling the kingdom on earth.

God's earnestness "fulfills the time," in "the fullness of time." That phrase, "the fullness of time," cited by Kierkegaard in this chapter's epigram, was coined by the apostle Paul. He was deeply immersed in understanding and communicating the significance of the life, death, resurrection, and ascension of Christ. Paul himself earnestly "laid hold" of God's earnestness that had "laid hold of him," leading him to spend his life for that

---

6. "Men From Earth" was a 1976 album by The Ozark Mountain Daredevils.

one purpose—God's earnestness for humanity (Phil 3:12). Therefore, Paul framed the gospel as God's movement *into* our earthly context *in Jesus*: "But when the fullness of time had come, God sent forth his Son, born of woman, born under the law, to redeem those who were under the law, so that we might receive adoption as sons." (Gal 4:4–5, ESV). If we were to summarize Paul's statement philosophically, it reveals that in and through Christ there was *an encounter* of the infinite with the finite, eternity with time, and freedom with necessity.

THE GOD-MAN "BRIDGED" THE POLARITIES OF HEAVEN AND EARTH, AND OF THE HUMAN BEING

This encounter between these opposite metaphysical poles should not be considered as an impersonal meeting. For Christ *is* the meeting of God's *personal* infinitude, eternality, and freedom with humanity's *personal* finitude, temporality, and necessity. What we must now try to see is why this meeting between these *opposite* poles, what Kierkegaard called "the infinite qualitative *distinction*" between God and man, was *possible*. Of course, "the God-man" is the key, for *God incarnate* is what happened "in the fullness of time" according to Paul. But we need to see *why* that provided the encounter. We must begin with Kierkegaard's definition of every person:

> "A human being is a synthesis of the infinite and the finite, of the temporal and the eternal, of freedom and necessity."[7]

We see in Kierkegaard's definition that Paul's coming of the kingdom of heaven in Christ in the fullness of time, which bridged the metaphysical poles between heaven and earth, *parallels* the needed bridging of the same poles within each individual person. We can therefore look at what happened in the fullness of time in two different ways. 1) Jesus, as the heavenly agent of the earthly kingdom, bridged the opposite poles of heaven and earth. 2) Jesus, as the God-man, bridged the opposite poles that human beings are.[8] The first demonstrates universal macrocosmic redemption, while the second demonstrates individual microcosmic redemption. And both exhibit the gospel's redemptive bridgings of *"the infinite and the finite, of the temporal and the eternal, of freedom and necessity,"* in "the fullness of time."

We need to bring these two bridgings back to our critique of the gospel as "going to heaven," a view that fails to bridge heaven and earth. To that end

---

7. Kierkegaard, SUD, 13.

8. Jacob's "ladder" of Genesis 28:12 is interesting to consider in relation to our subject here.

we posit a simple correlation between the macrocosmic proclamation of the kingdom of heaven arriving on earth and the microcosmic proclamation to "repent and believe in the gospel." In other words, Jesus is saying "align yourself—the synthesis of *your microcosm*—to the encounter of the "fullness of time," the arriving synthesis of *heaven and earth*." In many other parts of these readings, we will more fully consider how the synthesis achieved within Christ, the God-man, can be "communicated" to "synthesis-challenged" humans. But the overall point is that salvation is not leaving *our* synthesis or the *kingdom of God synthesis* of heaven and earth. We don't fully know what life will be like in "the resurrection," but we will be creatures, though of a new creation, fulfilling the synthesis that we already are, but which will then be fully united as it already is in Jesus the new 'adam' (Matt 22:30; 1 John 3:2; 1 Cor 15:47).

God's macrocosmic kingdom provides opportunity for microcosmic response to "the fullness of time," providing the "moment" to receive and willingly participate in the new, albeit apocalyptic arrangement of *heaven and earth*, as newly "adopted sons" who can find their maladjusted and warring "factions"— "the infinite and the finite, the temporal and the eternal, their freedom and necessity" redeemed in Christ. The old polarities dividing heaven and earth, and man's own being, find redemption in *the moment* of the macrocosmic/microcosmic apocalyptic Christ. Thus, the author of Hebrews writes of this ongoing moment,

> See that you do not refuse him who is speaking. For if they did not escape when they refused him who warned them on earth, much less will we escape if we reject him who warns from heaven. At that time his voice shook the earth, but now he has promised, "Yet once more I will shake not only the earth but also the heavens." This phrase, "Yet once more," indicates the removal of things that are shaken—that is, things that have been made—in order that the things that cannot be shaken may remain. Therefore, let us be grateful for receiving a kingdom that cannot be shaken, and thus let us offer to God acceptable worship, with reverence and awe, for our God is a consuming fire (Heb 12:25–29, ESV).

THE MOMENT IN THE FULLNESS OF TIME: THE COMING OF HEAVEN AND EARTH

To summarize this chapter, we will revisit its epigram from Kierkegaard:

> "If . . . time and eternity touch each other, then it must be in time, and now we have come to the moment . . . Only with the moment does history begin . . . A moment such as this must have a special name. Let us call it: 'the fullness of time.'"[9]

Kierkegaard follows Mark's lead, that if time and eternity are to meet, it must be in time: "after John was arrested . . . Jesus came into Galilee." At this point in Mark, we are only seeing the beginning of this meeting. But this meeting is "the moment" when "history begins," the fruition that requires "a special name"— "the fullness of time." What does Kierkegaard mean by this? It seems that the ever-subjective Kierkegaard is waxing existential here. There certainly was a space/time when and where Jesus came into Galilee, an objective historical time. But Kierkegaard seems to be emphasizing "the moment" wherein eternity and time touch for each individual. For Mark and Kierkegaard, and Jesus for that matter, that moment was *always* now: "The time is fulfilled, and the kingdom of God is at hand; repent and believe in the gospel."

Christ bridges the disparate elements of heaven and earth, and of the human being. But our stress has been on the fact that this has all occurred on earth, in the incarnate God-man Jesus the Christ, and one could even say the incarnation of heaven on earth in the arrival of the earthly kingdom of God. We therefore find a heaven/earth synthesis in world-history in the fulness of time. And we find a synthesis in Christ that fulfills our very being with a new becoming.

"Go to Heaven" and "Don't Look Down" provide valid critiques of Heaven, and Earth, when they are separated. But the gospel is of the uniting of *heaven and earth*, those poles outside of us and those within us. Thus, *everything* outside us and inside us calls us to this *meeting*, this *moment* in "the fullness of time" which is no *mere* moment.

> And now, the moment. A moment such as this is unique. To be sure, it is short and temporal, as the moment is; it is passing, as the moment is, past, as the moment is in the next moment, and yet it is decisive, and yet it is filled with the eternal. A moment such as this must have a special name. Let us call it: "*the fullness of time.*"[10]

---

9. Kierkegaard, CA, 87, 89; PF, 18.
10. Kierkegaard, PF, 18.

6

The Call to Contemporaneity with Jesus through the Middle Term of Death and the Dynamic of "Spirit"

Mark 1:16–20 (ESV)

16 Passing alongside the Sea of Galilee, he saw Simon and Andrew the brother of Simon casting a net into the sea, for they were fishermen. 17 And Jesus said to them, "Follow me, and I will make you become fishers of men." 18 And immediately they left their nets and followed him. 19 And going on a little farther, he saw James the son of Zebedee and John his brother, who were in their boat mending the nets. 20 And immediately he called them, and they left their father Zebedee in the boat with the hired servants and followed him.

Lord Jesus Christ, you who knew your fate beforehand and yet did not draw back, you who let yourself be born in poverty and lowliness and then, a sufferer, in poverty and lowliness carried the sin of the world until you, hated, forsaken, mocked, spat upon, finally even forsaken by God, bowed your head in that degrading death—but you lifted it again, you eternal victor, you did not conquer your enemies in life but in death conquered even death! Forever victorious,

you lifted your head again, you ascended one! Would that we might follow you!
—Soren Kierkegaard[1]

When Christ calls a man, he bids him come and die. —Dietrich Bonhoeffer[2]

Mark quickly moves from the preaching of Jesus in Galilee to his passing alongside its sea and his calling of four busy fishermen either actively fishing or mending their nets. Mark provides content to what "the moment" God orchestrates will bring to pass. So, we see Jesus saying to those upon whom the moment has come: *"follow me, and I will make you become fishers of men."* The emphasis is on the imperative, the call, even though the task or goal of "men-fishing" was stated. What that prospect could possibly mean is unexplained, and undoubtedly raised more unspoken questions in their minds than could be answered, even if they had taken the time to ponder it. Ironically, the content the moment reveals is without *particular* content. Dietrich Bonhoeffer aptly comments,

> What is said about the content of discipleship? Follow me, walk behind me! Going after him is something without specific content. It is truly not a program for one's life which would be sensible to implement . . . No further content is possible because Jesus is the only content. There is no other content besides Jesus. He himself is it.[3]

Bonhoeffer touches upon several of the most important aspects of this passage in Mark. The Christian life is centered upon a single-minded following of Christ. It is not a "sensible program" for one's life from a normal point of view. Christ is the only deliberation of following. But it is also important to note elements in Mark's account that present a "foreshadowing" of things that necessarily follow in the call to God's kingdom that collides with the kingdoms of man.[4]

---

1. Kierkegaard, FSE/JFY, 56.
2. Bonhoeffer, *Cost of Discipleship*, 89.
3. Bonhoeffer, *Discipleship*, 59.
4. ". . .Foreshadowing and retrospection are two ends of a thread or an earlier and later occurrence of a motif. They connect the narrative forward and backward: the foreshadowing anticipates an event that is coming; and when the event occurs, it recalls the earlier anticipation." Rhoads et al., *Mark As Story*, 49.

MARK'S FORESHADOWING OF WHAT DISCIPLESHIP BRINGS

Mark's motifs are woven into the "warp and woof" of his Gospel. Many are easy to miss, and when pointed out, may seem to be from the imagination of the person who "sees" them. Can every motif "seen" in Mark be proven? Probably not. But on the other hand, Mark certainly does use motifs, developing them through foreshadowing, repetition, and fruition. Therefore, the reader ought to be "suspicious" of Mark, whose compositional technique is seen by Wright as essentially "parabolic" and therefore requiring an attentive inquisitiveness.[5] So with these things in mind, we can consider one "reading" of the implications of Mark's account of Jesus "passing alongside the Sea of Galilee." Horne writes,

> In verse 10 we saw the Spirit descend upon Jesus as He came up from the banks of the Jordan. That same Spirit then drove him into the wilderness to be trained. The Holy Spirit, in a word, called Jesus. Now, Jesus, filled with the Holy Spirit, is the one who calls the disciples. They too are called from the shallows of the sea . . . The new creation is spreading. Just as the Spirit hovering over Jesus as He comes up from the waters hearkens back to Genesis 1:2, so we see now that the new creation continues with Jesus calling others from the water as Himself a life-giving Spirit.[6]

Imagination or implication? Mark would most likely reply, "*let the reader understand.*" So, following that lead, Mark's foreshadowing in the minor details of disciples leaving "their nets" and "their father" reveals that discipleship: 1) implies the primacy of Christ; 2) requires decisiveness; 3) brings a new occupation—or perhaps better a *preoccupation*; 4) relativizes all former values and relations; and 5) posits the *adoption* of "higher" values and new "familial" relations. Bonhoeffer observes what this "transvaluation of all values" means: "The disciple is thrown out of the relative security of life into complete insecurity . . . out of the foreseeable and calculable realm . . . into the completely unforeseeable, coincidental realm."[7]

---

5. Wright summarizes Mark's method with his parenthetical words in 13:14 "Let the reader understand," but which is linked to a theme of "understanding" throughout the gospel. See Wright, *New Testament*, 390–91.

6. Horne, *Victory According to Mark*, 39–40. Horne also points out that when Jesus calls Levi he is "sure to let us know that this too happened near the seashore" and that when Jesus chose the twelve, it was in the context of the mountain "by the sea." (See 2:13–14, 3:7, 13.)

7. Bonhoeffer, *Discipleship*, 58. I am using Nietzsche's term in a positive sense, whereas as he saw this as the Christian tactic, inherited from the Jews, which was the

So, these four fishermen simply answering the immediate call by following, when augmented by the foreshadowed implications, provides a sort of pictorial "shape" or framework of discipleship. But what are the nuts and bolts that hold the frame together? What is the "divine theory" of discipleship? Soren Kierkegaard provides a thorough account of what a disciple essentially is, and what is its inner dynamic. He held that there are essentially three factors of discipleship. The first is what he called "*contemporaneity with Christ*," the second concerns "*the middle term of discipleship*," and the third is "*spirit*." We will consider these three in order but with the second factor in two parts.

CONTEMPORANEITY WITH CHRIST

It goes without saying that to be a disciple of Jesus, one must be in some relation with him. The four fishermen were obviously contemporaries of Christ, but by *following* him they became contemporary with him in a more immediate and ultimate sense. Kierkegaard sees this as the essential shape of discipleship, necessary for "becoming a Christian." He writes,

> If you cannot prevail upon yourself to become a Christian in the situation of contemporaneity with him, or if he cannot move you and draw you to himself in the situation of contemporaneity, then you will never become a Christian.[8]

But how can one become *contemporary* with Jesus? It would seem we cannot because of our historical distance from him. But perhaps we may become "contemporary" with Christ because he was resurrected with a spiritual body and can therefore be with us, and we with him. That is true in one sense but misses what Kierkegaard meant. For him the key question was *which Christ* do we become contemporary with? The now glorified "lofty" Christ, or the earthly "lowly" life of Jesus. Kierkegaard saw the early life of Jesus as a "sacred history" which is not merely a part of the past, but something which is meant to become actual for us:

> Only the contemporary is actuality for me. That with which you are living simultaneously is actuality—for you. Thus, every human being is able to become contemporary only with the time inwhich he is living—and then with one more, with Christ's life

---

basis of the "dominant motive" of "ressentiment" of the "slave morality" of the "herdmen." See Kenny, *Philosophy in the Modern*, 237–239.

8. Kierkegaard, PC, 64.

upon the earth, for Christ's life upon the earth, the sacred history, stands alone by itself, outside history.⁹

Kierkegaard believed, in a manner of speaking for the sake of the shape of discipleship, that a true follower of Jesus' earthly life became *contemporary* with "the sacred history." He thought it the error of Christendom to concentrate on Christ as he became subsequently known in Christendom as the "God-man" and "Lord of Glory."

It does not seem that Kierkegaard commented on the similarity of this problem with one that Paul encountered in Corinth, namely, the self-designated "Apostles" who had apparently denied the necessity of costly discipleship in following the pattern of Jesus as Paul did, and which he thought essential for those of true faith (see 1 Cor 4:8–13). These spiritually advanced "kings" in Corinth seem to have had a type of "over-realized eschatology," although it's true nature is difficult to discern for lack of detail.[10] Whatever its precise nature, their errors at the least signify "uncritically perpetrating the norms and values of the pagan culture around them."[11]

In Kierkegaard's day, Danish Christendom consisted of the theoretical and practical denial of the necessity of discipleship after the pattern of Christ, and such "discipleship" was not merely the privilege of a small group as seems the case with Paul's "super-apostles," but was that of the masses. Therefore, Kierkegaard often referred to Christendom as paganism, or as even worse.[12] Kierkegaard speaks of their rejection of the very concept of discipleship, saying

> Imitation must be affirmed to press toward humility. This, quite simply, is how it is done. Everyone must be measured by the prototype, by the ideal. All this rubbish about its having been said only to the apostles and that it was intended only for the disciples, intended only for the first Christians, etc. etc. must go. Christ

---

9. Kierkegaard, PC, 64.

10. Fee surmises that their view of spirituality ". . . reflects an 'overrealized' eschatology. Paul's perspective, which he shares with the rest of the NT writers, is one of 'already but not yet' held in tension; theirs is one of 'already' with little room for the 'not yet.' Having received the Spirit, they have already arrived; for them spirituality means to have been transported into a whole new sphere of existence where they are 'above' the earthly, and especially 'fleshly,' existence of others." Fee, *First Epistle*, 172.

11. Hays, *First Corinthians*, 70.

12. "Even the consciousness of sin is not reached, and the only kinds of sins recognized are those that paganism also recognized—and life goes on happily in pagan peace of mind. By living in Christendom, however, men go beyond paganism, they go ahead and imagine that this peace of mind is—well, it cannot be otherwise in Christendom—consciousness of the forgiveness of sins, a notion that the clergy encourage the congregation to believe." Kierkegaard, SUD, 117.

wants admirers no more now than he did then, to say nothing of drivelers; he wants only disciples. The *disciple* is the criterion; imitation and Christ as the prototype must be affirmed.[13]

Kierkegaard saw contemporaneity with Christ as one's prototype, which would make "the disciple" the *criterion* for all Christians, as essential to all times this side of Jesus' return.

THE MIDDLE TERM OF DISCIPLESHIP

The middle term, simply put, is *death*. This includes, but is not limited to, actual physical death if that is required by following Christ's *life*. Thus, it more precisely signifies "death to self" or self-denial as the *means* between the goal of discipleship, and the disciple. At this point in Mark, the possibility of physical death is only *foreshadowed* in the uncertainty that accompanies "leaving the nets" of the former life. But that possibility may have been well-known by the hearers of Mark's gospel reading "after the fact" of the deaths of Jesus, the disciples, and others unknown to us.

"Death" as *the middle term* signifies the "placement" between following Jesus and self-denial. In other words, "death" is always *in-between* the gospel and any or all would-be disciples. Kierkegaard explains the term by saying,

> My listener, with regard to Christianity, there is nothing to which every person is by nature more inclined than to take it in vain. Neither is there anything that is at all Christian, not one single Christian qualification that by some slight modification, by removing some more specific middle term, does not become something entirely different, something about which one must say, "This has arisen in the heart of man"—and this is taken in vain. On the other hand, there is nothing against which Christianity has protected itself with greater vigilance and zeal than against being taken in vain. There is not one, not one Christian qualification into which Christianity does not first of all introduce the middle term: death, dying to [*at afdoc*]—in order to protect the essentially Christian from being taken in vain. It is said that "Christianity is gentle comfort, is this doctrine of the grounds of gentle comfort." Well it cannot be denied—that is, if you will first of all die, die to, but this is not so gentle![14]

---

13. Kierkegaard, FSE/JFY, 198–99.
14. Kierkegaard, FSE/JFY, 75–76.

Simply put, Kierkegaard contended that apart from accepting "the middle term," the would-be Christian's discipleship is "being taken in vain." Therefore, *the middle term* of "death" is *the given* that Christ's life is to be our pattern.

Kierkegaard believed it proper to view the entire life of Jesus as exemplifying the middle term of death. In a lengthy exposition of Matthew 7:14 called "Christ is the Way," Kierkegaard methodically and poignantly portrays the entire "narrow way" life of Christ in self-denial culminating in his death. Towards the beginning he says,

> Even if Christ had never said, "Strait is the gate and narrow is the way that leads to life," look at him and you see immediately: the way is narrow. But the fact that his life every single day, every hour, every moment expresses "the way of sorrow" is indeed a totally different continual and penetrating proclamation that the way is narrow than if his life had not expressed it and he had proclaimed a few times: the way is narrow. *Furthermore, you see here that the proclaiming of Christianity for a period of a half hour, by a man whose life every day, every hour of the day, every moment, expresses the opposite, is at the greatest possible distance from the true proclamation of Christianity.* Such a proclamation transforms Christianity into its very opposite.[15]

The reader will note that Kierkegaard contrasted the life of Christ with the "Christianity" of Danish Christendom. As always, Kierkegaard's proclamation of Christianity was aimed at what he saw as its nearly complete obverse. Kierkegaard's thought that the forgoing of contemporaneity with Jesus led to the loss of the *paradoxical* nature of the God-man and Christian life, and the possibility of offense arising from them. The pattern Jesus left for following began "in earnest" at his baptism when he chose God's narrow way that became increasingly narrower to the point of death. And this way *is narrow* because, in Bonhoeffer's words cited earlier, it does not exhibit, "*a program for one's life which would be sensible to implement.*" Sensible religion is the criterion for paganism, for the world. But Jesus (and Kierkegaard) thought otherwise:

> "Christianity is gentle comfort, is this doctrine of the grounds of gentle comfort." Well it cannot be denied—that is, if you will first of all die, die to, but this is not so gentle!"[16]

---

15. Kierkegaard, FSE/JFY, 57. (Emphasis mine.)
16. Kierkegaard, FSE/JFY, 76.

"Sensible" religion grasps after the consolations of "faith," but categorically rejects the middle term of discipleship. It stumbles over that rock of offense because it doubts the light side of the paradox. For the paradox is not that Christ and discipleship are *ways of death*. The paradox is that what *appear* to be ways of death are the ways of *life*. This is *"the open secret"* of the gospel—open because proclaimed in the light of day, secret because the many don't understand.

THE MIDDLE TERM OF DEATH: IS THERE A BRIGHT SIDE OF DEATH?

What then are some of the secrets of the light side of the paradox? Optimists in life say, "always look on the bright side of life." So, what might be the bright side of the middle term of death?

First and foremost, must be the fact that the narrow way is the way of love. Kierkegaard writes of Jesus "narrow way" that "*his whole life was nothing but an act of love.*"[17] It can easily be concluded that Jesus exemplified love, as portrayed in perhaps the greatest of Paul's writings, *1 Corinthians 13*, and in perhaps the greatest of Kierkegaard's writings, "*Works of Love.*" Those writings certainly portray the animating dynamic of the life of Jesus. M. Jamie Ferreira says that "Jesus Christ is the unique exemplar. The 'sheer action' that is Christian love was in Jesus."[18]

Second, the narrow way is ultimately the way to ascension. This is where the paradox becomes the greatest. This is because Kierkegaard sees the ascension of Christ to heaven following the resurrection as discontinuous with the cruciform life. In other words, the cruciform life does not logically lead to, or end in ascension, but rather it ends in death. Kierkegaard clarifies this by saying,

> Remember, the way was narrow until the end; death comes between—then follows the ascension. It is not at the midpoint on the way that he ascends to heaven; it is not even at the end of the way, because the way ends on the cross and in the grave. The Ascension is not a direct continuation of what went before, truly not.[19]

Third, the narrow way is not the way of doubt. Kierkegaard concludes his discussion by considering the paradox of the relation of doubt and giving

---

17. Kierkegaard, FSE/JFY, 60.
18. Ferreira, *Love's Grateful Striving*, 69.
19. Kierkegaard, FSE/JFY, 65.

one's life for Christ. He holds that life in the narrow way, *because* it required an inestimably *strong commitment* to it, essentially makes doubt fade away. This is indeed strong medicine for a doubting age such as ours, which has been especially on the increase since the modern "Enlightenment" period. Kierkegaard's basic thought regarding this plague of doubt is that it is precluded for those that will live in committed *imitation*. He believed that the *evidence* of Christianity lies in *imitation*."[20] Ironically, the Enlightenment brought doubt which "enlightened" humanity sought to refute with *reason*.[21] The error in this response was that the demonstration of the truth of Christianity was sought in human reason, rather than by *participation* in "the sacred history" of Christ's *lived* life. He explains how the tactic of "*offering reasons*" backfires, and *feeds* doubt rather than *kills* it.

> The demonstration of Christianity really lies in *imitation*. This was taken away. Then the need for "reasons" was felt, but these reasons, or that there are reasons, are already a kind of doubt—and thus doubt arose and lived on reasons. It was not observed that the more reasons one advances the more one nourishes doubt and the stronger it becomes, that offering doubt reasons in order to kill it is just like offering the tasty food it likes best of all to a hungry monster one wishes to eliminate. No, one must not offer reasons to doubt—at least if one's intention is to kill it—but one must do as Luther did, order it to shut its mouth and to keep quiet and offer no reasons.[22]

He then explains, whether convincingly or not, that *idleness* rather than *strenuousness* became characteristic of life in modernity, such that people could *play at things* like doubt. To explain this, he quotes Samson's riddle from the OT book of Judges: "out of the eater comes something to eat."[23] Kierkegaard is saying that the Ascension can only be removed from

---

20. Soren Kierkegaard, FSE/JFY, 69.

21. Newbigin more fully narrates this ironic outcome in *Proper Confidence*, 16–44.

22. Kierkegaard, FSE/JFY, 68. C. S. Lewis narrates how this psychological phenomenon that follows modernity's order of "making man the measure" affected him, saying: "I have found that nothing is more dangerous to one's own faith than the work of an apologist. No doctrine of that Faith seems to me so spectral, so unreal as one that I have just successfully defended in a public debate. For a moment, you see, it has seemed to rest on oneself: as a result, when you go away from that debate, it seems no stronger than a weak pillar. That is why we apologists take our lives into our hands and can be saved only by falling back continually from the web of our own argument, as from our intellectual counters, into the Reality—from Christian apologetics into Christ himself." Lewis, *God in the Dock*, 103.

23. See Judges 14:14.

the realm of doubt when one truly needs to do so. Surely this seems like a "Catch-22" type scenario. But he further presses his case:

> So, it is always with need in a human being: out of the eater comes something to eat; where there is need, it itself produces, as it were that which it needs. And the imitators truly needed his Ascension in order to endure the life they were leading— and therefore it is certain. But someone who sits in idleness and ease through the good days or is busily astir in busyness from morning to night but has never suffered anything for the sake of truth actually has no need. It is rather something he imagines or something he lets himself imagine for money as a curiosity— and so, of course, he doubts, since he has no need; or he invents some reasons, or someone else has kindness to hand him three reasons for—well, now, neither is that person's need especially great! And now you, my listener, what do you do? Do you doubt the Ascension? If so, then do as I do, say to yourself: No sense in making a fuss over that kind of doubt; I know very well its source and nature—namely, that I have coddled myself with respect to *imitation,* that my life is not exerted enough in this direction, that I have too easy a life, spare myself the dangers bound up with witnessing for truth and against untruth. Just do that![24]

It is interesting to note that Kierkegaard seems to be recognizing that the supposed acceptance of the "lofty" aspects of Christ by the subjects of lofty Christendom, such as the ascension, are not as certain as may be claimed. But again, he traces the source of the doubt more to the vacillations of the doubter than to the intellectual difficulties of the paradoxical God-man. And it is evident that Kierkegaard viewed the "theology of the cross" as the only sufficient answer in relation to both sources of doubt.[25]

SPIRIT: THE INTEGRAL DYNAMIC OF THE DISCIPLE

Underlying much of these thoughts of *commitment* and *imitation* lies the third and most integral element of discipleship, "*spirit*," which is the dynamic that accepts and "uses" the "middle term of death" to reach the goal of contemporaneous discipleship. In other words, the middle term creates and cultivates "spirit"- the essential quality of the disciple. "Spirit" was another sort of "middle term" to Kierkegaard, a "third" and necessary factor

---

24. Kierkegaard, FSE/JFY, 69.
25. See Forde, *On Being a Theologian,* 69–95.

of human personhood. He saw humans as "*a synthesis of the psychical and the physical; however, a synthesis is unthinkable if the two are not united by a third. This third is spirit.*"[26] Kierkegaard held that humans could live in "spiritlessness," an inadequate "too happy, too content . . . stagnation of spirit . . . too light-minded" non-response to life which becomes only "fate."[27]

What then is "spirit" positively, in contrast to that "spiritlessness?" First, "spirit" is not the Holy Spirit in man, though God undoubtedly relates to persons with their psyche and body through the "third" person of the Triune God. Second, "spirit" seems to indicate something like the will—perhaps something like "earnestness"—a favorite term of Kierkegaard's. Interestingly, C. S. Lewis presents a similar picture of the human as a trichotomous being. He writes,

> . . . the head rules the belly through the chest—the seat, as Alanus tells us, of Magnanimity—Sentiment—these are the indispensable liaison officers between cerebral man and visceral man.[28]

Lewis cites the Medieval theologian Alanus who frames the human triad as: head / "chest" / belly; and more specifically as cerebral man / "magnanimity"/ visceral man. It seems that Kierkegaard's middle term of spirit is in the same place as "the chest"—or "magnanimity"—perhaps demonstrating these terms as synonymous. Of course, Lewis saw "the chest" as inestimably important but tragically absent in modern man's *Abolition of Man*. For modern "education" has mass-produced "men without chests."[29] This modern "fall of man" is what Kierkegaard, a hundred years earlier, saw as the "spiritlessness" of the "mass-man." Lewis aptly describes this diagnosis:

> And all the time—such is the tragic-comedy of our situation—we continue to clamour for those very qualities we are rendering impossible. You can hardly open a periodical without coming across the statement that what our civilization needs is more 'drive,' or dynamism, or self-sacrifice, or 'creativity." In a sort of ghastly simplicity we remove the organ and demand the function. We make men without chests and expect of them virtue and enterprise. We laugh at honour and are shocked to find traitors in our midst. We castrate and bid the geldings be fruitful.[30]

---

26. Kierkegaard, CA, 43.
27. Kierkegaard, CA, 95–98.
28. Lewis, *Abolition of Man*, 34.
29. Lewis, *Abolition of Man*, 11–35.
30. Lewis, *Abolition of Man*, 35.

It is not difficult to see why "spirit" is the necessary human quality for a disciple of Christ, or why modernism's surgical removal of "spirit," well underway in Kierkegaard's day and rampant in Lewis', demonstrates that "discipleship" is perhaps *the* challenge that Christianity faces today. And that challenge can only be met by clearly proclaiming the requirement of "contemporaneity" with Christ's earthly life, the means of the "middle term of death," and the dynamic of "spirit" which meets the term and moves toward the goal.

Of course, none of this is easy. So, we will close the chapter with an encouragement from Kierkegaard which recognizes the difficulty of the situation, but nevertheless holds forth the way of "spirit" as overcoming the doubts the paradoxes present. I consider it to be "Kierkegaard's Wager"—much in the "spirit" of that of the great Blaise Pascal's from several centuries beforehand. It follows upon an excerpt cited above, some of which we recapitulate here:

> And now you, my listener, what do you do? Do you doubt the Ascension? If so, then do as I do, say to yourself: no sense in making a fuss over that kind of doubt; I know very well its source and nature—namely, that I have coddled myself with respect to imitation, that my life is not exerted enough in that direction, that I have too easy a life, spare myself the dangers bound up with witnessing for truth against untruth. Just do that! But above all do not become self-important by doubting; there is, I assure you, no basis for it either, since all such doubt is actually a self-indictment. No, make a confession to yourself and to God, and one of two things will happen—either you will be motivated to venture further out in the direction of imitation—and then certitude about the Ascension will probably come—or you will humble yourself, confess that you have coddled yourself . . . then you at least will not allow yourself to doubt . . . go out and become an imitator of Christ . . . only someone like that has a right to speak up—and none of these has doubted.[31]

---

31. Kierkegaard, FSE/JFY, 69–70.

7

"The First Day" in the Sacred History of the Contradiction

Foreshadows of Resistance and Faith, Fame and Infamy, Treason and Redemption

Mark 1:21–34 (ESV)

21 And they went into Capernaum, and immediately on the Sabbath he entered the synagogue and was teaching. 22 And they were astonished at his teaching, for he taught them as one who had authority, and not as the scribes. 23 And immediately there was in their synagogue a man with an unclean spirit. And he cried out, 24 "What have you to do with us, Jesus of Nazareth? Have you come to destroy us? I know who you are—the Holy One of God." 25 But Jesus rebuked him, saying, "Be silent, and come out of him!" 26 And the unclean spirit, convulsing him and crying out with a loud voice, came out of him. 27 And they were all amazed, so that they questioned among themselves, saying, "What is this? A new teaching with authority! He commands even the unclean spirits, and they obey him." 28 And at once his fame spread everywhere throughout all the surrounding region of Galilee. 29 And immediately he left the synagogue and entered the house of Simon and Andrew, with James and John. 30 Now Simon's mother-in-law lay ill with a fever, and immediately

they told him about her. 31 And he came and took her by the hand and lifted her up, and the fever left her, and she began to serve them. 32 That evening at sundown they brought to him all who were sick or oppressed by demons. 33 And the whole city was gathered together at the door. 34 And he healed many who were sick with various diseases, and cast out many demons. And he would not permit the demons to speak, because they knew him.

There is a surprising, and disconcerting, reticence in regard to Jesus. We don't figure Jesus out, we don't search Jesus out, we don't get Jesus on our terms. Jesus and the salvation that he embodied are not consumer items.
—Eugene Peterson[1]

The God-man is the sign of contradiction, and why? Because, replies Scripture, because he was to disclose the thoughts of hearts. Does all the modern thought about the speculative unity of God and man, all this that regards Christianity only as a teaching, does all this have the remotest resemblance to the essentially Christian? No, in the modern approach everything is made as direct as putting one's foot in a sock—and the Christian approach is the sign of contradiction that discloses the thoughts of hearts. —Soren Kierkegaard[2]

Soren Kierkegaard called the earthly life of Jesus "the sacred history." In Mark's frenetically paced focus on that history, we now come to the first *substantial* encounter of Jesus with people. What is interesting is the dearth of spoken words of Jesus. Examining a "red letter" Bible, one will find only six sentences spoken by Jesus in the first forty-five verses of our English translations. In comparison to the other gospel accounts, Mark's instances of Jesus speaking are the least in number and shortest in length. Mark, perhaps especially at the outset, seems most concerned to allow Jesus to be portrayed by his actions.

Why did Mark put the emphasis on the actions of Jesus in *the sacred history* of the unique person? It is probable that Mark intended to set Jesus apart from the many Greek philosophers that influenced Greco-Roman Culture through rationalism.[3] Therefore Mark basically bypassed our preeminent value of rationalism as wholly insufficient for recognizing who Jesus was. And in service of his emphasis, it seems that here at the outset of his

---

1. Peterson, *Christ Plays*, 183.
2. Soren Kierkegaard, PC, 126.
3. See Bruce, *New Testament History,* 41–55; Latourette, *History of Christianity*, 1:20–28.

gospel, Mark provides a "paradigmatic day" in the sacred history of Jesus.[4] This "day" patterns and foreshadows the entire gospel-communication of the *unique person* of Christ who requires *faith* that *excludes* mere "rational" response, as the pre-eminent divine/human agent of God's kingdom.

We will focus on the main aspects of this paradigmatic day by viewing them in relation to Jesus' own parable which "summarizes" his mission to Israel in Mark 12:1–12. This parable provides the following outline, 1) The Abrupt Arrival of the True Heir; 2) The Personal Authority of the Heir; 3) The Response of the Vineyard's Tenants.

THE ABRUPT ARRIVAL OF THE TRUE HEIR

Mark shows the arrival of Jesus to the human scene in immediacy. There is no beating around the bush for God's earnestness. Quoting the prophet Isaiah, John the baptizer had proclaimed to Israel that the coming Lord desired "straight paths." For Malachi had indeed previously declared to Israel that the One they were supposedly seeking was going to abruptly "*show up*" Mal 3:1–2).[5] So, here he is! And he "immediately" comes into the synagogue on the sabbath! He comes right to the center of Israelite religiosity, the synagogue. Granted, he did not come first to the representational center of Israel's religion, the Temple in Jerusalem. But the synagogue was the practical center of Jewish religious life.[6] This is especially fitting for Mark's immediate purpose here, to contrast Israel's "practical teaching" with that of Christ's.

This arrival of Jesus in the synagogue is paradigmatic of the prolonged "collision" that transpired throughout the ministry of Jesus. It foreshadows the imminent arrival of *the moment,* when God in his *earnestness* shows up as the true Son, the rightful heir of God's Israelite vineyard, and everyone *shall* have an opinion about it! The outcome of the opinion of the Israelite tenants of the vineyard appearance is not disclosed until Jesus presents *their* parable just before his death at *their* hands (Mark 12:1–11). At this beginning point, that "fate" is only foreshadowed. Regarding the results of the collision only now beginning, all turns upon the Son-as-heir being *the sign of contradiction*. And his "sign-ness" was not due to the philosophical content and wisdom of his teaching, but to the questions of who he was, the nature

---

4. Myers, *Binding the Strong Man,* 149.

5. Lewis writes, "For I am not sure, after all, whether one of the causes of our weak faith is not a secret wish that our faith should *not* be very strong. Is there some reservation in our minds? Some fear of what it might be like if our religion became *quite* real? C. S. Lewis, *Christian Reflections,* 43.

6. See Bruce, *New Testament History,* 143.

of God's kingdom, and the cross-shaped life of his followers. Kierkegaard explains the significance of "contradiction," saying, "*The God-man is the sign of contradiction, and why? Because, replies Scripture, because he was to disclose the thoughts of hearts.*"[7]

THE PERSONAL AUTHORITY OF THE HEIR

Of course, it was not immediately apparent that Jesus of Nazareth was the Son, the rightful heir. In fact, even though Malachi had predicted the coming of the Lord to their temple, this was not understood as signifying that Israel's God would come as the incarnate "God-man."[8] Jesus, the Heir of God's vineyard, appears at the first, to be a mere Rabbi—a teacher of Israel. But Mark intends to demonstrate that Jesus was a teacher unlike any other, ultimately pointing not so much to his teaching as though he merely brought a higher ethical system, but as the Heir of God's vineyard, and ultimately therefore of God's kingdom (1 Cor 15:24–28).[9]

So, beginning with what is more generally relatable to human custom, his teaching naturally includes the verbal *presentation* of intellectual content, although even here his manner rises to the higher level of *proclamation*. Nevertheless, Jesus taught *propositionally* about the Kingdom of God, which he saw as good *news* because it was no longer far off in the future but was now "*at hand*" (1:15). But even at this early point, his presentation was *astonishing* to those that heard (1:22). Gundry says that they were quite "knocked out" by his teaching, undoubtedly not expecting its power.[10] Their astonishment was due to their recognition of the "*authority*"

---

7. Kierkegaard, PC, 126.

8. Gerald Bray writes, "The Old Testament talked about the Word of God, the Spirit of God, and the Wisdom of God in ways that sounded personal, but the Jews understood those terms as poetic metaphors more than anything else." Bray, *God Has Spoken*, 34. Regarding Jewish expectations of a divine Messiah, N.T. Wright summarizes the evidence: "Certainly there is no reason to hypothesize any widespread belief that the coming Messiah would be anything other than an ordinary human being called by Israel's God to an extraordinary task." Wright, *New Testament*, 320.

9. Kierkegaard carefully distinguished Jesus as the ultimate *content* of Christian teaching which requires transcendent revelation to receive, and the Socratic method in which the teacher is merely a "midwife" for teaching content that is immanent to human experience and accessibility. PF and CUP are, respectively, about receiving the "teaching" of these two types of teachers.

10. Gundry's own translation is "awestruck." He explains: "'Were awestruck' translates a verb whose literal meaning is to be knocked out. Obviously, it carries a figurative meaning here, but a very strong one that underlines the authority with which Jesus taught." Gundry, *Mark*, Loc 328.

which accompanied his teaching. This was also something that surprised them since the usual scribal fare seems to have been "*without authority.*"[11] Gundry explains what particularly made the propositional teaching of Jesus authoritative, by pointing out the nature of Jesus' method which will be seen explicitly at a later point:

> In 7:1–13 Jesus will contrast God's commandment with scholarly tradition. This suggests that the scholars supported their teachings by citing the opinions of past scholars (as happens in rabbinic tradition). But here in chapter 1, Mark is content simply to pit Jesus' authoritative teaching against the unauthoritative teaching of scholars.[12]

In essence it seems that Mark's portrayal of the teaching method of Jesus parallels Matthew's where Jesus repeatedly declares "you have heard that it was said . . . but I say to you" (Matt 5:21–22 ESV). In other words, Jesus' teaching was not merely based in *an interpretation* of the old sayings, but in *his declaration* of new things. Jesus also declared present fulfillments of old predictions, as in Luke 4:21— "*Today this Scripture has been fulfilled in your hearing,*" and in his announcement of God's kingdom being "*at hand*" in Mark 1:15. Also, it must not be overlooked that the authority of Jesus was undoubtedly birthed in his complete dedication to the Father's will, being sealed at his baptism and confirmed in the wilderness temptations. His unwavering dedication set him on a collision course with the vineyard tenants of Israel because he wouldn't serve *them* as though it were *their* vineyard, even though he came to be "the servant of all" in *God's* vineyard (Mark 9:35, 10:45). But the coming collision is only foreshadowed here, and for the time being he is quite popular with this crowd in the synagogue.

Moving to the next aspect of his "new teaching," we find what was even more astonishing to them, namely his authority *as power* over the demons and sickness. This is also astonishing and *offensive* to modern hearers, because of our rationalistic anti-supernatural worldview. But remember that God's purpose is to remind us of our vocation as creatures in relation to our Creator, rather than continuing our charade as masters of our own fate. The intent is not to puzzle us as though our salvation depends on solving a cosmic riddle of "the God-man" we will never be able to comprehend, or

---

11. Ironically, Kierkegaard thought it important for there to be teaching that was "without authority," and presented much for edification under the rubrics of natural "icons of the natural world" that only speak silently of God's teaching. Of course, Jesus did the same. For an excellent treatment of Kierkegaard's method see Barnett, *From Despair to Faith*, 87–129.

12. Gundry, *Mark*, Loc 335.

even the riddle of our own selves, straddling "the infinite and the finite, . . . the temporal and the eternal . . . freedom and necessity."[13]

Mark denotes that this power is unleashed like a flood overcoming demonic powers, sicknesses, and diseases. *Immediately* in the synagogue appears a man "with an unclean spirit" which Jesus rebukes and exorcises. After leaving the synagogue and coming to the house of two of his disciples, he *immediately* heals Simon's mother-in-law. Subsequently, at sundown "the whole city" comes to their door and he "heals many" and "cast out many demons." It is worth noting that this paradigmatic day is framed with exorcisms of demons, and that their being qualified as "unclean spirits" signifies not merely a *raw power* of Jesus, but his *holy* power. The encounter of Jesus with Satan in the wilderness to test his holiness was only the beginning of the battle with demonic forces entrenched in the world. But as is seen, this hardly seems a battle, since the holy authority of Jesus is fully recognized by the demons, and fully unassailable as he casts them out. Of course, these "easy" victories are only possible because of the outcome of the first *difficult* battle in the wilderness and the final *most difficult* battle of the cross to come at the end, which is therefore foreshadowed here. It is also important to note that only the demons know that Jesus is "the Holy One of God" and that to them, even these early "skirmishes" signify the arrival of God's ultimate *earnestness*, paradoxically incarnate in the fully human Jesus of Nazareth who emptied himself of worldly power to obtain ultimate victory (Phil 2:6–11). Mark thereby explicitly shows that this conflict "in the heavenly realm," with the destiny of humankind hanging in the balance, has now overflowed into the earthly scene with the arrival of the Son, the *heir* of God's vineyard.

THE RESPONSE OF THE VINEYARD'S TENANTS

The "tragic" response of the tenants was already glimpsed in the reactions in the synagogue and at the house of Simon. It would steadily grow into a cosmic conflagration, casting "dark over the whole land" (Mark 15:33). The "chaos" to unfold was how salvation would come to the world.[14]

The magnitude of the conflict was foreshadowed in the powerful exorcisms of demons. For the opposition of the demons revealed their hidden entrenchment even in chosen Israel. That infiltration would soon be revealed when the demonic vapors would eventually rise to visibly inhabit

---

13. Kierkegaard, SUD, 13.

14. Speaking explicitly of Pauline theology Peter Leithart writes: "For many, the gospel Paul announces is no good news, it seems, but a threatening wave of chaos." Leithart, *Delivered From The Elements*, 42.

the treasonous tenants against the vineyard's rightful heir, Jesus. The cataclysmic was not yet because *their contradiction*—the heir—was still to be manifested. For now, the authority of the heir in a sense "aired" the demonic vapors, bringing to light the conflict to come in this first day of the new beginning, framed by the morn of the "sabbath" day (Mark 1:21) and the "sundown" of night (Mark 1:32). We might observe and conclude "and there was evening and morning, *the first day*" (Gen 1:5). Thus, the sacred history was encapsulated in a new-creational "first day."

As for more typical human responses in this paradigmatic day, we see *reasoning*, as those present "questioned among themselves, saying 'What is this?'" (1:27). Also seen is the *fame* of this wondrous Rabbi, which "spread everywhere" as the news of his activities was reported widely. The crowd is essentially flowing to him as it often does, toward what is new and novel. Of course, this was anything but novel, as lives were certainly being powerfully changed, at least regarding those suffering under demons and diseases. But in the shadows lurked *infamy*, because "the crowd" can easily become *the mob*. Mark *introduces* the crowd in a state of ambiguity *because* they were sure to change. Kierkegaard says,

> When Christianity came into the world, it did not need to call attention (even though it did so) to the fact that it was contrary to human nature and human understanding, for the world discovered that easily enough.[15]

Soon enough what is foreshadowed will become actual. But this is not merely a history lesson that Mark wants remembered. He is surely presenting a mirror in which his readers, crowds of sorts, might see themselves.

But there is one response Mark seems to focus on, that of Simon's mother-in-law. Jesus "*took her by the hand and lifted her up, and the fever left her, and she began to serve them*" *(1:30)*. Is this report merely to point out that Simon's mother-in-law acted like a mother-in-law? It seems more likely that Mark intends her to portray several things. Her "serving" probably foreshadows the gospel imperative that disciples are to follow Jesus in being "*the servant of all*," made plain later in 10:42–45. Also, it may foreshadow the motif of the "mother" and the "brethren"—the new "family" gathered around Jesus. This would be an especially important comfort to the early Christians in Mark's audience who in following Jesus had "*left house or brothers, or sisters or mother or father or children or lands, for my sake and the gospel*" (Mark 10:29). In essence Jesus, the four disciples, and now Simon's mother-in-law and whoever else was present as they ate, are probably

---

15. Kierkegaard, PSW, 167.

meant to foreshadow Jesus' new definition of *family*, to become normative in the kingdom of God.

The response of Simon's mother-in-law, being "singled out" by Mark, can also represent and foreshadow what Kierkegaard would consider "the single individual" who in *response* to God's grace leaves the crowd *by* exhibiting faith and love. Thus, in this paradigmatic day, Simon's home portrays the microcosmic church-home, the "home for the homeless"—to provide for the very real form of actual homelessness that can be presumed to be the experience of many in Mark's audience. As they are beaten and then (presumably) shunned from the synagogues, they find a home "nearby," just as Simon's house was nearby the synagogue and was already becoming Jesus' new "family" (See Mark 13:9).[16]

A "first day" of new creation, a paradigmatic day, foreshadowing what looms on the not so far-off horizon. War in the heavens was already growing intense in the unseen realm. Demonic raindrops threatened to germinate *the crisis* in the earthly vineyard of God and the heir. Yet that son arrived *full of grace*. Nevertheless, judgment accompanied him due to the recalcitrance of the tenants to serving the true heir.[17] The salvation of humanity lies in its confirmation by God that is received through atonement and forgiveness. But this "first day" as disclosed by Mark and Kierkegaard, reveals that when this salvation draws near, it becomes *the contradiction*—to those who would seize the vineyard that is not theirs. For it is only given to the heir because he would not serve them according to their plans, nor even his own as Gethsemane revealed, but only the will of the true owner.

> But since he draws the attention of all to himself, they of course might wish to try in the most diverse ways to win him over to their side, if he would only give up this exaggeration: to serve only one master.[18]

---

16. "The geographical and cultural diversity of the lands through which the Christian movement had spread, the social inferiority of the converts it had attracted, their possible economic deprivation, and the exclusivism required by the sectarian character of the movement of which they were a part were all contributing factors toward the predicament in which the addressees found themselves. . .." Elliott, *Home for the Homeless*, 101.

17. See John 1:14; 3:19; 9:39.

18. Soren Kierkegaard, FSE/JFY, 170.

8

Concluding Preface to "The First Day"

Glory in Solitude and the Glory Made Manifest

Mark 1:35–39 (KJV)

35 And in the morning, rising up a great while before day, he went out, and departed into a solitary place, and there prayed.

36 And Simon and they that were with him followed after him.

37 And when they had found him, they said unto him, All men seek for thee.

38 And he said unto them, Let us go into the next towns, that I may preach there also: for therefore came I forth.

39 And he preached in their synagogues throughout all Galilee, and cast out devils.

Looking over his shoulder he saw the whole island ablaze with blue, and across it and beyond it, even to the end of the world, his own enormous shadow. The sea, far calmer now than he had seen it yet, smoked towards heaven in huge dolomites and elephants of blue and purple vapour and a light wind, full of sweetness, lifted the hair on his forehead. The day was burning to death. Each moment the waters grew more level; something not far removed from silence began to be felt. He sat down cross-legged on the edge of the island, the desolate lord, it seemed, of this solemnity. For the first time it crossed his mind that he might have been sent to an uninhabited world, and the terror added, as it were, a razor-edge to all that profusion of pleasure. —C.S. Lewis[1]

O mad lover! It was not enough for you to take on our humanity. You had to die as well. Nor was death enough . . . You deep well of charity! It seems you are so madly in love with your creatures that you could not live without us. What could move you to such mercy? Not duty or any need, but only love. —Catherine of Sienna[2]

These words spake Jesus, and lifted up his eyes to heaven, and said, Father, the hour is come; glorify thy Son, that thy Son also may glorify thee . . . And I have declared unto them thy name, and will declare it: that the love wherewith thou hast loved me may be in them, and I in them . . . When Jesus had spoken these words, he went forth with his disciples over the brook Cedron, where was a garden, into the which he entered, and his disciples. —John 17:1, 26; 18:1 (KJV)

Now the unspeakable is like the murmuring of a brook. If you go buried in your own thoughts, if you are busy, then you do not notice it at all in passing. You are not aware that this murmuring exists. But if you stand still, then you discover it. And if you have discovered it, then you must stand still. And when you stand still, then it persuades you, then you must stop and listen attentively to it. And when you have stooped to listen to it, then it captures you. And when it has captured you, then you cannot break away from it, then you are overpowered. —Soren Kierkegaard[3]

In Mark's fast paced gospel of passionate activity, there appears to be little inactivity, although what little is shown is *passionate* "inactivity." In these early chapters of his Gospel, Mark allots merely one sentence, a brief interlude to the seemingly unceasing activity of Christ. But Mark's slim report, perhaps easily overlooked as a minor detail of the setting, is probably meant to reveal a repeated practice of Jesus (see Matt 6:6, 11; Luke 5:16). Mark conspicuously *highlights* this "spiritual retreat" by setting it in contrast to the "usual" frenetic pace of Jesus. Therefore Mark 1:21–34, which we saw as the paradigmatic day of Jesus, *includes* Jesus in solitude as an *essential* ingredient. For even more precisely, the scant episode reveals the vital but generally

---

1. C.S. Lewis, *Perelandra*, 38.
2. Cited in Macquarrie, *Two Worlds Are Ours*, 155.
3. Soren Kierkegaard, PH, 49.

unseen wellspring of *all* the days of Jesus. Soren Kierkegaard, speaking of this hidden wellspring of the deepest glory of being human writes,

> From whence comes love, where does it have its origin and its source; where is the place, its stronghold, from which it proceeds? Certainly, this place is hidden or is in that which is hidden. There is a place in a human being's most inward depths; from this place proceeds the life of love, for "from the heart proceeds life" . . . The hidden life of love is in the most inward depths, unfathomable, and still has an unfathomable relationship with the whole of existence. As the quiet lake is fed deep down by the flow of hidden springs, which no eye sees, so a human being's love is grounded, still more deeply, in God's love. If there were no spring at the bottom, if God were not love, then there would be neither a little lake nor man's love.[4]

It can safely be assumed that Jesus' life *in* the love of his Father flowed from those depths (John 17:26). Therefore, Jesus "*departing*" to the desolate hidden *place* of solitude and silence more accurately provides a glimpse of the *interior process* of Jesus, the inner workings of his soul.

Mark's Gospel later provides a fuller episode of the place of Jesus's wellspring in the expansive scene in the garden of Gethsemane, wherein he most deeply drank vitality from the source—the 'elan vital' of life. Interestingly, John's gospel finds it adequate to narrate that Jesus crossed over the brook Cedron and entered the garden, perhaps demonstrating that entrance to the *place* of glory—albeit now turned terrifying—was sufficient for the *passion* of Jesus to follow. For in that solitary garden Jesus *became* the desolate place. Even at the approach Jesus said, "*My soul is overwhelmed with sorrow to the point of death*" (Mark 14:34, NIV). But this was only one view of the place of glory for Jesus, though it had then become the place where the glory must fight for its "life" to overcome the threatening terror, the torturous death of the fallen world and God's wrath against its sin (Mark 14:41b; 2 Cor 5:21).

Yet we ought not think that his life entirely consisted in such conflict and sorrow, or that such a time overcame his vital relation to God (Mark 15:34, 37; cf. Luke 23:46). For the more "common" experience—the mundane *glory*—is what needs to be considered as the essence of Mark's first glimpse.

---

4. Soren Kierkegaard, WOL, 26, 27. Kierkegaard's allusion (in quotations) is to Proverbs 4:23.

THE GLORY OF BEING HUMAN

The first chapter epigram above, from C.S. Lewis, provides a glimpse of "*the glory of being human*" at a sunset.[5] It is a strange glory portrayed there, since it is an excerpt from the story of a fictitious Christ-figure named *Ransom* who had that day been transported by angelic means to the planet Venus. Up to that point his first day there had kept him occupied with "mundane" things like not drowning immediately upon landing in the planet's ocean, gaining "sea legs" for walking on the saving floating islands which rippled on the waves beneath, and foraging the bare necessities of water and food for continued survival. But at the end of the day, after he has surprisingly fared fairly well, he sees the alien sundown. And what happens portrays the imaginative genius of Lewis. He experiences "the glory of being human," millions of miles from his home.[6] That glory is not wholly dependent on "favorable" outward circumstances! Naturally, we all crave "security." But the first real lesson Ransom learns as he finds a respite of solitude following fairly dangerous and traumatic disorientation, is *the glory of being human*. In other words, he learned what Jesus knew, that the glory is *because* of being human in a world created by our Father. But the *sense* of that glory, needs to be guarded, rekindled, and preserved, because it is always under threat by circumstances, crowds, pain, and sorrow. That was why Jesus "went out, and departed *into a solitary place*, and there prayed," to maintain his vital *lifeline* to glory.

My reading of the meaning of the title of Terrence Malick's film "*The Thin Red Line*"— the red boundary line on a map that men war and kill and die over—is that it also signifies the vital and fragile lifeline, the "silver cord" of life (Eccl 12:6). There is one scene that seems to poignantly portray the glory of being human.[7] In that scene, Private Witt (played by Jim Caviezel) who also seems a sort of Christ figure, has selflessly volunteered for an especially dangerous scouting mission for the sake of his brothers in arms. Before long he discovers a large platoon of enemy soldiers quietly advancing down the wide but shallow river, heading directly toward the war-weary remnants of his own depleted platoon. Just as he begins to turn

---

5. "The Glory of Being Human" is the title of one of Kierkegaard's "Upbuilding Discourses." See Kierkegaard, SWK, ix.

6. He had graciously received some strong reminders of the glory earlier in the day, such as when he discovers he could drink from bladder type structures on the vegetation that contained drinkable and almost narcotically enhanced sea water for an exhilarating refreshment.

7. Malick's 1998 film portrays the lives of many different soldiers centered around one battle in the Guadalcanal Campaign during the Pacific Theatre of World War II.

back to warn them, he is detected and pursued. He frantically tries to make it back downstream to save his comrades. At one point, near exhaustion, he stumbles and collapses along the riverbank. Lying there on his back, the moment becomes suspended in time. Ironically, everything is infused with serenity. Looking up he sees the leaves basking in the warm sun and dancing by the gentle breeze, their branches exalted upward toward the bright blue sky above. A large group of bats silently hang from the leafy branches, silently looking back at him with their own large and wondrous eyes. Beneath him the sounds of the babbling water provide music for this scene of doxology. His eyes and face in response to all this plenitude portray *the glory of being human*. Though his death is probably imminent, he *knew* the glory of being human.

The odd incident from Lewis was also chosen for this meditation because Ransom's experience of glory was enhanced, just as the day had been enhanced, by the fact that "the day was burning to death." For Ransom the thought "crossed his mind that he might have been sent to an uninhabited world, and the terror added, as it were, a razor-edge to all that profusion of pleasure." Was this a prophecy that his days would soon burn to death? He had survived *one day* in this potentially uninhabited world. Was that survival a sign of his future, or an exception which at some point would be proven in death by some unknown terror. Yet, somehow, that did not mitigate, but rather sharpened, "all that profusion of pleasure" in the glory of being human.

Ransom, witnessing "the day burning to death" and perhaps also his own, knows "the profusion of pleasure" with a "razor-edge." Private Witt, facing probable immanent death, experienced the wondrous doxology of life. Jesus communed with the source of love in the desolate place that foreshadowed Gethsemane's dark night of his soul. All knew *the glory of being human*. The first two examples *are* fictitious, the third the reality of the God-man. But the imaginations of Lewis and Malick only portray what is the common grace of the glory of being human. Yet, that mundane glory requires "attention" to what Kierkegaard called *the unspeakable*.

The glory of being human is an essential fact of human existence. For that reason, the challenges disorientation presents to life do not remove that glory. Episodes of disorientation are rather a part of that glory. And if glory remains present even in such times of darkness and danger, it naturally also pervades the "normal" light of day. This points to the fact that the "normal" is, infused by God and the miraculous. Jesus called us to consider the glory of being human, seeing it through the everydayness of God's silent teachers, the lilies of the field and the birds of the air, whom Kierkegaard often considered as silent witnesses for God and the glory, speaking "without authority."[8] The call to consider them is the call from anxiety and cares, recognizing God's perpetual care, which simply *is*. Even in the moment a sparrow falls, God is there. For God exists for creatures only in the present moment. Forgetting this moment *when* God *is* and projecting ourselves into the *non-existent future*, only "*backfires*" on us, bringing anxiety into *the present*.

THE GLORY OF THE MOMENT

Kierkegaard saw the reality of "the moment" or "the instant" as of paramount importance for authentic and fulfilling human living. This was because humans commonly fall from living in the moment, and thereby fall into a world of "problems" additional to those already inherent in life. Basically, we "*invent ourselves*" many anxieties.[9] This is because we don't cherish, guard, and make the most of "the moment." In his book "The Concept of Anxiety," he says:

> If . . . time and eternity touch each other, then it must be in time, and now we have come to the moment. "The moment" is a figurative expression, and therefore it is not easy to deal with. However, it is a beautiful word to consider. Nothing is as swift as the blink of the eye, and yet it is commensurable with the content of the eternal.[10]

The importance of the moment is due to its brevity. It is here and gone literally in the blink of an eye. The significance of the moment is that it is the only point in history where time and eternity touch for temporal creatures such as we humans. That is why the moment must not become "lost" to us, because in a sense it is all we have. Kierkegaard believed that one of the greatest threats to the moment was speech. He explains,

> It is only by keeping silent that one meets the moment, and if one talks, if one merely says but one word, one misses the

---

8. Chris Barnett writes, "Kierkegaard makes clear from the start that the lilies and the birds are 'teachers,' but not of the usual sort. While human teachers instruct with words and confront their interlocutors, the lilies and the birds are silent. Persons look at them, but they direct their gaze elsewhere." Barnett adds that the lilies direct us to their passive reception of beauty as the key to the passive reception of the glory of being human: "Just by virtue of existing, regardless of any individual qualities or achievements, each human being is magnificent, wonderful." Barnett, *Despair to Faith*, 104–105.

9. See Kierkegaard's discourse, "The Anxieties We Invent Ourselves." Kierkegaard, SWK, 151–163.

10. Soren Kierkegaard, CA, 87.

moment. The moment exists only in silence. That is why it so rarely happens that human beings really get to understand when the moment has arrived, or how to make good use of it—because they cannot keep silent.[11]

The glory of being human is integrally related to recognizing and cherishing the glory of the moment. They go hand in hand, as do solitude and silence. They are the foundation of meaningful activity, without which our busy lives can be reduced to "knee-jerk" unthinking reactions dictated by circumstances, mere repetitions of the mundane without the glory. Solitude and silence are meant to be the spring from which flows the glory of life grounded in *the unspeakable*.

Jesus departed to the desolate place, not only for solitude and silence, but to pray. This shows that prayer, which *sometimes* includes speech, should not and need not disrupt the moment. Since the moment is *when* time and eternity meet, and God is the eternal, then breaking silence in speaking to God is not necessarily breaking the moment. But the prayer will need to be focused so that it is not creating future anxieties that draw us out of the present moment. The *wellspring* of life calls for a strength, namely faith, that the wellspring *is*, and prayer, to draw forth its vitality. Water of itself settles to the lowest point possible, due to its mass and gravity. But due to their geological placement, underground reservoirs of water will, because of their inherent physical potency, gush forth when given a course for movement. This is all a crude attempt to picture how prayer vitally connects us to God as our hidden wellspring, "constructing" the watercourse that channels the outflow from the depths—out into our visible world. And of course, this water is a symbol of the love of our God who is love and intends that love to come forth from God's hidden depths. This was the secret source of the life Jesus lived, and is meant through the Spirit to be ours also:

> On the last day of the feast, the great day, Jesus stood up and cried out, "If anyone thirsts, let him come to me and drink. Whoever believes in me, as the Scripture has said, 'Out of his heart will flow rivers of living water.'"[12]

The plain illustration of Jesus is undoubtedly better than all the attempts to describe the process, because it is the simple promise of the one "with authority," who no less pictorially, but more simply said what is required: thirst, faith, and drinking. And the "hangover" from this drinking will only be the constant flowing stream of "living water" which is

---

11. Kierkegaard, SWK, 188.
12. John 7:37–38; ESV.

presumably good for the one in whom it flows, and for the many to whom it flows. This is the way to "drink oneself sober" in which one does not "forget himself, drowning himself" but rather becomes "drunk" by the Spirit, as the apostles and others were at Pentecost (Acts 2:12–13).[13]

Mark composed his Gospel to include this easily overlooked but invaluable facet of Christ's life to encourage those who had chosen to follow Christ in the time of the Roman Empire. He wanted Christians to know the "secret" of the life of Jesus, being thereby strengthened in their hidden depths to persevere not only in the everydayness of their lives but also in the inevitable difficulties. He wanted them to *know* the glory of being human and follow Jesus' pattern of cultivating connection to the hidden place of God's love, drawing—so to speak—God's love from the wellspring to then overflow with God's healing waters for the nations.[14]

THE GLORY MADE MANIFEST

Simon and those with him found Jesus in the desolate place and informed him that "*everyone*" was looking for him. The answer of Jesus at first seems puzzling, that he intended to go elsewhere, *away* from those seeking him. But Mark shows that this was not an evasion of following God's will, since Jesus wanted to go to the other towns to fulfill his mission, saying "*for that is why I came out.*" Mark then reports that Jesus "*went throughout all Galilee, preaching in their synagogues and casting out demons.*" (Mark 1:39, ESV.)

But this short dialogue reveals something of great importance regarding the necessity of solitude and prayer. Apart from keeping the vital lifeline to God connected, through time apart from people, one will inevitably become directed by "the tyranny of others," the "urgent," and/or one's own self, rather than by the compulsion of God. C. S. Lewis said, "*The hardness of God is kinder than the softness of men, and His compulsion is our liberation.*"[15]

---

13. In his discourse "Becoming Sober" on 1 Peter 4:7, Kierkegaard wrote that "the secular mentality considers Christianity to be drunkenness and Christianity considers the secular mentality to be drunkenness." Kierkegaard, FSE/JFY, 96, 104–105.

14. Many Christians view their lives under a different metaphor wherein we are like water containers that are filled in times "alone with God" which then become emptied in pouring out that "water" in our times "away from God." Time "away from God" may be a bit of an exaggeration, but it is intended to make the point, that we tend to experience ourselves more as containers of water than as springs of water. The overall point of "the glory of being human" in relation to *times* of solitude and prayer is that the glory *always is*, just as the "spring" of *the Spirit always runs*. It is interesting that Paul's metaphors convey that what can hinder our being "*filled*" with the Spirit is "*quenching*" the Spirit (1 Thess 5:19).

15. Lewis, *Surprised by Joy*, 229.

This means that only the person compelled by God will be *free* from the bondage of serving herself, others, or circumstances, and thereby corrupt the nature of that "service" by such concessions. Sometimes human and divine concerns will coincide, but an "accidental" coincidence in this regard is obviously not the best way to "follow" God or ensure that one will not be following autonomous human desires. Jesus struck the correct balance because his connection with God was kept through solitude and prayer. He would indeed serve others, but as directed by God. Therefore, the "hardness" of Jesus in not catering to all human wishes was God's "kindness" to *them* (John 5:19–20). God's direction was also a kindness to Jesus, freeing him from following his own compulsion that could lead to selfishness or even self-destruction, which was perhaps what the Devil hoped to exploit in the wilderness temptations (Matt 4:1–11). Others-directed and self-directed "service" are idolatrous, depend on self-reliance, generally cause burnout, and do not accomplish God's will. Mark demonstrates this "tug-of-war" throughout his gospel as Jesus encounters various expectations, and ultimately shows that catering to them would only end in compromise and failure to achieve God's mission.

If speaking breaks silence and can thus potentially lose *the moment*, then it seems that the crowd is the most dangerous place regarding losing one's *sense* of God. But it's not merely the crowd noise. It is more-so the crowd pressure. Greater numbers seem to "promise" greater things, whether overpowering pressure or greater reward. Both gain traction by appealing to a person's desire for either safety or success, security, or power. The greater the number of people, the greater the temptation of losing one's wellspring and failing God's will (Matt 4:8–9).

But Jesus struck the balance between catering to the crowd and oneself, by actually "catering" to God's provision of the vital lifeline—*against* the crowd and the self—*for* the sake of the crowd and the self. For our God, the wellspring of love and life, is the one Catherine of Sienna rightly called "mad lover . . . deep well of charity!" God's love was not content to "live without us" and this is the love in which we find the glory in solitude, to be always counterbalanced by the glory made manifest. That is the love of our "spiritual director" whose kindness both constrains us against mere self-love and compels us in genuine love for others. And therefore, Jesus replied to Simon, "Let us go into the next towns, that I may preach there also, because for this purpose I have come forth" (Mark 1:38, NKJV).

It is especially important to stress that Jesus *came forth* as fully human. Only then can his earthly glories be fully seen as *the glory of being human*, and as the *prototype,* as Kierkegaard would say, for us. Baggett provides some invaluable insights in this regard:

> Jesus, as the revelation of what it means to be authentically human, demonstrated in his own life the possibilities for facing the reality of this world with honesty and courage. But Jesus did more than *face* reality. Jesus *embraced* reality. Reality was not simply "the way life is," those things he was up against in life and those circumstances that would ultimately take his life. Reality was "the way life is as *good*," as the gift of the Father . . . The goodness of God's creation was transparent to Jesus as one who perceived in his vision of reality the activity of the Spirit amid this world. Through the eyes of his own faith, grounded in his own most personal experience, Jesus could see signs of the Spirit all about him. When he saw flowers blooming in the field, or birds flying, or a lifeless sparrow on the ground, he was struck with the awesome reality of God's amazing care for each of his creatures . . . For Jesus, the presence and power of the Spirit in this world was something he perceived and experienced every day. And because he lived and moved and had his being in that reality, he could speak with great clarity not only about the things of this world, but also about the things that cannot be seen with the eyes of the flesh. And because he always viewed the reality of this world as a world loved by *Abba*, whose care for the creatures of the earth was constantly transparent, everything in this world was a window to the world of the Spirit.[16]

The glory of being human is part and parcel of being created by God. Jesus "coming forth" as fully human confirms this. The gospel brings "life more abundantly," the glory of being human (John 10:10). But human lostness can conclude that it must deny such glory, because in the core perversity of human be-ing, independence is craved. Deep down the creature knows that its glory can only be real if God is real. And so, to truly deny God, the creature must deny its own glory. G.K. Chesterton colorfully describes how this essentially *suicidal* denial of God and glory has become the underlying theme of modern humanity.

> Now, it has appeared to me unfair that humanity should be engaged perpetually in calling all those things bad which have been good enough to make other things better, in everlastingly kicking down the ladder by which it has climbed. It has appeared to me that progress should be something else besides a continual parricide; therefore, I have investigated the dust-heaps of humanity; and found treasures in all of them. I have found that humanity is not incidentally engaged, but eternally

---

16. Baggett, *Seeing Through The Eyes*, 344–45.

and systematically engaged, in throwing gold into the gutter and diamonds into the sea. I have found that every man is disposed to call the green leaf of the tree a little less green than it is, and the snow of Christmas a little less white than it is; therefore I have imagined that the main business of man, however humble, is defense.[17]

We can only follow such a diagnosis of humanity's response of *total recoil* from its own glory, by pointing again to the words of Jesus, *coming forth* from the Father in his earnestness as the incarnate beloved Son, and from the desolate place of solitude again *coming forth* to the disheveled and demonized crowd, the "mad lover" himself wholly possessed by *God's Spirit*, and saying: "for this purpose I have come forth"—for the glory of being human.

---

17. As cited in Belmonte, *Defiant Joy*, 42. I would like to thank a friend, Maretta Ernest, for pointing out this quote of Chesterton at the time that I was writing this section.

9

Mark's Leper and A Leper's Self-Contemplation

Jesus leprosus and the Gospel's Inversion of the Fortunate and the Unfortunate

Mark 1:40–45 (ESV)

40 And a leper came to him, imploring him, and kneeling said to him, "If you will, you can make me clean." 41 Moved with pity, he stretched out his hand and touched him and said to him, "I will; be clean." 42 And immediately the leprosy left him, and he was made clean. 43 And Jesus sternly charged him and sent him away at once, 44 and said to him, "See that you say nothing to anyone, but go, show yourself to the priest and offer for your cleansing what Moses commanded, for a proof to them." 45 But he went out and began to talk freely about it, and to spread the news, so that Jesus could no longer openly enter a town, but was out in desolate places, and people were coming to him from every quarter.

I am going to try to get rid of the gloomy thoughts and black moods that still live in me by writing something which will be called: A Leper's Self-Contemplation.
—Soren Kierkegaard[1]

1. Kierkegaard, SLW, 507.

Periissem nisi periissem [I would have perished had I not perished].
—J. G. Hamann[2]

Ah, stupid human language, who is entitled to compassion if not someone who is unfortunate, and yet it is the reverse, it is the unfortunate one who has compassion on the fortunate one. —Soren Kierkegaard[3]

Christ willed to be the socially insignificant one. —Soren Kierkegaard[4]

This section of Mark begins with the words "and a leper came to him." It seems that at one point in Kierkegaard's life, in answer to his constant "gloomy thoughts and black moods" a leper came before him. In this chapter we will juxtapose these two lepers to present a Kierkegaardian reading of this passage from Mark's gospel. We hope to show that both Mark and Kierkegaard presented the gospel significance of "a leper." It is interesting to note that though one wrote as an inspired apostle, and the other as a tortured poetic writer, both were enabled to write to pierce their reader's imaginations by encountering "a leper," namely their very own self. Perish the thought? Nay be enabled to embrace that "dark" thought. For there is life in the "perishing" that saves us from perishing in our gloomy thoughts, black moods, or the thought that we are simply fortunate—apart from first "becoming" a leper.

MARK'S FRAMEWORK FOR "A LEPER"

Mark's leper helps him develop themes he has already foreshadowed and will be implicit in this chapter's reading which largely will focus on Kierkegaard's leper. The theme of "the individual" was introduced by Mark as he "singled out" Simon's mother-in-law in 1:30–31. That theme was of course all-important to Kierkegaard. Here Mark greatly expands it as of great importance to his gospel also.[5] The theme of "touch"—we could say "a theology

---

2. Kierkegaard, SLW, 194. Kierkegaard says in his journal "*Periissem nisi periissem*" still is and will be my life motto. This is why I have been able to endure what long since would have killed someone else who was not dead." JP, VI:9, #6154. The Hong's write: "Possibly a reference to Kierkegaard's having learned late in June of Regine's engagement to Johan Frederik Schlegel." Hong & Hong, JP, V:520, n1005, cf. 236, #5666; 237, #5673.

3. Kierkegaard, SLW, 575.

4. Kierkegaard, PSW, 219.

5. Kierkegaard wrote, "*The single individual*"—*with this category the cause of Christ stands or falls.*" Kierkegaard, PSW, 309. Jesus himself was "the individual" par excellence, and it is only because he achieved true self-hood that God can give it to others.

of touching"—is also developed in this account. That theme was also introduced by Mark with Simon's mother-in-law, when Jesus "came and took her by the hand and lifted her up" (1:31). Jesus certainly had a "hands on" approach to ministry. In Mark's account of the leper this was not merely a method of healing but was deeply significant regarding Christ's holy ability to provide salvation by *touching* sinners whereas the OT laws for holiness (and health) in sum ministered "distance" (Heb 10:1–3). Worse, by the time of Jesus the law "norm" for "One Israel," that in *some* instances like leprosy required distance, had devolved into a system of "reality" that wholly *divided* Israelite society. For Israel's leaders for their own good systematized "distance" between the needy poor and the fortunate rich, far beyond what was necessary for health and holiness.[6]

The overarching theme of the identity of Jesus is of course also further developed. As an accompanying theme to that, we see in this account the explicit introduction of *holy subversion*: Jesus continually and *intentionally* bumps against "the system"—in this instance that of the priests—and *seeks* to subvert it.[7] Before this point in Mark this theme was only foreshadowed in the mention of John's arrest (1:14), and the emphasis on the drastically different and, to false authorities, "threatening" authority of Jesus, (1:22–26). That theme of holy subversion was also a theme of Kierkegaard's, leading one commentator to write of his creative writing, "every creative act is already a small destruction of the status quo."[8] We will now see why that was so with Kierkegaard.

"A LEPER'S SELF-CONTEMPLATION"

This literary gem of several pages lies hidden within Kierkegaard's massive 1845 book *Stages on Life's Way*, and is itself found within the largest part of that book called *"Guilty?"/ "Not Guilty?"*[9] *A Leper's Self-Contemplation* (hereafter ALSC) is certainly "a story of suffering," and aptly magnifies the subtitle of "Guilty?"/ "Not Guilty?" (185, hereafter GNG). For this reading, I will discuss ALSC under various headings that will serve to outline the complex narrative Kierkegaard has wittily penned.

---

6. See Kessler, *The Social History*, 28–29, 173–175.

7. Thus, Ched Myers describes Mark 1:40–2:15 as "Challenging the ideological hegemony of priest and scribe." Ched Myers, *Binding the Strong Man*, 152.

8. Solomon, *Continental Philosophy Since 1750*, 92.

9. Kierkegaard, SLW, 1, 185. In the remainder of this chapter the page references to GNG and SLW will generally be cited in the text above.

Before doing so, it is necessary to explicitly state that ALSC is both psychological and theological. This is implicit in the epigram—"I would have perished had I not perished." As is typical for Kierkegaard, most everything he presents is written dialectically, as though he had a sort of continual double vision. Thus, there is double meaning in "perish" which if taken literally would be nonsensical. The pseudonymous author, "Frater Taciturnus," states that ALSC is *psychological* because of his subtitle to GNG: "A Story of Suffering—An Imaginary Psychological Construction." But the real author, Kierkegaard, was writing what can be considered as "biblical psychology."

I propose this because Kierkegaard's 1845 *A Leper's Self-Contemplation* seems to thematically foreshadow the psychological/theological message of his 1849 *The Sickness Unto Death* which was subtitled "A Christian Psychological Exposition for Upbuilding and Awakening." In other words, in his contemplation, the social consequences of the leper's physical leprosy are meant to portray the struggle with "the sickness unto death." This does not mean that Kierkegaard belittles "real" sickness (or leprosy). What it means is that all "sicknesses" afflict their sufferers physically, socially, psychologically, and spiritually. The boundaries and battles "between" these domains overlap because of the physical/spiritual synthesis that humans simply are, though not always so simply. It is interesting that Kierkegaard's "preface" to GNG "geographically" describes a lake with terms of boundary and battle:

> The lake is not easy to approach, for it is surrounded by a rather wide stretch of quagmire. Here the boundary dispute between the lake and the land goes on night and day. There is something melancholy about this battle, of which, however, no trace of destruction gives any indication, for what the earth gradually wins from the lake is transformed into a smiling and exceedingly fertile meadow. Ah, but the poor lake that is disappearing in this way! (187).[10]

"I would have perished had I not perished." With Kierkegaard there is *always* more in the text than meets the eye. We hope to show why that's very instructive as we consider the multi-layered "self-contemplation" of Kierkegaard's leper. Therefore, in this reading we will need to keep track of several lines of meaning based in literal and figurative interpretations. The entire reading is based in the following basic premises.

---

10. Kierkegaard wrote of the "hidden," "quiet lake" of man's love which is fed by "the flow of hidden springs" of "God's love." One can't help wondering if this was "the poor lake that is disappearing" in Kierkegaard's perennial meditations on modern man's journey in the stages on life's way. See Kierkegaard, WOL, 27.

PREMISES FOR CONTEMPLATING "A LEPER'S SELF-CONTEMPLATION"

First, the topic of leprosy is amenable to both literal and figurative meanings, since the Scriptures often, though not without controversy, view leprosy as related to and reflective of the spiritual condition.[11]

Second, leprosy was an important biblical concern because it was a "sociocultural concern," not merely a biomedical one, since it was considered to be related to "communal integrity and holiness."[12]

Third, one could read double-meanings into many or most of Kierkegaard's writings, especially the pseudonymous ones. But he gives warrant to do so in ALSC by his admission that the reason he wrote the piece was *"to try to get rid of the gloomy thoughts and black moods that still live in me by writing something which will be called: A Leper's Self-Contemplation."*[13] Certainly this indicates that the leper's self-contemplation was Kierkegaard's.

Fourth, since ALSC is part of *Stages On Life's Way*, it figuratively "pictures" persons in aesthetic, ethical, and religious "stages" of human existence.

Fifth, real-life lepers are human beings who of necessity live in relation to life's "stages." Therefore, the literal and spiritual meanings ultimately find coherence in the overall "theological grammar" of leprosy. This will become more evident as we proceed and conclude.

With these preliminaries placed "on the table" we can now begin in earnest to contemplate *A Leper's Self-Contemplation* by considering a series of excerpts.[14]

"SIMON LEPROSUS WAS A JEW"[15]

Kierkegaard appends ALSC with that one "biographical" statement regarding Simon *leprosus*. We will see why this is vitally important as we consider this first excerpt:

---

11. "Various skin diseases with symptoms of rashes, scales, and sores, were plentiful. Those suffering from them were known as lepers, though the specific disease identified as leprosy in the modern world was rare." Baggett, *Seeing Through the Eyes*, 70.

12. Myers, *Binding the Strong Man*, 145.

13. Kierkegaard, SLW, 507.

14. Kierkegaard's "A Leper's Self-Contemplation" is merely one of a multitude of what could be called theatrical "stagings." The recent study of Hughes has demonstrated that this rhetorical method of "performance" so pervades Kierkegaard's authorship that it is the clue to the method and aim of the whole. See Hughes, Staging of Desire, 9–45. See also Simpson, *Truth is the Way*, 21.

15. Kierkegaard, SLW, 234.

> Simon! —Yes! —Simon! —Yes, who is calling? —Where are you Simon? —Here; with whom are you speaking? —With myself. Is it with yourself; how loathsome you are with your leprous skin, a plague upon all the living. Get away from me you abomination, flee out among the graves (ALSC, 232).

Kierkegaard starts by focusing on the name "Simon." What is interesting is the calling of his name in this soliloquy. "Who is calling" highlights the fact that Simon never *hears* the name Simon called. He is essentially *call-less* and *nameless*. Simon asks himself where he is. He is with himself, "away" from "the living" in a graveyard. He is *homeless* and without *community*. The implied question "Is it with yourself" highlights the fact that everything about his situation is perfectly justified, because he is a "loathsome . . . leprous . . . a plague . . . abomination." He is essentially *unclean*. The significance of all these things for "Simon *leprosus* . . . a Jew," is that he is for all practical purposes a *Gentile*. He was call-less, nameless, homeless, community-less, and unclean.

Simon seems to deliver his soliloquy while seated on a gravestone in *the wilderness*, his home is among the graves of the dead, who are his society. "Simon *leprosus* was a Jew" was Kierkegaard's ironic summation of Simon's Jewish identity, for he was an exile *from* Israel, *in* Israel. The statement was of negation rather than affirmation. Of course, all the elements that formed his non-identity are normally affirmed by being part of the Jewish community. Madeline L'Engle points out through the psalmist how integral community was to the Jews.

> In the Psalms . . . we often don't know whether the psalmist is talking of himself, or of the community. And for the psalmist there is very little difference. He is who he is because he belongs to the people chosen by God. Without his community, he has no identity.[16]

In sum, Simon leprosus the Jew was denied all the most essential characteristics of Jews. Kierkegaard's ALSC helps us to *begin* to understand the "desperation" of Mark's leper who *"came"* to Jesus, implored him, and knelt before him saying: "If you will, you can make me clean" Mark 1:40). The desperation, the "despair"—Kierkegaard's choice word in *The Sickness Unto Death*, runs very deep, as we shall see.[17]

---

16. Madeline L'Engle, *Irrational Season*, 157.

17. Hugh Pyper summarizes Kierkegaard's view of despair: "For Kierkegaard . . . despair is to be perpetually dying, to die and yet not to die, to die death. 'Life is death we're lengthy at,' wrote Emily Dickinson, in her own gnomic summary of this insight." Pyper, "Cities of the Dead," 131.

THE LAMENT OF SIMON LEPROSUS

> *Why must I fill the desert with my shrieking and keep company with wild animals and while away the time for them with my howling? This is no exclamation, this is a good question; I ask the one who himself said that it is not good for a person to be without companionship. Are these, then, my companions, are these the equals I am supposed to seek: the hungry monsters, or the dead, who are not afraid of being infected?* (ALSC, 233).

These initial pictures of Simon's manner of existence further enflesh the words we read of Mark's leper. Just as we need to see our own selves in "the mirror" of God's word, so also, we need to see other people in their real flesh and blood existence. Therefore, Kierkegaard calls us to see the leper through God's mirror and to stop *not seeing* him according to the limited views our society permits. For Godly empathy would teach us that Simon leprosus is a person whose only communications are shrieks and howlings to dead people, and wild "monsters" who were unsuitable for human companionship from the beginning (Gen 2:18–25).

We should note that Kierkegaard's unfulfilled life-long "love affair" with Regine Olsen was never far below the surface of many of his writings and is certainly showing itself here. That transparency reveals that Kierkegaard was voicing his own loneliness, despair, and unfaith, that contributed to the "gloomy thoughts and black moods" he was trying to exorcise in his "leper's self-contemplation." He confessed in his journal "If I had had faith, I would have stayed with Regine."[18] And since Kierkegaard held that the way to overcome despair was through faith, which we will explore more fully below, it follows that his lack of faith to marry only increased his despair and loneliness. Another allusion to Regine is probably hidden in the fact that he failed to marry *the one* who was "not afraid of being infected" by his melancholy, which further magnifies his regret. And talk about an even deeper allusion to the faith-relation to Christ, *the One* who cannot be infected by we lepers. The real-life analogies to Kierkegaard's life demonstrate the struggles common to man living between necessity and freedom, the temporal and the eternal, the finite and the infinite.

Therefore, Kierkegaard's leper, inhabiting a graveyard wilderness existence, speaks to our psychological, social, and spiritual realities—our existential realities. And until this day, the "age of anxiety" then being born has only exponentially increased and shows no signs of slowing down or even leveling. Perhaps Kierkegaard alludes to an unclean *fellowship of the infected*

---

18. Kierkegaard, JP: V: 233, #5664.

when he mentions his dead companions and wild equals, in comparison to Christendom's *fellowship of the fortunate*, the so-called non-infected. But it may be that true lepers "enjoyed" a sort of forced fellowship, as their quarantine cast the needy together where they *might* receive some physical provisions from society, but certainly no fellowship with society (see Num 5:2–3).[19] Thus we even see a "community" of ten lepers coming to Jesus in one gospel account (Luke 17:11–19).

SALVE

The self-contemplation of the leper takes a very interesting and abrupt turn at this point. It turns out that Simon has a companion after all, another leper named *Manasse*. But as we learn about him, he may be the alter-ego of Simon, the Mr. Hyde to Dr. Jekyll. Their diametrical difference is due to the way they would use the "salve" that Simon has created. So, we continue with another excerpt:

> *Where has Manasse gone? (With raised voice) Manasse! — (Is silent for a moment.) So he has gone off to the city, after all. Yes, I know. I concocted a salve by which all the mutilation turns inward so that no one can see it, and the priest must pronounce us healthy. I taught him to use it; I told him that the disease did not thereby terminate, that it turned it inward, and that one's breath could infect another so that he would become visibly leprous. That made him jubilant. He hates life; he curses men; he wants to have revenge. He runs off to the city; he is breathing poison on all of them. Manasse, Manasse, why did you give the devil a place in your soul—was it not enough that your body was leprous?* (ALSC, 233).

The story works well at the literal level, and much can be gained by considering it that way. The ingredients that contribute to its realism are the facts of the very real banishment of lepers from society and the resentment that can breed in the banished. If such a salve were "concocted" it could certainly have the different "applications" we see above. It seems that Simon's intent was deceptive but understandable. He would use it to hide the leprosy that prevented the priest's declaration that would enable his *careful* return to society, in which he would be *considerate* of the uninfected. But Manasse's use was downright diabolical, and he fully knew and delighted in that. He wanted "revenge" on those who banished him from life. He hated "life" as he knew it, to the point that he hated the normal lives of society

---

19. See Bock's comparison of the similar social treatment of lepers with AIDS patients. Bock, *Luke*, 101–102; 282.

and would be "jubilant" if they became infected and "died," just as he was "dead." It must be remembered that at some level, Manasse was hating them for their "cleanliness" regarding leprosy. The salve seems to be a way that Kierkegaard reveals the "soul-temptations" of envy, hatred, hostility, and alienation, that can ensue from the tragic situation of people like Mark's leper who were quarantined from society. It illustrates the spiritual trial of real-life lepers and points to the gravity of trials and temptations that "spiritual lepers" endure.

SIMON'S TEMPTATION, REPENTANCE, AND REDEMPTION, PART 1

The seminary-trained Kierkegaard would have been familiar with an important theological German word, "anfechtung," which signifies the overwhelming experience of *spiritual trial/temptation* which effects the entire psychical/physical person.[20] We have already seen the physical/spiritual trial that ALSC is illustrating. But it seems there is another dialectic embedded here. I believe it is probable that the salve that *differently* tempts ALSC's *two* lepers is meant to signify what tempts *one* Simon *leprosus,* who "Simon" and "Manasse" portray two sides of. And therefore, the salve reveals two different responses to the same trial/temptation and two different types of despair in either a Dr Jekyll or a Mr. Hyde. This is supported by that fact that Simon is repentant over the attitudes and actions of *Manasse*. "Dr. Jekyll" is content to use his science to gain the "normal" comforts of humanity and society, while "Mr. Hyde" is driven to the abnormal madness of antisocial revenge. Thus, it seems possible that Kierkegaard was portraying very different responses to the spiritual trial/temptation he was facing as a "leper" of sorts. There was also a greater question, not which of the two ways to choose, but whether it was possible to escape both ways.

Of course, the redemptive cleansing of *any* sort of leper was shown by Jesus: "*Moved with pity, he stretched out his hand and touched him and said to him, "I will; be clean." And immediately the leprosy left him, and he was made clean*" *(Mark 1:41–42).* To see how Simon leprosus, the Kierkegaardian "spiritual leper" was made clean, we must first consider his repentance over what Manasse "did" which in the story signifies the confession and repentance of Simon.

> *Manasse, Manasse, why did you give the devil a place in your soul—was it not enough that your body was leprous?* (ALSC, 233).

---

20. See Janz, *Westminster Handbook,* 1–5.

The greater spiritual temptation is here made explicit as a welcoming of *the demonic* to the inner person. Earlier I mentioned that "at some level, Manasse was hating the "normal people" for their "cleanliness" regarding leprosy. But note that Simon seems to "own" his leprosy as itself a "demonic" beginning, when he says, "was it not enough?" to simply *be* leprous. Kierkegaard is either repeating the view that leprosy was caused by sin, or simply showing his authorial hand by implying that the "leprosy" that Simon was speaking of *is* sin—the sickness unto death. The latter seems more likely. This perhaps shows how this story of the leper in "Guilty?"/ "Not Guilty?" fulfills its epigram: "I would have perished had I not perished." In other words, Simon evaded *the sickness unto death* by dying to *sin* altogether. He will throw away the source of his temptation of "not willing what is right," the falsely covering salve.[21]

> *I will throw away the rest of the salve so that I may never be tempted. God of Father Abraham, let me forget how it is prepared!* (ALSC, 233).

At this point we can consider the likelihood that the "salve" that covers the leprosy and turns it inward signifies the inadequate covering (or atonement) of "fig leaves," such as those Adam and Eve "concocted" to cover their nakedness (Gen 3:7). Thus, Simon leprosus, the Jew, was tempted to use his salve to abandon the faith of Abraham in two different ways: 1) To falsely cover his infection (sin) with his salve and be considered clean by the priest and his society to become "fortunate" again; or 2) To falsely cover but also more fully "employ" his infection to spread it and kill the "fortunates" who had oppressed him.

INTERLUDE: INTRODUCING THE CRITERION OF THE FORTUNATE AND THE UNFORTUNATE

At this point we need to note that there was one temptation that Simon had already overcome, if this "leprosy" is sin, namely, to deny it altogether. This reveals an important factor regarding Kierkegaard's situation. Kierkegaard admits that his sin is sin, as we saw above in his "owning" of his leprous body. He thereby distinguishes himself from "the fortunate"—which would be those in Christendom who were without a true knowledge of sin and therefore in "the despair that is ignorant of being in despair" (SUD, 42). Kierkegaard further explains that "most men are categorized by a dialectic

---

21. Kierkegaard, SUD, 95. Hereafter in this chapter the references will generally be cited in the text.

of indifference and live a life so far from the good (faith) that is almost too spiritless to be called sin—indeed, almost too spiritless to be called despair" (SUD, 101). Speaking of the criterion of God *and sin* he says, "what an infinite accent falls on the self by having God as the criterion!" (SUD, 79).

Therefore, it seems that the "fortunate" of society who are not "leprous" are those not *conscious* of sin, because they are without God as their criterion. This signifies that *they* are the *truly* leprous ones, and *they* are the *truly unfortunate*. This reveals Kierkegaard's inversion of the fortunate and the unfortunate which he develops forcefully, as we hope to show.

SIMON'S TEMPTATION, REPENTANCE, AND REDEMPTION, PART 2

We can now consider in more detail Simon's two temptations regarding the salve, by introducing a formula from *The Sickness Unto Death*.

> Sin is: *before God, or with the conception of God, in despair not to will to be oneself, or in despair to will to be oneself.* Thus sin is intensified weakness or intensified defiance: sin is the intensification of despair (SUD, 77).

This formula reveals two temptations that need to be overcome *after* having God as one's criterion and recognizing one's sin:

- The first is: *before God, or with the conception of God, in despair not to will to be oneself.*
- The second is: *before God, or with the conception of God . . . in despair to will to be oneself.*

The first temptation was of Simon *as Simon* and is as follows: Simon, *in despair*, did not will to be himself, a leper. This is shown by the fact that he concocted the salve to hide his leprosy. Again, this is the hiding of the self that Adam and Eve vainly attempted in the garden to cover their nakedness and shame. This is the despairing sin of "intensified weakness." So, the challenge this temptation presented to Simon was to "own" his leprosy rather than cover it with his salve. This would mean that he was willing to be an unfortunate. We saw above that he "passed" the test of this temptation when he said that he would "*throw away the rest of the salve so that I may never be tempted. God of Father Abraham, let me forget how it is prepared!*" (ALSC, 233).

The second temptation was of Simon *as Manasse* and is as follows. Manasse, in *despair*, willed to be himself, a leper. Because he willed this *in despair*, he desires to weaponize his leprosy against his adversaries, God's priest, and all the "fortunate" without need of the declaration of "cleanliness." Manasse's desire to thus use his leprosy was an aggravated sin of "intensified defiance," an increase of the demonic aspect of sin. Remember that the first level is merely sin, *as sin*, which Simon "owned" when he admitted that leprosy *itself* gave "enough" place to the devil. But this second level is sin as a *more fully realized defiance*.

These comparisons of ALSC and SUD seem to demonstrate a substantial degree of inner coherence that exists between them. This is interesting since SUD was written in 1849 while ALSC was written in 1845. It seems that the latter more realized formulations of despair and sin were foreshadowed in the earlier formulation. Kierkegaard in 1845 seemed to be trying to work these things out at the personal level, struggling with his own vicious cycle of sin and despair, and the temptation of using what he called salve. That struggle seems to have prepared him to write of its "theory" in 1849.

Before leaving SUD, we note another interesting correlation that perhaps reveals a dialectic regarding the "salve" of ALSC and something SUD calls "inclosing reserve." For Simon's salve that turns the infection *inward* seems much like the weak despair of not willing to be oneself, a sinner. Yet the *outward* hostility of Manasse seems much like the defiant despair that wills to be itself, a sinner. Therefore, the *infectious breath* seems to be an action based in the ironic *manifestation* of "inclosing reserve." So, perhaps there was a third temptation that is easy to miss because we see the either/or but miss the both/and. For the both/and is the struggle of being *both* Simon *and* Manasse in a confusion of persons, such as in the melancholy "boundary" battle we saw earlier with the lake. Thus, in Kierkegaard's description of the second temptation—in despair willing to be a sinner—there seems to be an unwillingness at the same time, which is the reason for the torment. Otherwise, why the complaint? The torment would be absorbed in the realization of pure evil *as good*. So possibly this is the both/and of willing despair but suffering torment that makes the sickness unto death become a hell.

In other words, and to summarize, perhaps the either/or dialectic of *either* Simon *or* Manasse reveals a deeper both/and dialectic: the melancholy border fluctuation between Simon and Manasse's question of having *both* delightful *and* remorseful torment. Did the suicidal Kierkegaard think he had experienced the ingredients of hell? It might well be possible, given the *"gloomy thoughts and black moods that still live in me"* which he was trying to "exorcise" by writing ALSC. In any case, here is Kierkegaard's summary of the hellish state for the reader to contemplate:

> But the more spiritual despair becomes, the more attention it pays with demonic cleverness to keeping despair closed up in inclosing reserve, and the more attention it pays to neutralizing the externalities, making them as insignificant and inconsequential as possible . . . to ensure having . . . a world *ex*-clusively for itself, a world where the self in despair is restlessly and tormentedly engaged in willing to be itself . . . Rebelling against all existence, it feels that it has obtained evidence against it, against its goodness. The person in despair believes that he himself is the evidence, and that is what he wants to be, and therefore he wants to be himself, himself in his torment, in order to protest against all existence with this torment (SUD 73–74).

Marius Timmann Mjalland summarizes SUD and perhaps shows how Kierkegaard's "gloomy thoughts and black moods" that birthed ALSC demonstrates the dialectical double despair of Simon/Manasse when he writes,

> . . . despair is profoundly *suicidal* in these two respects: (1) Despairingly not willing to be oneself, hence seeking to "rid himself of [*blive af med*] the relating himself," without being able to; and (2) in despair willing to be oneself, hence being incessantly occupied with oneself to the exclusion of otherness. Kierkegaard calls the latter "inclosing reserve," and this tendency is deeply rooted in despair—as it is in his understanding of suicide as mutinying against God." . . . Despair is an effort aimed at getting rid of oneself while not being able to get rid of oneself.[22]

This diagnosis of the double despair of Simon/Manasse reveals the one cure of this temptation common to "spiritual" lepers who are conscious of their leprosy (sin). As already mentioned, but not fully explained, the remedy is revealed in Kierkegaard's epigram to GNG "I would have perished had I not perished." Simon Podmore provides an excellent explanation of the dynamic in that cure which we will further relate to Simon leprosus just below.

> Kierkegaard's life motto can thus be read . . . First, the notion that it is via a metaphorical submission to "death" that the self will transcend the reach of absolute death. Secondly, that "dying to" is a *process,* which causes the self to be negated, to vanish, to become as nothing *before God.* And it is precisely by this "disappearing"—or by coming to what *The Sickness unto Death* calls a self-resting "transparently [*gjennemsigtigt*— 'see through'] in the power that established it" . . . that the self will not be

---

22. Mjaaland, "Suicide and Despair," 84–85.

"annihilated" before God, even though the thought of existing before God is fraught by the anxious prospect of the biblical injunction that to see God is to die (Exod. 33:20).[23]

As Simon, he is a leper who has "owned" his sin and realizes what that means before God. He is "*in despair*" to will to be himself—a leper—a sinner, before God, because that would mean that he could not see God without dying, as Podmore has stated. We saw earlier how Simon leprosus overcame this first aspect of temptation, denial, that the salve provided opportunity for.

As Manasse, he is a leper who has "owned" his sin and realizes what that means before God. He "*in despair*" wills to be himself —a leper—a sinner before God, so that he will defy the God who would "annihilate" him, to the point that he would annihilate God or himself in that despairing defiance. In short, he "*hates life; he curses men; he wants to have revenge*" and further gave "*the devil a place in his soul.*" Manasse is the *evangelistic* antitheist. Manasse is not merely "against all existence." He is more accurately against anything that does not conform to his view of existence. In other words, he embodies "Satan's monomaniacal quest for absolute individualism" that wills to "invent the universe out of the self."[24]

So how did Simon *leprosus* overcome both the crusading *Manasse* and the cowering *Simon*? We saw his repentance earlier when Simon repents over the salve he created and what Manasse has willed. And the faith that gave rise to his repentance becomes more explicit in the next words of his we will see. To understand where the faith came from, we must again remember that Kierkegaard's Simon was a *Jew*. Therefore, Jesus, who is willing to touch the leper, is intimated to Simon through *Father Abraham* who like Jesus is "not afraid of lepers."

> *Father Abraham, when I die, I shall awaken in your bosom; then I shall eat with the purest of the pure—you, after all, are not afraid of lepers. Isaac and Jacob, you are not afraid to sit at table with someone who was leprous and loathed by men.*

Ultimately Simon's faith was birthed from the compassion and love of God Simon intuited as Abraham's who thus "mediates" Christ's love to him.

In sum, God's love enabled Simon *leprosus* to overcome the uses of the "salve" by the anti-human *Manasse* and the false-human *Simon*. The love of God made a way that enabled him to "perish"—to the double-despairs of weakly *not willing* and defiantly *willing* to be one's leprous self before

---

23. Podmore, "To Die and Yet," 44–45.
24. Tanner, *Anxiety in Eden*, 165–166.

God—and yet not perish, through the love that provided God's true covering of *cleanness*. That love births the faith that rests in God "in which there is no despair at all: in relating itself to itself and in willing to be itself, the self rests transparently in the power that established it" (SUD, 131). A less technical definition of faith than that of Kierkegaard's pseudonymous author of *Sickness Unto Death* is provided by C. Stephen Evans:[25]

> Faith is the cure that enables a person to accept the concrete being that he is, warts and all, and to move toward becoming the ideal person God has created him to be, since for God all things are possible. The person who stands before God in faith can begin to overcome the self-deception that is endemic to human life. If I can trustingly reveal myself to God, I have no reason to hide the truth from myself or ultimately from other humans as well.[26]

It is interesting that Simon, coming out of the spiritual trial in faith, can thereby fulfill both the figurative and literal readings for redeemed lepers. This is because the faith of real people coheres with the restoration of fellowship in the true family of God and in the eschatological Kingdom of God, here called "Abraham's bosom." The "table fellowship" Simon thinks he will only receive hereafter but hopes for in the present earthly life is "provided" for in Messiah's cleansing of Mark's leper. That was one reason why Jesus sternly pressed him to go to the priest for the proof of cleansing and be welcomed back to society, or at least *a new family* (Mark 1:43–44). Another reason for the priestly proof would be to testify that Jesus, who was not a priest, had both touched and cleansed a leper, in violation of the priestly system, to subvert it and the Jewish society built thereupon.[27]

Therefore, the "table fellowship" Simon *leprosus* envisioned was provided in Mark's new family in Christ that prefigured the redemption of human society. But the society of the fortunate must go through the "perishing" we saw above to enter God's new society of the *redefined* fortunate—which will still appear as a society of the unfortunate to those who have not also "perished" by becoming lepers. Thus, Simon *leprosus* through his eschatological faith and Mark's leper, perhaps finally seen in Mark 14:3 living in *a society* at table fellowship, both participated in the eschatological kingdom of Father Abraham, albeit as a few raindrops participate in an approaching thunderstorm.

---

25. "The pseudonym Anti-Climacus was invented to represent the highest expression of Christianity—a position to which Soren aspired." Backhouse, *A Single Life*, 255.

26. Evans, *Kierkegaard's Christian Psychology*, 120.

27. Myers, *Binding the Strong Man*, 152–154.

INTRODUCING THE MISSION OF SIMON LEPROSUS

At this point we reach a place where we need to consider how those undergoing spiritual trials and temptations to weak and/or defiant despair should *Christianly* relate to the larger society. Of course, Kierkegaard provides us with an example as person/Christian who "owned" his sin (leprosy) in a society that generally did not. Inasmuch as ALSC is autobiographical, he believed that by "coming clean" about his spiritual leprosy he would appear as an "unfortunate leper," and unnecessarily so, in the view of Christian Denmark where salvation was simply a given and surely nothing to be despaired over. The question then becomes whether Kierkegaard's temptation was the Simon/Manasse dilemma between *weakly* desiring to cover his "leprosy" to be accepted in the already "clean" society, or *defiantly* desiring to cover his sin to "infect" others with his leprosy, the consciousness of sin. This aspect of the reading transforms Manasse's apparently diabolical aim into a truly evangelistic one. And therefore, it seems that Kierkegaard "became" Manasse, for two reasons.

First, in his "Christian Discourses" he does not so much claim to be a Christian as play along with the fiction that all of Denmark was Christian—only to then infiltrate society secretly as a heathen—because they (and he) were actually heathens or "lepers" in his analogy.[28]

Second, he thereby intentionally and defiantly spread his "infectious breath" throughout all his "Christian society," to "wound from behind" those who thought they were clean, but were in his mind, lepers just as he was.

In both tactics, his aim was to be a true Christian witness of the necessity to become a despairing leper like him in order to be cleansed by Jesus, the one true priest. So perhaps his temptation was ultimately whether his sin-despairing consciousness would spread his "leprosy" for the sake of his own hate and revenge at the society he was alienated from, or whether he would spread it for the sake of the love of Christ who *only* touches the unclean. He "became a sinner," a leper, *for* them. Even through his final "attack" he claimed he was not a Christian, just as they were not (see Isa 6:5).

---

28. Evans writes, "Instead of directly attacking the illusion by claiming that other people were not true Christians, Kierkegaard adopted the ironical method of taking other people at their word, accepting the illusion as 'good money.' He then engaged them in a Socratic manner." Evans, *Kierkegaard's Christian Psychology*, 117–118. Backhouse helpfully and convincingly discusses Kierkegaard's refusal to claim the title "Christian," even in his later writings in the famed "Attack on Christendom." Backhouse, "Politics as Indirect Communication," 58–60. Also see Christman, "Lewis and Kierkegaard" for a fuller treatment of his missional method for reaching post-Christian pagans.

SIMON'S MEDITATION ON THE CRITERION OF HUMAN COMPASSION

> *You dead who are sleeping around me, wake up, just for a moment; listen to a word, just one word: Greet Abraham from me so that he has a place prepared among the blessed for the one who was not permitted to have a place among men* (233).

Simon continues to contemplate his lot in life as he looks away from his graveyard community, the bodies of those now departed, toward the hope of "Abraham's Bosom" where he will one day receive *there* what he was denied *here*. He asks the departed to speak to Abraham for him. This seems to allude to Jesus' story of another outcast—Lazarus the beggar—who sat destitute at the rich man's door in this life, but found their roles reversed in the afterlife, again pictured in relation to "Abraham's bosom" (Luke 17:19–31). The *reversal* of roles of the fortunate and the unfortunate is thus subtly introduced. This *inversion* is integrally related to a further criterion of who is fortunate or unfortunate: the presence of absence of *compassion*. Simon's lack of receiving compassion (and what it provides) is intimated in his request, the humility of which in a sense qualifies him as one of the "meek" who will inherit the promised land (Matt 5:5). It is worth noting that the ground upon which his hope is based, expressed in this desire to be remembered by Abraham, is because Abraham's bosom is the place of *realized* compassion, the community of the *blessed* (the fortunate). Simon's greeting also seems to evoke the desire of the repentant thief on the cross for Jesus to remember him when he comes in his kingdom (Luke 23:42). Of course, Jesus assured him of a place in "paradise" beginning even "today."

Simon's future hope where he might receive compassion highlights its absence in the here and now. Simon vividly describes what he sees instead. The fortunate continually take advantage of the unfortunate. He sadly concludes,

> *What is human compassion anyhow? Who is entitled to it if not the unfortunate one, and how is it paid to him? The poverty-stricken man falls into the hands of the moneylender, who ultimately helps him into captivity as a slave . . . But if there is a danger, they drive the unfortunate one out into the desert in order not to hear his screaming, which could disturb the music and dancing and opulence and pass judgment on compassion—the human compassion that wants to deceive God and the unfortunate one . . . So look in vain for compassion in the city and among the fortunate, look for it out here in the desert* (233–234).

Simon's meditation shows that if the fortunate can use the unfortunate they will "accommodate" them into their society, as slaves. But if the unfortunate are a danger to their society, they drive them out. Simon therefore sees the fortunate as without compassion.

THE PRIESTLY COMPASSION OF SIMON LEPROSUS ON "THE FORTUNATE"

In what can only be considered an ironic redemptive move, Simon evidences the thoroughness of his repentance and the paradox of salvation. Rather than seeking to exact revenge on the fortunate, he realizes that he, *as a leper*, is instrumental for *their* salvation. Simon writes,

> *If no one has compassion on me, no wonder then, that compassion has fled as I have out among the graves, where I sit comforted as one who offers his life to save others, comforted as one who has compassion on the fortunate. God of Father Abraham, give them new wine and grain in abundance, and happy times; build their barns bigger and give them surplus bigger than their barns* (234).

Since the salvation of the fortunate is not found where they are and was found by Simon where he is—in the social isolation of the consciously "leprous"—this situation inverts all. This is the truth that was implicit in his meditation on the inverted destinies in Abraham's bosom. This is the truth that where compassion is, salvation has preceded, and where it is not, salvation is not. This is the truth that salvation has fled from the fortunate because they mistook it as theirs by birthright. So, it has fled to where Simon dwells, outside their society, in the community among the graves of the dead who now know these truths. And Simon already lives in this place of death, where he sits *"comforted as one who offers his life to save others, comforted as one who has compassion on the fortunate."* He compassionately testifies to them where their salvation lies, namely, in the compassion that has fled with him to the place of those counted as dead. And he is not only counted as dead by them, but he also now counts himself "dead" and gives his life for theirs.

Kierkegaard's "scene among the graves at dawn," described thus as the "play" opens, now seems revealed as overtly eschatological and perhaps alludes to Jesus' resurrection morning of Mark 16:2–8. The now *transfigured* and *redemptive* grave scene seems to "fulfill" the epigram of GNG, "I would have perished had I not perished," and thus proclaims the ultimate inversion of the fortunate and the unfortunate, or respectively the "living" and the "dead." For the now "dead" Simon, "sitting on a stone" (a gravestone) during his contemplation, comes to receive ahead of time and therefore proclaims the life of the blessed community to come. By sitting on that gravestone he is from that place enabled to challenge the "fortunate" to dismantle their avoidance culture as "the testimony to the human achievement of constructing meaning in the face of death."[29] Instead they are to "found" their present community "not on human mutuality" such as the fortunate trade in, but in Christ's injunction to "love his neighbor, to love him as he is, even if he is, as he must be, one of the dead who inhabit this city of the dead."[30] That love of neighbor participates in the community of the blessed dead which is still to come:

> The New Jerusalem, the city where mourning is done with, the city peopled by the dead raised in Christ, is where true community and the true polis can be established.[31]

Now, in even further subversive inversion, Simon *leprosus* prays for "the fortunate" as *their* priest. He prays what at first seems a blessing that they could agree to: more fortunateness! But this is a "thought that wounds from behind" wherein what seems a promise delivers an unexpected negation.[32] The "hidden" negation is present in the fact that the "blessing" is based on Jesus's parable of *the rich fool* in Luke 12:13–21, who had sought salvation through an increased abundance of worldly gain. But salvation does not consist in such fortunateness, and so the parable of Jesus "wounds from behind," revealing the rich man as a fool. "Then comes the sting" because that night, when he could finally rest with full barns, his "fortunate" life was forfeit.[33] Therefore, Simon's priestly blessing of the fortunate will only come through their becoming unfortunate like him, a "leper" who is not infected by *the infection of the fortunate*.

> *Hear the prayer of him whose body is infected and unclean, an abomination to the priests, a horror to the people, a trap for the happy; hear him if his heart is still not infected* (234).

29. Pyper, "Cities of the Dead," 128, cf. 137.
30. Pyper, "Cities of the Dead," 135.
31. Pyper, "Cities of the Dead," 135, 137.
32. Kierkegaard explains the method of his discourses called "Thoughts that Wound from Behind—For Edification," saying: ". . . the text shall be so chosen that it looks like a gospel, and also is such, but then comes the sting. No. 1. 'What shall we have who have forsaken all.' The satirical point for us in this question—for us who have not yet forsaken anything. No. 2. All things for our good—*if* we love God. (Irony) Kierkegaard, CD, 166.
33. Kierkegaard, CD, 166.

Simon concludes his gravestone prayer confessing his leprosy, and what it signifies to the fortunate, namely, "a horror." But it is also "a trap for the happy," as we have just noted. He implores God to hear him, if his heart is "still not infected" by *their view* of what fortunate is. Simon now *personifies* the inversion of the fortunate and the unfortunate, and his earlier confession of repentance is replaced by his new confession of salvation— " I would have perished had I not perished"—revealing a paradoxical beatitude: *Blessed are those who perish, for they will not perish*. As for the fortunate, they will perish, unless they perish to their fortunateness. Unless they own their "leprosy" as the sickness unto death as Simon did, and through Jesus' touch are restored to the life that does not die. Pyper writes,

> What is necessary, Kierkegaard asserts, is not to evade death, but truly to undergo it. For Kierkegaard, the human problem is not how to gain eternal life. Eternity is the heart of who we are and is the source of our anguish. The problem that we have is our inability to die. That problem is overcome in Christ. His victory for us is that he underwent death, took death upon himself in its entirety, thus enabling the believer to truly die with him rather than to be condemned to an eternity of dying.[34]

SIMON LEPROSUS AS A CHRISTIAN

Kierkegaard ends Simon's self-contemplation with another ironic thought-experiment in which he further shows his hand regarding the real thrust of the entire "parable" for the "Christians of Denmark. He says,

> *Simon leprosus was a Jew; if he had lived in Christianity, he would have found an utterly different kind of sympathy. Whenever in the course of the year there is a sermon about the ten lepers, the pastor affirms that he, too, has felt like a leper—but when it comes to typhoid . . .* (234)

Kierkegaard's point seems to be that had Simon lived in Christianity it would *not* have been different, and that if the "Christian" fortunate sense a danger from the unfortunate, the unfortunate would be driven out to the desert to live with Simon *leprosus*.

By noting Kierkegaard's inverted telling of the cleansing of a leper, who is "cleansed" by more fully "becoming a leper," we ironically see that the spiritualizing reading we generally followed in a very real sense coheres

---

34. Pyper, "Cities of the Dead," 134. Pyper poignantly summarize how Christ saves from "the sickness unto death."

with the literal reading that salvation is *literally* "good news for the poor," the unfortunate, and the fortunate who are willing to "throw their lot" in with them, in the place where compassion has fled.

CONCLUSION: CHRIST INCOGNITO AS JESUS LEPROSUS

At this point we turn to the account of Mark's leper to consider how Christ relates to the place where compassion is and how that relates to human society's estimation of Christ.

> *And Jesus sternly charged him and sent him away at once, and said to him, "See that you say nothing to anyone, but go, show yourself to the priest and offer for your cleansing what Moses commanded, for a proof to them." But he went out and began to talk freely about it, and to spread the news, so that Jesus could no longer openly enter a town, but was out in desolate places, and people were coming to him from every quarter* (Mark 1:43–45, ESV).

Jesus here and elsewhere instructed persons to not spread the news of what he had done. This has puzzled many and produced numerous explanations. Kierkegaard offers a reading of Jesus' desire for secrecy that nicely coheres with the truth underlying the question, *who is fortunate and who is unfortunate?*

Mark's gospel portrays Jesus inverting the expectations of Israel, as regards who the Messiah would be, namely, the significant one for the solely fortunate ones, Israel. Of course, this expectation of Israel was an apostasy or inversion from the scope of God's covenant with Abraham that in his seed all the nations of the earth would be blessed (Gen 22:18). So, what Jesus did was to increasingly become the unfortunate one, the insignificant one, become like Kierkegaard's Simon *leprosus*. Kierkegaard wrote,

> We fabricate that Christ really would have liked to be *directly* recognizable as the extraordinary he was, but that blind infatuation of his contemporaries iniquitously refused to understand him. In other words, we betray that we utterly fail to understand what it means to be an incognito. It was Christ's free resolve from eternity to want to become incognito.[35]

---

35. Kierkegaard, PC, 128–29. It could seem that Kierkegaard viewed Christ's desire to be incognito as mostly for epistemological reasons regarding human "knowledge." But there is a deeper reason that God desires true knowledge which is deeply theological, namely the love of God and God's desire to be loved by humans. His somewhat well-known tale of "the mighty King who falls in love with a simple peasant" illustrates

Kierkegaard shows that Jesus' method of secrecy was not an ad hoc mid-stream *adjustment*. It was the outworking of an *eternal resolve* called for by the perennial tendency of humans to turn God's gifts and callings meant to ultimately benefit all into tools for self-advance often achieved by the oppression of others.[36] Kierkegaard saw Christendom following this tendency just as Israel had at the time of Jesus and in earlier periods. Nordentoft writes,

> Kierkegaard is especially interested in the socially oppressing effect which the content of religious belief can have when it is shaped into an institutionalized bourgeois and clerical ideology. The Church has allied itself with the state and the ruling class in society, and the Christianity of "Christendom" is therefore not only a deception directed against Christianity, but at the same time also against the people to whom Christianity especially addresses itself, "the proletariat . . . the suffering, the poor, the sick, the lepers, the mad and so forth, the sinners, the criminals."[37]

Christianity therefore demonstrates the need for all to engage in "self-contemplation" as Simon leprosus did. And of course, Jesus came forth to provoke that as we saw in chapter 3 and will further explicate in the following chapter. The method for that provocation is to *invert* the "normal" human estimations of who God's anointed Christ is which is always closely related to who the fortunate and unfortunate are. When gospel-inversion takes place, "salvation" "moves" from being the status of the fortunate to being that of those considered unfortunate. And compassion, the sign of salvation which should always be in/among the fortunate because of Abraham's covenant given to Israel for all—if it is not "there"—therefore "moves" to being among/in the unfortunate. Thus Jesus, who personified God's compassion, increasingly "moved" from *being* the "fortunate" famed miracle worker and possible "Christ" nearly acclaimed by all, to *becoming* declaimed as the "unfortunate" blasphemous Jewish apostate (Mark 1:28; 15:13).

Therefore, in Mark's gospel Jesus increasingly became "incognito." Thus, he *became* the forsaken one, the dangerous one, the one ultimately driven out into the "community of the dead"—the greatest "unfortunates"—the loathsome "leprous" sinners crucified outside the "fortunate" chosen city of Jerusalem, and "outside" of humanity, itself according to the

---

God's eternal resolve. See Evans, *Kierkegaard's Christian Psychology*, 127. See also Hughes, *Staging of Desire*, 1–7. The tale is in Kierkegaard, PF, 26–30.

36. See Jonathan Sacks, *Not in God's Name*, for a masterful psychoanalysis of this destructive pathology of humankind.

37. Nordentoft, *Kierkegaard's Psychology*, 253.

Roman Empire's intent of crucifixion.[38] Most scholars agree that when Jesus touched the leper, he did not become unclean. Rather the leper became clean. That is true in a christological sense. But in a sociological sense, the gospel truth is that when Jesus touched the leper, he *became* a leper. And this does not mean that he became "sin" on the cross only, christologically, to atone for sin. Rather, it means that to the world, sociologically, Christ appears as Jesus *leprosus*. Thus, when Mark narrates, "*Jesus could no longer openly enter a town, but was out in desolate places*" we could read that dialectically to signify an increase in the false fame he shunned and therefore also an increase in being increasingly shunned and incognito. Ironically, as "*people were coming to him from every quarter*" he became Jesus *leprosus*, the unfortunate. Kierkegaard's Simon *leprosus* sees the ironic salvific inversions in which we find Jesus:

> Ah, stupid human language, who is entitled to compassion if not someone who is unfortunate, and yet it is the reverse, it is the unfortunate one who has compassion on the fortunate one.[39]

And that is why the author of Hebrews wrote of the Christian's participation in Christ's inversion, writing, "Therefore let us go to him outside the camp and bear the reproach he endured" (Heb 13:13, ESV). Several scholars nicely tie together what this imaginative text based in OT imagery means for Christians living in relation to the incarnate *incognito* life of Christ and the call for our *imitation*. In more familiar and richer theological terms, they ask,

> . . . what does this incognito mission have to do with the *imitatio Christi* and *imago Dei*? At the very least, the idea of "Christ incognito" implies that our own embracing of anonymity is likely to bring us into harmony with the incarnate *imago Dei*. To be sure, by embracing anonymity, we will have more in common with the family of God—the great cloud of witnesses" visible only to the eyes of faith—the vast majority of whom have not been memorialized in any way."[40]

And therefore, the incarnate one—and those given to follow—together participate in the kenotic self-emptying of God who inverts the

---

38. See Wright, *Day the Revolution*, 52–69, for a presentation of the horrible dehumanizing purpose of crucifixion.
39. Kierkegaard, SLW, 575.
40. Sirvent & Reyburn, "The Spotlight," 298.

normal expectations: "it is the unfortunate one who has compassion on the fortunate one."[41]

I expect that I have not infallibly or wholly explicated the rich, ironic, inversive, dialectical messages of Mark's Jesus *leprosus* or Kierkegaard's *Simon leprosus*. Since our reading is of a paradoxical gospel and the apostle and genius who have "staged" its explosive subversions and inversions, I cannot claim to be sufficient for such things. Therefore, the reading is only offered in hope that its lengthy meditation has conveyed some manner of proximity to the gospel-spirit of holy subversion. The gospel's apocalypse will "scatter the proud" while gathering the unfortunates longing for the blessed community of "Abraham's bosom." Enacting the apocalyptic inversions, Christ seeks and gathers the world's unclean "lepers" into a holy army of infectious healers, giving themselves for the sake of "the fortunate" who will only be saved by also becoming "lepers" and being "made clean" by the infectious touch of Jesus *leprosus*.

---

41. Kierkegaard, SLW, 575.

10

"Your Sins are Forgiven!"

"The Happy Passion" and Unhappy Revolutions at the First-Century Crossroad and the 1840s Fork

Mark 2:1–12 (ESV)

And when he returned to Capernaum after some days, it was reported that he was at home. 2 And many were gathered together, so that there was no more room, not even at the door. And he was preaching the word to them. 3 And they came, bringing to him a paralytic carried by four men. 4 And when they could not get near him because of the crowd, they removed the roof above him, and when they had made an opening, they let down the bed on which the paralytic lay. 5 And when Jesus saw their faith, he said to the paralytic, "Son, your sins are forgiven." 6 Now some of the scribes were sitting there, questioning in their hearts, 7 "Why does this man speak like that? He is blaspheming! Who can forgive sins but God alone?" 8 And immediately Jesus, perceiving in his spirit that they thus questioned within themselves, said to them, "Why do you question these things in your hearts? 9 Which is easier, to say to the paralytic, 'Your sins are forgiven,' or to say, 'Rise, take up your bed and walk'? 10 But that you may know that the Son of Man has authority on earth to forgive sins"—he said to the paralytic— 11 "I say to you, rise, pick up your bed, and go home." 12 And he rose and immediately picked up his bed and went out before them all, so that they were all amazed and glorified God, saying, "We never saw anything like this!"

It comes to pass when Reason and the Paradox encounter one another happily in the Moment, when the Reason sets itself aside and the Paradox bestows itself. The third entity in which this union is realized (for it is not realized in the reason, since it is set aside; nor in the Paradox, which bestows itself—hence it is realized *in* something) is that happy passion to which we will now assign a name . . . We shall call this happy passion: *Faith*. —Soren Kierkegaard[1]

MARK'S ELONGATING FORESHADOWS

At this point in Mark, as his narrative continues, several of the things foreshadowed earlier are seen developing. The episode of the healing of a paralytic takes place in Simon's home, and Mark's statement that Jesus was there "*at home*" seems significant. Of course, he had returned there *incognito*, due to the healed leper's exuberant publicizing of what Jesus did for him. But the mention of Jesus being at home probably signals another stage in the development of the new family of Jesus, consisting of his followers. This could be his "headquarters," but it is likely that Mark's "family" motif is being developed.

The paralytic who is the center of this episode can be seen as another "individual" as Mark increasingly portrays individuals encountering Jesus and thereby developing the motifs of faith and discipleship. This focus on individuals always presupposes the ever-present "crowd" from which these individuals are distinguished and become selves in relation to God as Kierkegaard would say.

The story of the scribes also presents a development in the theme of the Israelite "tenants," as already discussed on Mark 1:21–34. In this section the scribes, though silent, come into the foreground through the response of Jesus to the *thoughts of their hearts*. The focus of Jesus on their inward state and workings, opens a window on the inner workings that lead to outer results, which of course eventually lead to the crucifixion of Jesus. The scribes are the "negative" of "the individual" who comes to a true faith-response to Jesus, shown by their contrasting initial response of offense and eventual willing to be themselves *in despair*.

---

1. As cited in Rosas, Scripture *in the Thought*, 77.

At this point in Mark, we see the mission and ministry of Jesus becoming a decisional crossroad which begins with mere thoughts that eventually become actions and settled ways, and not merely those of a few, but of towns, nations, and civilizations.

A HEALING THAT REVEALS AND KINDLES HAPPY OR UNHAPPY PASSIONS

Human passion in relation to faith is central in this house scene. The house was full of people passionately desiring to see or receive something from Jesus. A paralytic passionately desiring healing is lowered through the roof after his four friends passionately break its barrier to lower him, bed, and all, to Jesus. Of course, Jesus sees his passion as evidence of faith, and passionately declares to the paralytic "your sins are forgiven." The scribes of the Jewish law present an interesting "dialectic" of passion in *unfaith*. They were "passionate" enough to be there and become a near-constant presence in Mark's gospel-story. But their body language of "sitting there," "speaks" of their passion to sit in judgment on Jesus, as though that is their reason for existence. In their silent judgment they were not without "passionate" *thoughts* and were quite "cool" toward Jesus. They were like the Bible commentators Kierkegaard critiqued, for being without any sincere desire to be receptive to what God might be doing. Apart from their being needed for the gospel history, they may serve in Mark's gospel as a sort of a "readers warning" to those "now" thereby observing its scenes.

Jesus of course perceives their thoughts, and the true nature of their passions and unfaith. He intuited their problem with Jesus forgiving the paralytic since only God could forgive sins. The only "logical" answer was that Jesus was "blaspheming." It may seem that the scribes were innocently following their "reason," but we will see that their fallen "passions" were what truly led them. For Jesus came to bring all things to God's light, including the pre-existing passions. And that disclosure is generally achieved not by directly pointing at the fallen passions, but by bringing the wholly positive gospel in his person and actions: the *light* which reveals what is in the dark. Thus, this positive healing and declaration of forgiveness participate in the light which reveals the dark passions and what lies beneath them. These positive acts are meant to provide the possibility of faith, what Kierkegaard called "the happy passion." But invariably, the positive gospel also provides the crossroad where offense is the other road taken, whether of individuals, villages, countries, empires, or all of humanity.

SINNERS AT THE CROSSROAD OF PARADOX AND PECULIARITY

In the previous chapter we saw that Jesus came *incognito*, regarding who he was. And as his ministry progressed, he became *more* incognito, not less. This is because Jesus and the life he calls his followers to, appear to be paradoxical to reason and peculiar to society. Nevertheless, it is only through encountering those "unreasonable" elements that one also encounters the possibility of the gospel, which always also presents the possibility of offense, and is thus also a crossroad. Kierkegaard writes,

> Just as the concept "faith" is an altogether distinctively Christian term, so in turn is "offense" an altogether distinctively Christian term relating to faith. The possibility of offense is the crossroad, or it is like standing at the crossroad. From the possibility of offense, one turns either to offense or to faith, but one never comes to faith except from the possibility of offense. Essentially offense is related to the composite of God and man, or to the God-man.[2]

The ironically "offensive" aspects of Jesus, such as healing a helpless and hopeless paralytic, and doing so by forgiving his sins, *appear* to support the idea that the paradox and peculiarity of Jesus are such solely because of human reason. But, as stated above, "passion" is the *real* determinative factor. The scribes surely thought that their "questioning" was *dispassionate*, shown as such by the neutrality of their posture as they were just "sitting there." But they were not without passion, and were in fact ruled by it, though they distracted themselves from the truth of *their selves*.

The fetishization of "reason" in the modern Enlightenment also distracted humans from the real issue, the fallen passions. William Barrett reports that a "wit" said that David Hume was "like a man who goes outside his house and looks through the window to see if he is at home."[3] Hume thought that the clue to true human knowing was found in unraveling "the puzzles of sensation" when the "truth" was more accurately determined by human *sensuality* or desire.[4] That Jesus appears as paradoxical to reason does several things simultaneously. It "attacks" reason as the false criterion of man—the supposed "purely rational" measure of all things; and it reveals the "passions" that oft lay beneath it as the iceberg of the volitional life.

---

2. Kierkegaard, PC, 81.
3. Barrett, *Death of the Soul*, 46. Barrett did not name this "wit."
4. Barrett, *Death of the Soul*, 33, cf. 42–48.

Therefore, Jesus was resolved to appear as incognito and reveal and divide human "reason" as oftentimes *passion* incognito (Heb 4:12–13). And this always presents the possibility of offense, but also God's desired possibility of faith. Reason and passion are revealed and set in their true hierarchy by the wedge of "paradox and peculiarity."[5] When Jesus declared to the paralytic, "Son, your sins are forgiven" he set a "hidden" depth charge for faith or offense inside the scribes' lives that they fully sensed and reacted to. Because of their basic human passions, they "must have an opinion about it." For the questions arising in their hearts were not merely related to "reason" but to the whole fabric of life that founded their "unhappy passion" of *unfaith*. But what was their "fabric of life?" How did it become the most important thing to them and determine the "answering" passion which would eventually lead to their fervent conspiracy to kill Jesus? More generally, how do the passions of life come from this "social fabric" for any of us, and more importantly, relate to the gospel's new *possibility* which is *not part* of that social fabric?

THE SOCIAL IMAGINARY, GOD'S POSSIBILITY, AND "THE HAPPY PASSION"

The truth is that a "wedge" driven in to divide reason and passion reveals the need of a deeper wedge between the pre-existing social fabric and God's new social possibility. For God's possibility is paradox and peculiar because it does not "naturally" fit into our social fabric. This "social fabric" has been called "the social imaginary."[6] It should be obvious that "imagination" is part of it, and as such relates to possibility. What can't be imagined can't be conceived of as possible. The scribes could not imagine the possibility that Jesus could forgive sins, nor how that related to God's new social fabric. Therefore, the reason the gospel brings offense is because it is not related to the "meaningful" preexisting categories of human society. And therefore, Jesus is only considered a question to be answered by our reason. But as we

---

5. Mahn has provided an important discussion of this question, and holds that what Kierkegaard often meant by paradox was "peculiarity," namely the fact that the person of Christ, and the way that is required to follow him, is "peculiar" to what is normal, the social mores, the social imaginary. He also presents valuable reasons that demonstrate that the gospel does not present an intellectual test for salvation. Mahn, *Fortunate Fallibility*, 158–161.

6. A well-known and now oft-quoted phrase popularized by the philosopher Charles Taylor, which describes the pre-cognitive way that individuals exist within their culture, through subconscious "shared" imagination that "narrates" what is meaningful in any given society. See Smith, *How (Not) To Be Secular*, 143.

have tried to show, we are more determined by our passions than our reason. But what lies beneath our passions? The answer is *the social imaginary*, our shared *pre-cognitive social imagination* that pre-determines what we value. The imaginary conveniently provides the idea that we have *reasoned* our way to its fabric of meaningful life. The imaginary makes us seem to be primarily "thinking things." But the truth is that we are primarily "desiring things," creatures sold out to "passion," and thus, "loving things," though generally loving the *wrong* things.[7] It is the "social imaginary" which makes it very difficult for those within it to imagine something "outside" it. The essential question is whether there is another "passion," a "happy" one in fact, that can be positively "witnessed" of and so create willingness to receive God's new possibility against the impossibilities of the old it reveals.[8] Kierkegaard writes,

> It comes to pass when Reason and the Paradox encounter one another happily in the Moment, when the Reason sets itself aside and the Paradox bestows itself. The third entity in which this union is realized (for it is not realized in the reason, since it is set aside; nor in the Paradox, which bestows itself—hence it is realized *in* something) is that happy passion to which we will now assign a name . . . We shall call this happy passion: *Faith*.[9]

Faith is the result of passion meeting God's possibility where there was previously only impossibility. Faith is thus God's "happy passion."

THE FIRST-CENTURY CROSSROAD: FOLLOW JESUS OR FIGHT ROME?

We will now consider where the rejection of God's "happy passion" leads. At this crossroad in Capernaum the result of the wrong road chosen was already becoming decided because of the pre-existing sinful passions that lay hidden to their hosts but fully visible to Jesus. Mark's foreshadowing in the thoughts of offended scribes provides a "prophesy" of where Israel's unredeemed passions would lead. Thus, the possibility of offense leads to actual offense and to the further possibility of God's judgment. The judgment of God that accompanied "the Jewish War," wherein Jerusalem was terribly destroyed by the Romans in 66–70 AD, is "the writing on the wall"

---

7. See Smith, *Desiring the Kingdom*, 39–71; *You Are What*, 1–25.

8. See Christman, *Gospel in the Dock*, 146–155, on what I called "The Gospel of Culture."

9. As cited in Rosas, Scripture *in the Thought*, 77.

at this point. The leaders of Israel along with most of the Jews rejected Jesus' "gathering" of them under his wings and instead elected themselves to pursue a "holy war" against Rome. This led to self-destruction and the spiritual desolation of their house (Matt 23:37–38).[10] The prayer of "Simon leprosus" for the blessing of "the fortunate" to fill their barns, seen in the previous chapter, was alluding to Jesus' words concerning this coming judgment (Mark 8:35–37, Matt 23:32).

Mark showed that mere thoughts rising in Capernaum would grow to erupt in destruction, death, and spiritual desolation. Obviously, a mustard seed of faith would have grown better results. Mark, and the Scriptures as a whole, stress that small beginnings, whether of faith or offense, grow and bear their natural fruits, either of abundant life or death.

But we also must see a further prophesy of a more-distant coming offense at "the Inviter." For in the coming Christendom, passionate thoughts would again arise in some of its "scribes." Those thoughts seemed to them "reason," which then took on a life of its own, and ironically baptized modern "Christianized" humankind into its own course of anxiety, destruction, and desolation.[11] And this all began by *yet another* generation questioning Jesus' healing of the paralytic *by saying* "your sins are forgiven."

THE 1840S FORK OF MODERNITY: FOLLOW KIERKEGAARD'S CHRISTIANITY OR MARX'S REVOLUTION?

It is interesting that Kierkegaard's nickname when young was "the fork."[12] In this section we will see that "the fork" grew to mercifully "spear" the "rising thoughts" of socialism and communism with the sword of the gospel. But seemingly demonic ill-winds and sinful human gravity were behind the tides of a growing false sociology that flooded the modern and now postmodern West. Its wake left the bitter fruits of "the death of God," namely,

---

10. See Christman, *Gospel in the Dock*, 178–180.

11. Lesslie Newbigin masterfully charted the ironic course of modern humanity from faith to desolation in the following steps: the rejection of faith as the way of knowledge led to the embrace of doubt as the way to certainty, which then led to nihilism. See Newbigin, *Proper Confidence*, 1–44.

12. "According to his sister's account this stems from an incident in which he was asked what he would most like to be, and he answered, 'A fork.' 'Why?' 'Well, then I could 'spear' anything I wanted on the dinner table.' 'But what if we come after you?' 'Then I'll spear you.' Kirmmse, *Encounters with Kierkegaard*, 1.

and ironically, the suicide of man and perhaps non-ironically the genocide of many created in the "dead" God's image.[13]

Theologian Paul Tyson has argued that Kierkegaard's Christian thought and writings represented a "fork in the road" for the entire modern West in the 1840s: the road not taken was Kierkegaard's "theologically defined and doxologically centered sociology;" the road taken was Marx's "secularized, functionally atheist, and materialist" sociology.[14] We could say that the fork was the choice between humankind following its own passion for autonomy rather than the "happy passion" of faith in Christ. Of course, that "happy passion" is based in Jesus' provocative statement to the paralytic "your sins are forgiven," rather than merely saying "rise." For the fork between Kierkegaard's and Marx's sociology is the fork between *God's possibility*, namely, "your sins are forgiven," and *man's possibility* which primitive religion was attempting to say all along but didn't have the words for until the "death of God," namely, to "rise." In Christianity, "your sins are forgiven" is the basis of a God-given theological sociology. In the new sociology, "rise" epitomizes human potential in a world void of God. Hence, humankind *must* become religionless, but ironically—only to *deify itself*—as the center and goal of all human existence. Thus, Marx explains the all-important criticism of religion:

> Criticism has plucked the imaginary flowers from the chains not so much that man may bear chains without any imagination or comfort, but so that he may throw away the chains and pluck the living flowers. The criticism of religion disillusions man so that he may think, act, and fashion his own reality as a disillusioned man come to his senses; so that he may revolve around himself as his real sun. Religion is only the illusory sun which revolves around man as long as he does not revolve around himself.[15]

It seems Marx held that the Copernican revolution would be completed by realizing a geocentric cosmology in which everything is determined by and thus revolves around man at the center of all purposeful existence. This seems to ego-centrically "save" the geocentric view through the use of

---

13. Westphal explains that Nietzsche's "death of God," and Kierkegaard's "disappearance of Christianity from Christendom," were both descriptions of the "religious event" that coincided with the "sociological event" of "the emergence of mass society, the crowd, the public, the herd." Westphal, *Kierkegaard's Critique*, 43.

14. Tyson, *Kierkegaard's Theological Sociology*, 7, cf. 31–40: "Kierkegaard at the 1840s Fork." Of course, it is probably only hindsight looking at a "what if" of history which can now make it appear that there was a "fork" in history, in light of the "secularized, functionally atheist, and materialist" sociology that "won the day."

15. As cited in Westphal, *Suspicion and Faith*, 139.

human "growth steroids." And Kierkegaard would have none of its demonic "self-deification." When Jesus says "your sins are forgiven" it is because God is the center of all. But Marx and the humanity he represents would have none of that. This signals the cataclysmic collision of Christendom and its rebellious offspring, "the world come of age" through the Enlightenment which ironically replaced true Christian humanism with "anti-humanism."[16] Kierkegaard provides a short statement that paraphrases and summarizes Marx's criticism as "that frightful sigh (from hell) uttered by socialism: God is the evil; just get rid of him and we will get relief."[17] Kierkegaard saw the ongoing collision between de-Christianized Christendom and its atheistic, demonic prodigal son "come of age" as effecting the catastrophic "age of disintegration" (6255). In elaboration of this age he writes,

> That it was an age of disintegration—that "the System" itself signified, not as the systematicians were pleased to understand, that the consummation had been achieved, but that "the System" itself, as an overripe fruit, pointed to decline. That it was an age of disintegration—and consequently not as politicians were pleased to think, that "government" was the evil, an assumption which would have been a curious contradiction from the standpoint of "the single individual," but that "the crowd," "the public," etc. were the evil which corresponds consistently with "the single individual." That it was a time of disintegration—that it was not nationalities that should be advanced but Christianity in relation to "the single individual," and the task: to change it into individuals (6255).

Kierkegaard's emphasis on "the single individual" points to the basic human problem of "personal sinfulness" rather than the socialist/communist approach of blaming societal "disintegration" wholly on societal "systemic" sins rather than on human "individual" sinfulness. The Marxist sociology vainly thought that above-surface maintenance of the societal field of noxious weeds (rooted deeply in the sinful human ground) would transform it into a fruitful vineyard. But the true "master gardener" says,

---

16. Barry Harvey sees the term "world come of age," which may have entered the modern world of theological discourse via Dietrich Bonhoeffer's controversial usage in his influential "Letters and Papers from Prison," as useful to point out "the ultimate irony associated with the myth of a world come of age, creating the instruments of its own demise." Harvey, *Taking Hold*, 16; cf. Chapter 2: "The Ironic Myth of a World Come of Age" (58–87). The term "anti-humanism" is specifically drawn from Jen's Zimmermann's chapter "The Rise of Anti-Humanism" in Zimmermann, *Incarnational Humanism*, 163–204.

17. Kierkegaard, JP, VI:61, #6256. Further references in this chapter will be cited in the text above, by giving the entry number (not the page number).

first make the soil good (Mark 4:8). In another metaphor he says to "make the tree good" and the fruit will follow (Matt 12:33). For the ground and tree in those parables picture the all-necessary "influence" of God, since branches severed from the vine can do nothing—other than ultimately self-reap fire and destruction—as much of Israel learned in the Jewish War discussed above (John 15:1–6). Therefore, Kierkegaard speaks of the completely wrong self-diagnosis and mis-prescription that was winning the day at the 1840s fork:

> For the generation is sick, spiritually, sick unto death. But just as the patient, when he himself is supposed to point to the area where he suffers, frequently points to an utterly wrong place, so also the generation. It believes—yes, it is both laughable and lamentable—it believes that a new administration will help. But as a matter of fact it is the eternal that is needed. Some stronger evidence is needed than socialism's belief that God is the evil, and so it says itself, for the demonic always contains the truth in reverse (6256).

"The eternal" (God) was what was needed for the "sick" (sinful) patient, but the Marxian socialists, like Mark's scribes, were offended at that diagnosis and prescription, and therefore "sat" in judgment (Mark 2:6). And as the scribes eventually attacked, so also Kierkegaard calls the God-abolishing prescriptions of socialism and communism "attacks of passion, attacks by the offended" (6257). Note that Kierkegaard did not say this was an attack based in true "reason."

Of course, the ultimate irony is that the socialist prescription of the annulment of God necessarily leads to the establishment of man *as God*, and self-deification does not result in a benevolent loving God of true justice but in a deified "humanity" whose justice, as human, all-too-human, tends toward and becomes "wrath"—which does not work the righteous of God" (Jas 1:20).

It is interesting that Marx, like Nietzsche, was up-front about the *religious* self-deification *inherent* in atheistic sociology. Kierkegaard thus observed something that needs to be fully recognized and wrestled with even today in our secular, supposedly religiously neutral world. Kierkegaard intuited the shift of politics to religion, which of course implies that humans innately know that "the eternal" is necessary, though as that knowledge was expressed in the Marxian sociology, it became idolatrous and demonic—a pattern Paul revealed in his letter to the Romans (1:18–23). Kierkegaard writes,

What lay at the root of the catastrophe will then become apparent, that it is the opposite of the Reformation, which appeared to be a religious movement and proved to be political; now everything appears to be politics but will turn out to be a religious movement . . . then, like mushrooms after a rain, demonically tainted characters will appear who soon presumptuously make themselves apostles on a par with "the apostles," a few also assuming the task of perfecting Christianity, soon even becoming religious founders themselves, inventors of a new religion which will gratify the times and the world . . . the most dangerous comes when these demonics themselves become apostles—something like thieves passing themselves off as policemen—even founders of religion, who will get a dreadful foothold in an age which is critical in such a way that from the standpoint of the eternal is eternally true to say of it: What is needed is religiousness—that is, true religiousness; whereas from the standpoint of the demonic, the same age will say of itself: It is religiousness we need—namely demonic religiousness (6256, 6257).

Kierkegaard mentions how leaders of this movement will assume the task of perfecting Christianity by gratifying the times and the world. An example of this is provided in a study of Nazism, which is appropriate since fascism is born of the same sort of ideological power structure. For in this "new religion," rather than a conversion of people to the gospel, there is a conversion of the Bible to the people. Matthew Kirkpatrick writes of several German church leaders who enabled this process, saying, "Seeberg, as with so many others, stood alongside Althaus in affirming natural theology that ultimately legitimated the Nazi regime and the 'conversion' of the Bible to fit the age."[18] The truth is that any self-deifying strategies—whether fascist, socialist, communist, or capitalist—proposed to "save" societies and even all of humanity, are grown in the same corrupt soil of human ideological power where unjust societies have always grown and flourished. And if they somehow use some perfected "Christianity" to do so, it will surely be *fitted* to the "attacks of passion, attacks by the offended" of the world, but *ill-fitted* to "eternity."

It is important to add one very large qualification to this descriptive introduction to the 1840s fork for modernity, which will undoubtedly lie beneath "readings" to come in latter portions of this series. That qualification is to point out a degree of commonality between Kierkegaard and Marx, and the need for some true "sociology" because of the reality of injustice in societies and humanity at large. When Kierkegaard wrote in his journal that

18. Kirkpatrick, *Attacks on Christendom*, 61.

"the generation is sick, spiritually, sick unto death" he *was* obviously speaking of *societal sinfulness*. And that sickness was not *caused* by the Marxian sociology. Rather it was due to the self-dissipation of Christendom. There were powerful external changes taking place "outside," but a pre-existing internal sickness which had been increasingly manifesting itself in outward symptoms. Marx was a perceptive critic of the sickness of "Christian" society. Merold Westphal helps us to understand the context and content of his critique:

> Religion is, according to the Marxian atheism, "the opium of the people" . . . This verdict is as central to Marx's view of religion as it is familiar. The degree to which we understand it will be the degree to which we understand his critique. But the meaning of the metaphor is not self-evident, especially in a time when it is possible to speak of the recreational use of drugs. For Marx, religion and opium are painkillers that are not only addictive but even worse since they treat symptoms rather than diseases. While there may be medically hopeless situations in which narcotics play a useful role, religion invariably distracts attention from a social disease that *can* be treated and cured. Rather than a desperate response to genuine hopelessness, it is the diabolical creation of *unnecessary* hopelessness concerning the human social order.[19]

Westphal's explanation should make us think about Jesus and the paralytic in Mark 2:1–13. In the eyes of Marx, religion would say "your sins are forgiven" but leave him paralyzed. This would create the addiction to religion, while nevertheless leaving the desperate in a situation of paralysis, yet "mercifully" pacified by the narcotic *carrot* of "eternal life." Of course, to Marx, the paralytic was the present human social order, which through "forgiveness" is distracted from its miserable sickness unto death. And if there is no God, no eternal life, and no sin, this is a "diabolical *unnecessary* hopelessness concerning the human social order." But Kierkegaard believed that Jesus did in fact *heal* the paralytic. But sadly, Christendom had resulted in a situation where most say "We never *see* anything like this"—namely *societal healing* (see Mark 2:12). Westphal further clarifies why this failure represents a situation that not only a Marx would bemoan and condemn, but even, or especially, an Amos.

> Even if there is a God, or especially if there is a God like the one described in the Bible, when religion functions as Marx describes, killing the pains of injustice rather than challenging

---

19. Westphal, *Suspicion and Faith*, 123.

its right to exist, it deserves the diatribes he directs against it. At least that is what the prophet Amos would have said.[20]

Kierkegaard would fully agree, and therefore frenetically presented his tailor-made diatribes against the Christianity-impoverished religion and society of "Golden Age Denmark" in his "Attack on Christendom," toward the end of his relatively short life.

We must now briefly turn back to the worm in the "healing ointment" of Marx, which is that many symptoms of the sickness of the age were "the epiphenomena of a spiritual condition rather than of economic structure."[21] And the self-deification that was necessary for treatment amounts to *the replacement God*, the narcotic "idol," with "idols worthy of worship that we know we have fashioned ourselves, and in our image."[22] Of course, the charge that religion was man's construction of idols in his own image was the basis of Feuerbach's atheism. And Feuerbach's surgical detection of that unholy heart of religion was the basis of his own atheism that had greatly influenced Marx's sociology and those to follow in "the world come of age." Thus, Marx ironically became guilty of creating an idol in his own image, even though he critiqued religion for doing the same. Only this idol was not called "God" and therefore he thought it was not only permissible but necessary. For this idol, man become God, was considered a necessity following upon the "death of God." Lest we be too hard on Marx we must admit that his idol-making project made perfect sense within his "social imaginary," *if in reality there was no God*, which to him was a given.[23] To Marx, since there was no real God, man would have to replace him with that for which "God" was created by man to begin with, as the heavenly symbol of the earthly reality of man.[24] But this "God" had "died" as a meaningful symbol

---

20. Westphal, *Suspicion and Faith*, 139.

21. Westphal, *Kierkegaard's Critique*, 43.

22. Tyson, *Kierkegaard's Theological Sociology*, 10, n6; cf. 5–9.

23. This necessity has been made explicit by some, both in the past and the present, as evidenced by Simon Critchley's citation of Oscar Wilde and his book proposing a contemporary societal realization of the "Confraternity" of Wilde: "When I think of religion at all, I feel as if I would like to found an order for those who *cannot* believe: the Confraternity of the Faithless, one might call it . . . Everything to be true must become a religion." Critchley, *Faith of the Faithless*, 3.

24. Marx wrote: "Man has found in the imaginary reality of heaven where he looked for a superman only the reflection of his own self. He will therefore no longer be inclined to find only the appearance of himself, the non-man, where he seeks and must seek his true reality." As cited in Westphal, *Suspicion and Faith*, 136.

for society, something Nietzsche actually lamented, knowing the magnitude of the challenge of replacing what "God" had provided humanity.[25]

Kierkegaard agreed that the "God" of Christendom was dead, because true *Christianity* had disappeared from it, and had been "replaced" with a human construct (or idol) which had failed society and resulted in social injustice. But Kierkegaard would not agree that the true God was dead, and therefore the need was not replacement but following Christ as the only way toward true social justice. For the true God sent Christ to both forgive (individual sin) and bring "rising" healing (social justice). And therefore, the "worm in the ointment" of Marx and the atheistic sociologists who followed in his train, is revealed through the horrific anti-human results of self-deification. Jens Zimmermann summarizes that the humanism the Marxist sociologists aimed at failed and continues to do so because it lacks "*any transcendent telos* for self-creation . . . any conception what humanity is to look like" and becomes "simply an invitation for the powerful to trample the weak into submission."[26] Westphal summarizes the reality, irony, and tragedy that were centered in Marx himself, at the 1840s fork he had arrived at—not Kierkegaard's writings—but the answer that remained unfound in his theological studies as a "Young Hegelian" saying,

> Surely Marx is right that the disturbance of such religious faith will be politically disruptive. Despite his Jewish roots, which were not very deep, he seems oblivious to the fact that such a disturbance could itself be religiously motivated and to the historical fact that before there was a Feuerbach there was a Amos.[27]

THE ROAD LESS TRAVELLED

The way modern humanity could to have gone at the 1840s fork is evident. Of course, Kierkegaard said that life must be lived forward but can only be

---

25. Henriksen writes of Nietzsche's lamenting recognition: "In *The Madman* the major figure is the only one who notices how the cold dark night is drawing in. With the sun as the image of what God was, he asks: 'What happened when we tied loose the sun from the earth? Is it not turning colder? Are we not falling, upward, downward? Is there any direction upward and downward any more?'" Henriksen, *Reconstruction of Religion*, 165.

26. Zimmermann, *Incarnational Humanism*, 188–189.

27. Westphal, *Suspicion and Faith*, 136, cf. 135 on the "Young Hegelians." For a detailed narration of Marx's theological windings and turnings see Van Leeuwen, *Critique of Heaven*.

understood by looking backward.[28] Therefore the crossroads at the 1840s fork can be understood by looking back and recognizing that "the happy passion" was not only missed but rejected. By faith, rather than offense, humanity could have gone forth as Abraham did, not knowing where to, but knowing that it was nevertheless toward the "land of promise . . . for a city which hath foundations, whose builder and maker is God" (see Hebrews 11:8–10, KJV).

Throughout this chapter we have seen the danger when human thoughts, rising from offense at God and his Christ, present tragic unforeseen possibilities. The offended don't realize the crossroads at which they stand, nor how far their unchecked thoughts will lead when followed. The monotheists of Israel certainly did not foresee that their thoughts would lead them to craft an idol, *their* "holy war" and lead them and God's chosen city to destruction by Rome and desolation before God. The atheistic "apostles" of socialism certainly did not think that their offense at God would lead them to craft an idol, *their* "just society," into an ideological power that would cause Lenin to deem it *reasonable* to destroy "three-fourths of mankind" if "the last quarter should become communist."[29]

Nevertheless, the offense that presents a crossroads always provides the possibility of the happier passion, called faith, which does not result in an opiate that somewhat kills the pain but not the disease. In contrast, God's possibility brings the reaction "they were all amazed and glorified God, saying, 'We never saw anything like this!'" For they saw the paralyzed human "rise" from his hopeless situation to go "home" to the place that would now be different, *because* his sins were forgiven.

---

28. Dru, *The Soul of Kierkegaard*, 89.
29. As cited in Sandoz, *Political Apocalypse*, 22.

11

Jesus and Kierkegaard on Gaining the World

"It is not the Healthy but the Sick . . . there is no Bliss except in Despair, Hurry Up and Despair"

Mark 2:13–17 (NIV)

13 Once again Jesus went out beside the lake. A large crowd came to him, and he began to teach them. 14 As he walked along, he saw Levi son of Alphaeus sitting at the tax collector's booth. "Follow me," Jesus told him, and Levi got up and followed him.

15 While Jesus was having dinner at Levi's house, many tax collectors and sinners were eating with him and his disciples, for there were many who followed him. 16 When the teachers of the law who were Pharisees saw him eating with the sinners and tax collectors, they asked his disciples: "Why does he eat with tax collectors and sinners?"

17 On hearing this, Jesus said to them, "It is not the healthy who need a doctor, but the sick. I have not come to call the righteous, but sinners."

There is no bliss except in despair, hurry up and despair, you will find no happiness until you do.[1]

Thus also, in Christian terminology death is indeed the state of deepest spiritual wretchedness, and yet the cure is simply to die, to die to the world. —Anti-Climacus[2]

God creates out of nothing, wonderful you say: yes, to be sure, but he does what is still more wonderful: he makes saints out of sinners. —Soren Kierkegaard[3]

PECULIAR CROSSROADS/PECULIAR PEOPLE

This chapter further elucidates Mark's "crossroad" motif. Flannery O'Connor wrote that the regional writer operates at "the peculiar crossroads where time and place and eternity somehow meet" and therefore creates stories that illuminate "the eternal crossroads" that Mark perhaps first set in story form.[4] Thus, Levi the "regional" Jewish tax collector for Rome is Mark's "next" individual shown in relation to "the eternal crossroads." In fact Levi, like the paralytic in the previous account, becomes part of that crossroad for others.

The "peculiar" stories of the individuals encountering Jesus and becoming part of Mark's "eternal crossroads" were chosen because they would certainly provoke strong "crossroad" attitudes of either antipathy or sympathy. In this case, we can surmise that unless Mark's audience had already been influenced by the Christian movement, his story of Levi the tax collector would generally have evoked *antipathy*. This was because those that made their living collecting taxes *from* Jews for the Roman Empire would evoke great hatred. And since Levi was a Jew this would make him not only an enemy, but a traitor. Mark therefore *literally* invited his hearers/readers to recognize and reconsider their attitudes and actions toward what he portrays: "As the blind man is touched twice, so also the ideal audience is invited to be touched twice to see clearly, to take a second and more profound look."[5] At a minimum, Mark's audience would be invited to sympathize with people they would normally have considered quite negatively.

---

1. Kierkegaard, as paraphrased by Signe Laessoe in Kirmmse, *Encounters with Kierkegaard*, 57.
2. Kierkegaard, SUD, 6.
3. Dru, *Soul of Kierkegaard,* 50–51, 59. (Selections are from 1836, 1839.)
4. As cited in Driskell and Brittain, *The Eternal Crossroads,* 1, cf. 22–23.
5. Rhoads, et. al., *Mark As Story,* 140.

Of course, this *literary* invitation may well have been accompanied by a *literal* invitation. For Mark's "audience" in group settings likely included persons *of the sinful* "categories" stigmatized by the culture, possibly even seated near "the fortunate" at table fellowship.[6] Therefore, Mark presented Jesus as the example (or prototype) to be followed in relations to others in the new Christian community, because of God's gospel for "sinners." The obstacle the gospel community was to overcome was the sad reality of the outcasts of society, those who would have been a rightful concern of Marx, as seen in the previous chapter. Societies tend to care most about those who "fit in," as was seen in relation to Mark's leper. Mark thus presents the various social "categories" of people who encountered Jesus—to parallel those encountering him in and through the Marcan community—and thereby continue the gospel-call of hospitable welcome to all.

This development of the gospel-community accompanies and embellishes the redemptively *significant* account of Jesus' calling of Levi. For that call parallels his calling of the four fishermen: both took place "alongside/ *beside the sea*" and both were answered by immediate response (see ESV). But the incongruity of the parallel calls would be obvious to Mark's audience. Fisherman, though not of the upper class, were not of the despised class. So, Mark here shows Jesus eating with "many tax collectors and sinners" in his house, much to the disapproval of "teachers who were Pharisees." Jesus (and Mark) was determined that his growing family would not reflect the "fleshly" separations of society (2 Cor 5:16). Jesus' "creation" of a new family/society demonstrates that he did not aim to *press* its new manners and customs upon the larger society. The aim was to create "a city on a hill" which serves as a sign and witness of the kingdom which can "leaven" and "raise," through its social-dynamic, the entire "lump" of society (Matt 5:14; 13:33, 28:18).[7] But Jesus did *press* the criterion for his society by positing the threshold to its "family door" as the forgiveness of sin, implied in the fact that he graciously ate even with unrepentant sinners.[8] He came as the physician for the sick, not for the righteous. In the vernacular of Kierkegaard's day and ours "the righteous" might better be considered the fortunate, the successful, *the normal*.

---

6. See the commentary of R. Alan Streett on Luke's account of Levi where he discusses the table fellowship in the house services in the early church, and which can certainly also be applied to Mark's account. Streett, *Subversive Meals*, 135–141.

7. We again point out what Marx missed, that *true* Christianity is not to be the "opiate" to pacify the guilty consciences of "the fortunate" or to provide a painkiller for the hopelessness of "the unfortunate." See Westphal, *Suspicion and Faith*, 138.

8. See Witherington, *Gospel of Mark*, loc. 1828–1836.

"THERE IS NO BLISS EXCEPT IN DESPAIR; HURRY UP AND DESPAIR"

Kierkegaard was never seen as normal by most everyone, something he readily admitted. One example is shown in the short statement included in this chapter's title, "There is no bliss except in despair, hurry up and despair."[9] This provocative statement is a paraphrase penned by one of Kierkegaard's readers, disapprovingly summarizing part of Kierkegaard's first major work, *Either/Or*. His critical reader also added these words to the paraphrase, "you will find no happiness until you do." By hearing the message but not recognizing the significance of that vital qualification, his paraphraser summarized that Kierkegaard's *Either/Or* "contains a dissatisfaction with life that can only be the product of a warped life."[10]

Of course, it is true that Kierkegaard's life was melancholy and despairing. Throughout his life he was generally a misfit in relation to society and even to himself. But he preached those oddities as though he was the achiever, which would certainly seem "warped." His conflict with society was especially aggravated toward the end of his life, when he more obviously and vigorously "attacked" Christendom." For all along he had been clandestinely critiquing it. Thus, like Levi, he was more than simply a misfit, and more than merely an enemy, but also a sort of traitor to his people. But some did hear his arguments. According to reports of his funeral some protested the "violation" of Kierkegaard's person and message through the official pomp and reverence given a declared rebel by the established church.[11] Of course these protesters may have been, as one report had it, "composed primarily of young people and a large number of obscure personages . . . there were no dignitaries present."[12] Jorgen Bukdahl more honestly identifies these supporters as "the poor and simple people" who "escorted the coffin out to Assistens Cemetery" demonstrating that Kierkegaard, like Jesus, had to some extent become successfully "incognito" along with the unfortunate, the lowly "sinners" of his day.[13]

Kierkegaard's message in *Either/Or*, which was accurately paraphrased: "There is no bliss except in despair, hurry up and despair, you will find no happiness until you do," parallels Jesus' own words that he "only" came for the sick and not for the "healthy." For the Pharisees and other self-righteous

---

9. Kirmmse, *Encounters with Kierkegaard*, 57, 285 n6. (From the 1843 letter of Signe Laessoe to Hans Christian Anderson.)

10. Kirmmse, *Encounters with Kierkegaard*, 57.

11. See Garff, *Soren Kierkegaard*, 798.

12. Garff, *Soren Kierkegaard*, xvii.

13. Bukdahl, *Soren Kierkegaard*, 129.

people "will find no happiness" i.e., *righteousness*, unless they "hurry up and despair" i.e., become sick, or a *sinner*.

Kierkegaard's unhappy reader and paraphraser was offended that the "happy" people of Denmark needed to *despair* to find happiness and considered Kierkegaard's idea "the product of a warped life." Kierkegaard's point, proven. And the idea of Jesus, that one needed to "become a sinner" to become righteous, was similarly rejected and considered the product of a person who was blasphemous (2:7), unclean (2:16), unlawful (2:24), insane (3:21), demon-possessed (3:22), a local working-class simpleton (6:3), undignified (10:13), unauthorized (11:28), unfaithful to Israel (12:14), and unfaithful to the temple (14:58). "God's people" of Denmark and Israel certainly found the idea of needing to become "despairing" and "sick" deeply offensive to their personal and societal lives. And their offense indicated their belief that *they* did not need to "despair" and "become sick." Again, point proven.

In subsequent sections of this chapter, we will consider what further happens to the already low reputations of "sick" people when they come to Jesus, and the subsequent requirement to meet that challenge as *a second movement of faith*. But in the next section, we will consider why the gospel of salvation initially calls for a consciousness of sin and despair as *a first movement of faith*.

THE SICKNESS UNTO DEATH AND "THE PHILISTINE-BOURGEOIS MENTALITY"

In *The Sickness Unto Death*, Kierkegaard further characterizes the "Christians" he addressed in his *Christian Discourses* as essentially pagans.[14] In order to further understand this characterization, we first need to recognize a threefold "formula" that underlies the gospel "paradoxes" under consideration in this chapter.

1. "The sickness unto death is despair."[15]

2. "Despair is interpreted as a sickness, not as a cure."[16]

3. "The cure is simply to die, to die to the world."[17]

---

14. See in chapter 9, in the section "Simon's Temptation, Repentance, and Redemption, Part 2." In this section we will further deepen the understanding of "the first temptation" of Simon *leprosus*, which was the despair of not willing to be a sinner.

15. Kierkegaard, SUD, 11. Something Kierkegaard's paraphraser may not have understood, perhaps despairingly.

16. Kierkegaard, SUD, 6. What Kierkegaard's paraphraser seems to have not recognized and stumbled over.

17. Kierkegaard, SUD, 6. Very much another way of stating the motto of GNG, "I

Now we may consider Kierkegaard's further characterization of Denmark's "pagans" as "the philistine-bourgeois mentality" which is a "determinist, fatalist" necessitarianism which lacks possibility:

> It is quite different with the philistine-bourgeois mentality, that is triviality, which also essentially lacks possibility. The philistine-bourgeois mentality is spiritlessness; determinism and fatalism are despair of spirit, but spiritlessness is also despair. The philistine-bourgeois mentality lacks every qualification of spirit and is completely wrapped up in probability . . . therefore it lacks the possibility of becoming aware of God . . . he lives within a certain trivial compendium of experiences of how things go, what is possible, what usually happens. In this way, the philistine-bourgeois mentality has lost his self and God . . . The philistine-bourgeois mentality thinks that it controls possibility, that it has tricked this prodigious elasticity into the trap or madhouse of probability, thinks that it holds it prisoner; it leads possibility around imprisoned in the cage of probability, exhibits it, imagines itself to be the master, does not perceive that precisely thereby it has imprisoned itself in the thralldom of spiritlessness and is the most wretched of all.[18]

To summarize Kierkegaard's point, the philistine-bourgeois mentality is triviality and spiritlessness; lacks possibility—even of God; has lost itself; is in the despair of not knowing it is in despair; and is therefore in the most wretched condition.

In *The Concept of Anxiety*, we read "in spiritlessness there is no anxiety, because it is too happy, too content, and too spiritless for that."[19] Jason Mahn lists the various terms Kierkegaard uses to characterize this low spiritual quality of modern post-Christian life: "'the crowd,' 'Christendom,' 'speculation,' 'the present age,' 'philistines,' or, most commonly 'the spiritless.'"[20] He then adds that anxiety (despair) is also lacking, and clarifies that this lack of consciousness further removes them from the cure. Thus, they are in the most wretched condition of all because they are not conscious of their wretchedness. They suffer the despair of not being conscious of their despair which is fatal, a sickness unto death. In other

---

would have perished had I not perished." Kierkegaard, SLW, 194.

18. Kierkegaard, SUD, 40–42.

19. Kierkegaard, CA, 95. This is then qualified regarding the "spiritlessness" of Christian "pagans" in that true pre-Christian paganism "is qualified *toward* spirit" while post-Christian "paganism" is "*away* from spirit . . . To that extent, paganism is much to be preferred."

20. Mahn, *Fortunate Fallibility*, 80. Also see Christman, "Lewis and Kierkegaard."

words, a person cannot be cured if they do not know they are sick, and sick unto death. Hence, they are in the most despairing condition of all, not looking for a cure to the mortal disease they unknowingly have. Mahn summarizes that, "The spiritless are doubly removed from the Christian cure and so must (1) become capable of sinning before (2) learning to trust the Physician's guidance."[21] This mirrors the situation of the Pharisees in Mark. For they exhibited the spiritless philistine-bourgeois mentality of the sickness unto death—at the lowest level of not knowing they were in despair—and therefore needed to "become sinners" to receive the gospel's cure. Mahn notes that they are "doubly removed from the Christian cure," confirming the subsequent necessity of the "second-movement" which will be considered in the next section. Kierkegaard shows them as falling short of even the first movement:

> Most men are characterized by a dialectic of indifference and live a life so far from the good (faith) that it is almost too spiritless to be called sin—indeed almost too spiritless to be called despair. It is certainly true that there is no merit in being a sinner in the strictest sense of the word. But on the other hand, how in the world can an essential sin-consciousness be found in a life so immersed in triviality and silly aping of "the others" that it can hardly be called sin, a life that is too spiritless to be called sin and is worthy only, as Scripture says, of being "spewed out."[22]

This spiritlessness is without any real hope, because it lacks possibility and replaces it with the crowd's pseudo-provision of numerical comfort gained with "the others." These non-selves need to learn "to hope and fear—or to fear and hope—by rendering possible that which surpasses . . . But the philistine-bourgeoise mentality does not have imagination, does not want it, abhors it."[23] Like Kierkegaard's "Christian" pagans, the Pharisees fell to "aping" one another in the false comfort of their self-justifying herd. Simply put, they were not determined by God or a responsive "spirit" and only revealed their need to "become a sinner" in the "first movement of faith."

---

21. Mahn, *Fortunate Fallibility*, 81. "Become capable" does not imply innocence, but rather, evasion and self-deception.

22. Kierkegaard, SUD, 101.

23. Kierkegaard, SUD, 41.

THE SICKNESS UNTO DEATH AND THE "SECOND MOVEMENT OF FAITH"

The second movement of faith is something we saw Simon *leprosus* achieving when we considered him in chapter 9.[24] What we will see here is another consideration of how his faith overcame the higher levels of despair. The reader may remember that he overcame *two temptations* to despair that *followed* upon "the first movement of faith," of becoming sick, a sinner, before God. These two temptations were (1) in despair *not willing* to be oneself—a sinner, and (2) in despair *defiantly willing* to be oneself—a sinner. It seems that we see here *a third temptation*: the willing to be oneself—a sinner, not in defiance but in a *pseudo-faith*. And since that is a false faith, that is still *in despair*, and the overcoming of that could only be by true faith.

Kierkegaard's *Fear and Trembling* presents and differentiates between faith and false-faith in Johannes de Silentio's meditations on God's faith-trial of Abraham to sacrifice Isaac, the child of promise—*his future* according to the promise (Gen 22). Kierkegaard depicted that trial as whether Abraham would sacrifice Isaac as the "knight of infinite resignation" or as the "knight of faith." And what is interesting is that his *Fear and Trembling* presents the ways of these two knights in relation to the philistine-bourgeoise mentality. Kierkegaard's view is that the knight of infinite resignation falsely "overcomes" the bourgeoisie mentality through a disdain of life by exercising a *stoic* "faith" of non-attachment.[25] In contrast, the knight of faith truly overcomes the philistine-bourgeoise mentality not merely through a stoic disdain, but through his real faith in a future *reception* of the *this-worldly* promises of God. In fact, he rightly *ought* to be *relatively attached to the relative good*, though not *absolutely* attached thereto. For that absolute relation is reserved for the absolute good, namely God.[26]

Ironically, this makes the life of the knight of faith outwardly *appear* the same as life within the philistine-bourgeoise mentality.[27] The knight of

---

24. In the section "Simon's Temptation, Repentance, and Redemption, Part 2."

25. Westphal writes, "In infinite resignation, which is a 'substitute for faith,' I 'find myself and again rest in myself' (*FT*, 35)." Westphal, *Kierkegaard's Concept of Faith*, 37. See Kierkegaard FT, 48–49, where we read "The act of resignation does not require faith."

26. See Kierkegaard, CUP, 407.

27. Kierkegaard's pseudonymous author of *Fear and Trembling* writes of his unfulfilled quest to find the knight of faith, and what his imagination perceives him to be: "I have not found anyone like that; meanwhile I may very well imagine him . . . 'Good Lord, is this the man, is this really the one—he looks just like a tax collector!' . . . He belongs entirely to the world; no bourgeois philistine could belong to it more. Nothing of that distant and aristocratic nature by which the knight of the infinite is recognized.

infinite resignation was "content" to give up Isaac, the earthly future. But the knight of faith hoped to receive Isaac back in this life, receiving the future promised by God.[28] And of course, Abraham did receive Isaac back, as from the dead, just as Mark's disciples—who resign everything for Jesus and the gospel and thus die to the world—will "receive a hundredfold now in this time (see Mark 10:29–30; cf. Gal 6:14). This "hundredfold" fulfillment of such "worldly" things *appears* to be an endorsement of "the philistine-bourgeoise mentality." But it is not, because the latter is a faithless disdain of both the absolute relation to the absolute good and the relative relation to the worldly goods. Thus, we see in this second movement of faith, *from resignation to faith*, the fulfillment of the formula we numerated above: "(1) The sickness unto death is despair; (2) Despair is interpreted as a sickness, not as a cure; (3) The cure is simply to die, to die to the world." For those three items are overcome, respectively, by recognizing the despair, not being resigned to despair as the cure, and by faith becoming rightly related to the relative and the absolute through "death" to the world.

In chapter 9, Simon *leprosus* seems to have been too much the knight of infinite resignation since his hope for the future was in the main wholly deferred to Abraham's bosom.[29] But Mark did not emphasize the this-worldly reception of the promises of God for nothing. Rather, his emphasis was because there may be substantial realization of the promises of the kingdom in *this* life— albeit paradoxically as we will see in the next sections— and to kindle and cultivate that realization through the shaping of Christian discipleship and fellowship for true community. Thus, Mark shows Jesus, the prototype for discipleship and fellowship, "eating with the sinners and tax collectors." On that note we will begin to consider the paradoxical outworking of the second movement of faith, in which we will see the process

---

He finds pleasure in everything, takes part in everything, and every time he does it with an assiduousness that marks the worldly man who is attached to such things . . . and yet this man has made and is at every moment is making the movement of infinity. He drains the deep sadness of life in infinite resignation, he knows the blessedness of infinity, he has felt the pain of renouncing everything, the most precious thing in the world, and *yet the finite tastes just as good to him as to the one who never knew anything higher* . . . *he has this security that makes him delight in it as if finitude were the surest thing of all.*" Kierkegaard, FT, 38–40.

28. Westphal writes, "The two knights serve two very different gods. The knight of faith makes that 'one more movement,' the faith that he will get the beloved (Isaac or the princess) back *in this life,* and this movement is made (a) 'by virtue of the absurd' and (b) 'by virtue of the fact that for God all things are possible' (*FT,* 46)." Westphal, *Kierkegaard's Concept of Faith,* 36.

29. Though we also saw that Simon *leprosus* represented a believer struggling in the spiritual trial/temptation regarding the real possibility of this-worldly participation in God's promises.

by which God superintends it through the "invitation" of Christ incognito. This ensures that his "family" is also incognito, and yet is also able to enjoy life more fully than do those of the spiritless philistine-bourgeoise mentality.

CHRIST'S PARADOXICAL INVITATION TO THE FELLOWSHIP OF SUFFERING THAT GAINS THE WORLD

As persons become conscious of their despair and become sinners before the divine physician in the first movement of faith, how does Christ then enable them to make the second movement of faith? The answer is, at least largely, through the "outward pressures" and "worldly shape" that redemption takes in the community of God. As individuals come to Christ, their life at the first looks like the prodigal son's did in Jesus' well-known parable (Luke 15:11–32). When he came to "his right mind" he didn't return home to immediately begin the "happily ever-after" life. Instead, he found the "older brother" and his scorn. Similarly, Levi the tax-collector's "return" to home was met by the Pharisees. Yes, as the prodigal son was met by his loving father, so also Levi was met by Jesus. But the party-spoiler, the elder brother's Pharisaic counterpart was also there.

Situating this scene in the visible world of Mark's day, the Pharisaic "older brother" was someone Mark's returned prodigals would tangibly see and encounter in their lives. And the Heavenly Father of these returned prodigals was as visible to them as "Father Abraham" was to Simon *leprosus*, in other words, *invisible*. This again raises the question of what "Isaac" signifies to all believers, namely their dying to the world and what it would promise for the future. Is any worldly inheritance for returned prodigals wholly "delayed" until heaven? Is the "feast" at the father's table merely Marx's opiate, to kill the present pain of earthly famine and hopelessness, as we saw in chapter 10?

The answer is that the prodigal's "return" is not a restoration to their native society where they would not receive these "goods," but a welcome to God's new family where they will, albeit in possibly transfigured forms. But there will be definite and important changes of living environment and worldly goods, such as that shown by Mark's nameless leper who previously lived away from society and "Simon the leper" then living in his house with company (Mark 1:40; 14:3). When individuals became disciples, they entered a wholly new life in relation to society. And that change was certainly not a welcome to the bourgeois-philistine society! It was rather a banning from it. Therefore, Kierkegaard portrayed the call of Jesus in this way:

> Come here now, all you who labor and are burdened, *that is*, if you feel the need, (even if you are of all who suffer the most miserable,)

if you feel the need to be helped *in this way*, that is, *helped into even greater misery*—then come here, *he will help you.*[30]

Thus, a Levi, a Kierkegaard, and all other laboring and burdened prodigals, are promised *even greater misery* by the divine inviter. The truth of the welcome to the Christian community is its "Catch-22" paradox of what do not appear to be *good-news* societal consequences for those invited *and for the inviter* since both always become scandalous on the account of the other in a "vicious cycle" of offense: As Jesus attracts "the outcasts" to himself *he* becomes more scandalous (the incognito)! As the outcasts are attracted to Jesus, *they* become more scandalous! Thus, the gospel is certainly not what *seems* to be a win-win situation to the philistine-bourgeoise mentality which is "doubly-removed from the cure." For the cure is paradoxically *provided* in the two movements of faith: "becoming sick/a sinner" and coming to the "greater misery" of fellowship at the table of the "scandalous" community. Thus, Christian salvation is not about being reconciled to the native homeland but being welcomed to a new one. For Christians are truly born again, not just spiritually but also bodily, as members of the new community/kingdom of God (John 3:1–5; Mark 10:29–31; 1 Cor 12:12–13). It is also worth mentioning that that is why true Christianity is politically disruptive and does not merely distribute Marx's opiate to perpetuate a "harmonious" society of the guilty fortunate and the hopeless outcasts. Kierkegaard further explains that rather than providing an opiate, Christianity provides an offense:

> Christianity does indeed proclaim itself to be comfort, cure, and healing—that being so, people turn to it as they turn to a friend in need, thank it as they thank a helper, because by the help of it or by its help they believe they will be able to bear the suffering under which they sigh. And then—the very opposite happens. They go to the Word to seek help—and then come to suffer on account of the Word.[31]

With those words Kierkegaard explains the fact of the offense, noting how those coming to Christ experience it. With the last sentence he begins to explain why this is the case, namely that the offense comes when one follows the word of this particular physician, Christ:

> When in sickness I go to a physician, he may find it necessary to prescribe a very painful treatment—there is no

---

30. Soren Kierkegaard, PC, 56. (Parenthesis and italics added for clarity and emphasis.) Kierkegaard is making an ironic statement to the effect that Jesus the inviter of the miserable is offering to them an even greater misery.

31. Kierkegaard, PC, 114.

self-contradiction in my submitting to it. No, but if on the other hand I suddenly find myself in trouble, an object of persecution, because, because I have gone to *that* physician: well, then there is self-contradiction. The physician has perhaps announced he can help me with regard to the illness from which I suffer, and perhaps he can really do that—but there is an *aber* (but) that I had not thought of at all. The fact that I get involved with this physician, attach myself to him—that is what makes me an object of persecution; here is the possibility of offense.[32]

Thus, in the "second movement of faith" the knight of faith paradoxically receives "Isaac" back, gaining the promise in this life— "houses and brothers and sisters and mothers and children and lands"—albeit "with persecutions, and in the age to come eternal life" (Mark 10:30). But does this ultimately still open the door, albeit a difficult one, for a "double-minded" seeking of God for the sake of reward?[33]

"DOES JOB (THE KNIGHT OF FAITH) SERVE GOD FOR NAUGHT?"

Jason Mahn writes, "We might even read *Practice* as posing the question of the Accuser in the book of Job: Does Job serve God for naught? In other words: Can a person offer God proper praise even without receiving social, material, or spiritual benefits?"[34] Therefore, we will consider three ways Kierkegaard's understanding of "the invitation" does not succumb to the mercenary motive but rather overcomes Satan's accusation.

First, the second movement of faith certainly finds reward, as Mark 10:30–32 promises, but that reward is not "worldly" in the sense that the philistine-bourgeoise mentality is.[35] This is because, as was mentioned above, the relation to the world of the Christian in the "second movement of faith" remains relatively related to the relative and does not live in absolute

---

32. Kierkegaard, PC, 115.
33. A main concern of Kierkegaard, PH, 68–78.
34. Mahn, *Fortunate Fallibility*, 140. "Practice" signifies *Practice in Christianity*.
35 "They would experience support from each other, knowing that their trusted efforts to live the values of the rule of God would be just as misunderstood by and hidden from the world as Jesus' faithfulness was." Rhoads, et. al., *Mark as Story*, 146. The reality underlying this statement is what leads historian Rodney Stark to write, "What is almost always missed is that Christianity often puts the food on the table! It makes life better here and now. Not merely in psychological ways, as faith in an attractive afterlife can do, but in terms of concrete worldly benefits. Consider that a study based on ancient tombstones has established that early Christians outlived their pagan neighbors!" Stark, *Triumph of Christianity*, 105.

relation to the relative. Nevertheless, the paradox is that followers of Christ do, in a more wholesome sense, receive the world, much to the surprise of Kierkegaard's pseudonymous author of *Fear and Trembling* in a way that overcomes what he called "the reward-disease."[36]

Second, in the second movement of faith Christ's disciples as a community become signs of contradiction, and the possibility of offense for others, thereby ensuring their authenticity as witnesses to Christ. They enter what Paul called *the fellowship of his sufferings* which is certainly not any form of "worldly" reward to the philistine-bourgeoise mentality (Phil 3:10).

Third, faith increasingly leads the disciple toward the love of God *as* the only reward. Paul's *fellowship-centered* desire (eros) is the prime example that demonstrates the Christian normativity of *the love of God* as its own reward.[37] It is significant that in Paul's confession of the faith, hope, and love, that abide in the longing to "know fully" and be "fully known" by God, *love* is the "greatest" because it never ends (1 Cor 13:8, 13).

In Carl Hughes' important in-depth study of Kierkegaard's entire authorship, he demonstrates that the infinite love of God was its beckoning lodestar "inciting ever-greater desire for God and ever-more compassionate love for human beings."[38] So also, the ultimate ground and scandal of the community is the eternal love, the "dance," of the Triune God.[39] And the "Inviter" ensures that the sick, the sinners, and the despairing, will find the paradoxical "help" of "greater misery," in the fellowship of suffering that is consummated by participation in the abiding community's dance in God's infinite love.

We conclude that Mark's "table fellowship" of sinners— "the sick"— first glimpsed through Simon's mother-in-law (1:30–31), provides: a critique of the philistine-bourgeoise mentality, whether "Jewish" or "Christian;" a picture of the this-worldly realization of the new community; and a promise of the ultimate hope of the resurrection fellowship. Kierkegaard prays a benediction to these significant paradoxes and worldly inversions: *Lord, give us weak eyes for things of little worth, and eyes clear-sighted in all of your truth.*[40] For "the cure is simply to die, to die to the world."[41]

---

36. Kierkegaard, PH, 68. Thus "Johannes de Silentio" exclaims "Good Lord, is this the man, is this really the one—he looks just like a tax collector . . . he thinks that his wife surely will have a special hot meal for him when he comes home." Kierkegaard, FT, 39. (See 1 Tim 6:17–18.)

37. See Fredrickson, *Eros and the Christ,* 129–143.

38. Hughes, *Kierkegaard and the Staging,* 200.

39. Lewis, *Mere Christianity,* IV:4.

40. Kierkegaard, SUD, 3.

41. Kierkegaard, SUD, 6.

12

"Thy Disciples Fast Not?"

Fasting Disciples and Feasting Christendom: Either/Or?

Mark 2:18–22 (NIV)

18 Now John's disciples and the Pharisees were fasting. Some people came and asked Jesus, "How is it that John's disciples and the disciples of the Pharisees are fasting, but yours are not?" 19 Jesus answered, "How can the guests of the bridegroom fast while he is with them? They cannot, so long as they have him with them. 20 But the time will come when the bridegroom will be taken from them, and on that day they will fast. 21 "No one sews a patch of unshrunk cloth on an old garment. Otherwise, the new piece will pull away from the old, making the tear worse. 22 And no one pours new wine into old wineskins. Otherwise, the wine will burst the skins, and both the wine and the wineskins will be ruined. No, they pour new wine into new wineskins."

This is the road we all have to take—over the Bridge of Sighs into eternity . . . I am not Christian severity contrasted with Christian leniency. I am . . . mere human honesty. —Soren Kierkegaard[1]

---

1. As cited by Auden in Kierkegaard, LTK, 30, 3.

Did the seemingly austere Kierkegaard miss the gospel's cue that the new kingdom of God would be marked by feasting, rather than fasting? Or did the disciples eating on a regular fast day merely signify a transient celebratory mood during the brief halcyon days of Jesus' early ministry, to be subsequently followed by the mood of continual fasting? What is proper, to feast or to fast, during the time between the coming and return of Christ? Or is the question even one of an *Either/Or*?

KIERKEGAARD AND CHRISTIANITY: A MATCH MADE IN HEAVEN OR IN PERSONAL DISSATISFACTION?

As noted in the previous chapter, one reader of Kierkegaard's *Either/Or?* remarked that "*the entire book contains a dissatisfaction with life that can only be the product of a warped life.*"[2] Pushing this suspicion further, is it possible that the book revealed something even more telling, that Kierkegaard's dissatisfaction eventually found a home in Christianity because the faith itself is quite amenable to ascetic world-denial? Is Jesus the "pale Galilean" who has "conquered" *feasting* so that all his followers must live an ever-ascetic life of fasting which is a morbid "feeding on the fulness of death"?[3] Even though the previous chapter showed Christianity as otherwise, we will nevertheless consider the case that modern-day philosopher Mark Taylor presents regarding Kierkegaard and his Christian faith.

> By opposing essence to existence and eternity to time, Kierkegaard reduces historical processes to inessentiality. Time no longer possesses intrinsic value but is significant only to the extent that it points beyond itself to a transcendent eternity. In this situation, "consciousness of life, of its existence and activity is only the agonized suffering over this existence and activity, for therein it is conscious that its essence is only its opposite, is conscious only of its own nothingness." This awareness of one's inessentiality leads to a passionate self-negation through which the temporal subject seeks to regain essential being by means of reconciliation with the divine object."[4]

We can use Taylor's accusation as the basis for asking: "Was Kierkegaard's '*road we all have to take—over the Bridge of Sighs into eternity*' but an

2. Kirmmse, *Encounters With Kierkegaard*, 57.

3. "Thou hast conquered, O pale Galilean; the world has grown grey from thy breath; We have drunken of things Lethean, and fed on the fulness of death." From Swinburne, *Hymn to Proserpine*.

4. As cited in Roberts, "Introduction," xiv.

escapist denial that enabled the 'warped life' of his ascetic self-estranged spirit to find a kindred spirit in the gospel of the "pale Galilean?" In answer, we will first briefly consider a criticism of Taylor's view of Kierkegaard, then try to show that Jesus, his gospel, and Kierkegaard all presented *fasting and feasting* as a dialectical necessity for those following Jesus.

Robert Perkins cites Taylor as a modern example of the myth that Kierkegaard's emphasis upon the individual was formulated in a social and political vacuum and therefore a mistaken and unworkable theory of human existence on the universal scale.[5] In other words, Taylor held that Kierkegaard's individualism has no relevance to the human project qua humanity. The only way to "live" is to deny and ultimately escape life. Thus "fasting" would seem to be the quintessence of Kierkegaard's life-view. But we have earlier seen that Kierkegaard saw Christianity as "existence-communication," with the existence to be communicated, that of Christ's. Therefore, the gospel answer can probably best be found by considering how Jesus himself related to life-situations and the "moods" or responses they call for in fasting or feasting.

This section of Mark opens with Jesus being asked why his disciples were not keeping the regular fast day as the disciples of John the Baptist and of the Pharisees did. The question seems to be a general one asked by unspecified "people," as if to show that the disciples of Jesus were already becoming known for their peculiarity regarding customary practices. Jesus answers with an allegorical but scripturally based story, which he then explains with two illustrations. His story of how the bridegroom's "guests" behave at a wedding depicts the significance of his presence as the anointed Messiah of God's kingdom. For Isaiah 25:6–9 speaks of the coming kingdom as a rich feast for all peoples, a text that seems to provide the background for Jesus' parable of the wedding feast in Matthew 22:1–14.

FASTING AND FEASTING: FITTING PATCHES AND CONTAINING NEW WINE

Of course, Jesus knew that he was bringing the kingdom and that his table fellowships *signified* the kingdom. But we are not told whether Jesus instructed the disciples to not fast. Perhaps Jesus simply led the way by eating, which is perhaps probable, given that he always modelled the proper practice for God's kingdom. In any case, it is probable that the disciples themselves had no idea that eating rather than fasting had the significance that it did.

---

5. See Perkins, "Introduction," xii-xvii.

The regular fast days were special times when Israelites "commemorated all the tragic times that had happened in their history."[6] Jesus used the discrepancy between the feasting of his disciples and the fasting of other disciples, to illustrate and dramatize the fact that fellowship with him was a foretaste of the glory of the coming Kingdom of God. A contrast was drawn between the days of glory to come and the tragic days of the past, raising the question of how to behave in the meantime. Ought one fast, or feast?

His answer was that since "the bridegroom" was there, feasting was not only appropriate, but required. His illustrations of new patches and old garments, new wine and old wineskins, were more christological than historical since *he* was determining present history. The proper practice was determined by what was now proper since he, the bridegroom of Israel, was present. The fitted patch and new wine in this instance signify feasting, which was then appropriate because of the "wedding." But if one doesn't recognize the significance of a new occurrence that changes the present situation, one will act as though the new has not arrived. In short, the presence of Jesus signifies that it is appropriate to *feast*, while to continue to *fast* is to act as though the bridegroom is absent. By calling himself the bridegroom of Israel, Jesus was also identifying himself with Yahweh, who in several OT texts was betrothed to Israel, though "she" had become unfaithful and played the harlot.[7]

Jesus says that if the bridegroom is *with* his guests, they *can't* fast. But when the bridegroom is *"taken from them"* they will fast "on that day." This certainly alludes to the death of Christ and the times of trial and persecution to follow as narrated in Mark 13:9–13, and in Matthew 22:1–14, when the *"servants"* of the King who held the wedding feast for his son, are *"mistreated and killed"* by the invited guests who would not attend. In that "day" fasting will be appropriate. So now that Jesus has been taken away is perpetual fasting the order of "the day?"

THE QUESTION OF KIERKEGAARD'S CONTEMPORANEITY WITH CHRIST: FASTING OR FEASTING?

In chapter 6 we considered Kierkegaard's view that *contemporaneity with Christ through the middle term of death* was the necessary path for discipleship. And that "middle term of death" signifies "dying to" self in conformity

---

6. Wright, *Matthew for Everyone*, 1:101.
7. Ortlund, *Whoredom: God's Unfaithful Wife*, 137–139; cf. Garland, *Theology of Mark*, 114.

to Christ's life which the disciple then becomes "contemporaneous" with. We must now consider how *present* contemporaneity with Christ relates to Christ's present "location": are we to fast over his apparent "absence" or feast in his "presence" by being "contemporary" with him?

First, Kierkegaard held that the time of living contemporaneously with Christ is always *now*—the present day of disciples living between the time of Jesus' earthly life and his future return. That time consists of living in the situation Jesus predicted: "*The time will come when the bridegroom will be taken from them, and on that day they will fast.*" That then-coming day was what Kierkegaard believed Danish Christendom had somehow transcended, overcoming the need for contemporaneity with Christ. Therefore, there was no need for fasting. But the time of contemporaneity is always now, *and consists in* identifying with *the lowliness of Christ*, his "inglorious" humanity, the pattern of life that is to be followed.[8] Thus contemporaneity is with Christ's historical lowliness, not his present loftiness. What had happened was that after 1800 years, Christendom only identified with *the loftiness of Christ*, his glorious divinity that is to be celebrated. Kierkegaard described the situation:

> There is incessant preaching in Christendom about what happened after Christ's death, how he triumphed, and his teachings triumphantly conquered the whole world—in short, we hear nothing but sermons that could more appropriately end with "Hurrah" than with "Amen." No, Christ's life here on earth is the paradigm; I and every Christian are to strive to model our lives in likeness to it.[9]

The life of Christ on earth certainly included times of feasting, as can been seen in Mark. It also included some difficult times, but the presence of Jesus seems to have prevented the need for much or continual fasting. But after Jesus ascended, they were "in the world as Jesus was," as *living paradoxes* in relation to "normal lives" and therefore remained "contemporary" with Jesus in lowliness and as incognito. And *that* contemporaneity would inevitably be accompanied by the need for fasting, for they were at odds with the world.

---

8. "Only the contemporary is actuality for me. That with which you are living simultaneously is actuality—for you. Thus every human being is able to become contemporary only with the time in which he is living—and then with one more, with Christ's life upon the earth, for Christ's life upon the earth, the sacred history, stands alone by itself, outside history." Kierkegaard, PC, 64.

9. Kierkegaard, PC, 107.

Second, Kierkegaard's emphasis on contemporaneity's middle term of death was due to its absence in the over-realized eschatology of Danish Christendom. In other words, Christendom for the most part identified with the loftiness of Jesus, the aspects of his life that made him appear "esteemed *and desirable.*" But that is the reverse image of the early church in lowliness. Because of this shift to concentrating on Christ's loftiness, the result was that Jesus now had multitudes of *admirers,* but not many *imitators:*

> Christ came to the world with the purpose of saving the world, also with the purpose—this in turn is implicit in his first purpose—of being *the prototype,* of leaving footprints for the person who wanted to join him, who then might become an *imitator*; this indeed corresponds to "footprints." That is why he let himself be born in lowliness and thereupon lived poor, abandoned, despised, abased. . .Understood in that way, there was unconditionally nothing to admire, unless one wanted to admire poverty, misery, contempt, etc. He was not even exempted from the worst—being pitied, a pitiable object of sympathy. No, there was truly not the least thing to admire. Nor was there in the situation of contemporaneity any occasion for admiring because Christ had only the same conditions to offer the person who joined him—and on those conditions no admirer has ever wanted to join; the same conditions: to become poor, despised, insulted, mocked, and if possible, even a little more, considering that in addition one was an adherent of such a despised individual. whom every sensible person shunned. . .Thus, Christianly understood, in this world loftiness is abasement. So, Christ entered on high, but his life and works on earth are what he left for imitation: that true loftiness is abasement or that abasement is true loftiness.[10]

In the mention of Christ entering on high, Kierkegaard was drawing on Jesus' words "*when I am lifted up from the earth I will draw all to myself.*" Together with his explanation of the need for *imitation* rather than *admiration,* for lowliness rather than loftiness, these do not present an ascetic denial of the world, but rather that Christ-followers enter a *living* fellowship of self-giving for the true *life* of the world. Christ and his followers may appear as ascetic world-deniers, but they are more accurately passionate world-lovers (Heb 12:2). Moreover, a convincing case can be made that Kierkegaard became a joyful "evangelist" of the good news which makes its true hearers joyful.[11]

10. Kierkegaard, PC, 238, 240–41, 259.
11. Pyper, *Joy of Kierkegaard,* 1, 13–14.

THE PARADOXICAL DIALECTIC OF FASTING AND FEASTING IN CHRISTIAN LIFE

Being able to see self-giving world-lovers rather than self-denying world-deniers is based on the truth that following Christ through the "*middle term of death*" is to live within a paradoxical dialectic of Christian living wherein opposites—suffering and joy, fasting and feasting—coincide to *together overcome* the present world while also inheriting "abundant" life in this world and "eternal life" in the age to come (Mark 10:30). But is talk of "overcoming the world" and "inheriting the world to come" just another sign of a world-denying asceticism? Sylvia Walsh explains how Kierkegaard's conception of the Christian life is essentially not an ascetic denial of the world:

> Dying to worldliness means dying to one's selfish attachment to the worldly. It is an overcoming of the "vital power" and dominance of the finite or worldly in the sense that one is no longer absolutely attached to it or essentially has one's life in it. This does not mean, however, that one literally denies oneself the things of the world or avoids intercourse with the world, becoming, as it were, "otherworldly." The ideal task of the existing individual is to maintain an absolute relation to the absolute while continuing to live in the finite. The difference is that one no longer has one's life essentially in the finite. Climacus expressly contrasts this understanding of "dying to" to the medieval ascetic way of renouncing the world. One does not become indifferent to the finite or express renunciation of it in outward forms. The ethical-religious individual's separation from worldliness is *incognito* since he or she continues to look and act like human beings. Dying to worldliness is essentially an inward movement that cannot be directly, unambiguously, or unconditionally expressed in outward forms and identified with or by external actions.[12]

Christian living in contemporaneity with Christ in self-denial can therefore practice both *fasting and feasting*, in the dialectic of suffering and joy combined in *one Christian existence* wherein all things work together for good (Rom 8:28). This is not an escape from the world, but a way of transformed living in the world through the vital connection to the infinite—participation in what Kierkegaard saw as the "longing" which is "the umbilical cord to the higher life."[13] This *incognito* existence will appear to

---

12. Walsh, *Living Christianly*, 87–88. "Climacus" is a reference to the pseudonymous "author" of Kierkegaard's CUP:1.

13. As cited by Taylor in Roberts, "Introduction," xiv.

be puzzling to those with a merely temporal view that misses the kingdom, such as those who asked Jesus why his disciples did not fast, but instead feasted. Simply put, the disciples were simply and "already" living in a *bigger* world, open to the presence of the future, being enabled to fast *while* feasting, and vice-versa. Thus, while *feasting and fasting* in a world-affirming life, they would traverse *"over the Bridge of Sighs into eternity."*

In conclusion, one might say that "feasting" and "fasting" are the two parts of the one dialectic of joy and suffering in the matrix of the Christian life. Both are essential under the present conditions of life, wherein feasting and fasting are both *central* practices of joy and suffering, the two poles of the one magnet of life. Of course, God as eternal joy in Christ became suffering to provide an essential "synthesis" for finite creatures apt to either gravitate toward suffering or levitate toward joy to the exclusion of the other pole. Kierkegaard called these imbalances despair *over* the earthly, and despair *of* the eternal. But despair is to be "overcome" by living the dialectic of earth and heaven by "resting transparently" in Christ, who as the God-man is, lived, and thus provides the middle ground between the poles of human existence for all.[14]

---

14. Kierkegaard, SUD, 60, 131.

13

The Sabbath Dialectic

God Made the Sabbath for Man—On the Sabbath Man Plotted Death for the Son of Man

Mark 2:23–3:6 (ESV)

2:23 One Sabbath he was going through the grainfields, and as they made their way, his disciples began to pluck heads of grain. 24 And the Pharisees were saying to him, "Look, why are they doing what is not lawful on the Sabbath?" 25 And he said to them, "Have you never read what David did, when he was in need and was hungry, he and those who were with him: 26 how he entered the house of God, in the time of Abiathar the high priest, and ate the bread of the Presence, which it is not lawful for any but the priests to eat, and also gave it to those who were with him?" 27 And he said to them, "The Sabbath was made for man, not man for the Sabbath. 28 So the Son of Man is lord even of the Sabbath."

3:1 Again he entered the synagogue, and a man was there with a withered hand. 2 And they watched Jesus, to see whether he would heal him on the Sabbath, so that they might accuse him. 3 And he said to the man with the withered hand, "Come here." 4 And he said to them, "Is it lawful on the Sabbath to do good or to do harm, to save life or to kill?" But they were silent. 5 And he looked around at them with anger, grieved at their hardness of heart, and said to the man, "Stretch out your hand." He stretched it out, and his hand was restored. 6 The Pharisees went out and immediately held counsel with the Herodians against him, how to destroy him.

"Jesus thrown everything off balance." —The Misfit[1]

"Away with that man from the earth, he does not deserve to live"... Without change since the time of our Lord Jesus Christ. —Soren Kierkegaard[2]

"God in heaven, have mercy on me, God of Abraham, have mercy on me; if I have no father on earth, then you be my father!" —Johannes de Silentio[3]

Flannery O'Connor, in one of her famous (or to some, *infamous*) short stories called "A Good Man is Hard to Find," masterfully presents an escaped nihilistic serial killer known as "The Misfit" and a Southern superficially "Christian" grandmother engaged in a life and death struggle that transcends mere life and death. Their struggle is microcosmic of the universal struggle for cosmic balance that has transpired since the time, in the Misfit's words, *"Jesus thrown everything off balance."* In essence, their struggle shows two *misfit* people wrestling with spiritual forces greater than themselves while vainly trying to maintain the "balance" of their lives either in conformity to or collision with society. The irony is that their attempts to *maintain balance* struggle with the one who came to *bring balance* by throwing the human "normality" of living apart from God *off balance*. O'Connor's story parts the curtain separating invisible transcendent realities from the visible immanent ones to reveal a dialectical struggle between demonic and human invasive imbalance masquerading as balance and God's true restorative balance.

THE SABBATH FOR ALL BECAME FOR THE FEW

O'Connor's fictitious episode shadows the cosmic dimensions of Mark's first depiction of acute collision between the restorer of God's *gracious order* and man's *destructive disorder* which is misconstrued as "balance." Mark thus reveals the dialectical struggle between balance and imbalance. The specific dispute was over what activities are "proper" on the sabbath. God instituted the sabbath so that humanity could achieve a balanced practice between

---

1. O'Connor, *The Complete Stories*, 131.
2. Kierkegaard, AC, 279.
3. Kierkegaard, FT, 10. "*Johannes de Silentio*" was Kierkegaard's pseudonymous "author" of *Fear and Trembling*.

activity and resting for their own sake and for the creation they were to steward wisely and mercifully. According to many Scriptures, creation either sings or laments in response to the faithful stewardship of the sons of God (Rom 8:19).[4]

But humankind fell from that faithful stewardship by seeking to be wise apart from their creator and the givenness of their role. This prefigured the path that Israel followed, as depicted in the parable of the man who planted a vineyard and hired stewards who rebelled and claimed it as their own (Mark 12:1–12). Of course, after humankind's original fall from sabbath relations, God chose Israel and instituted the weekly sabbath-rest and other "commandments" to renew and re-order human stewardship toward God's original intent.

By the time Jesus arrived, this re-ordering had become disorder. Because of the fall of Israel that repeated that of humanity in Eden, God's "behold, it was very good" was turned into "cursed." The good sabbath structure meant to enhance the lives of all became the means of a corrupt system that promoted and preserved the status-quo of the few. Mark's Pharisees saw that the disciples plucking heads of grains on the sabbath, if applied wholesale throughout their society would undermine their privileged lives. The sabbath, meant to be a life-giving social structure, became all-important as a powerful means of social corruption in Israel. Similarly, Christendom became corrupt. In time, some desired its complete eradication. Thus, Voltaire declared: "*If you want to kill Christianity, you must abolish Sunday.*"[5] In a sense the Pharisees and Christendom became seduced by the power inherent in the sabbath. This also held true for the Jewish Temple and "the church." Jesus and his true disciples posed "a real and present danger" to the world of Israel and Christendom.

What the disciples were doing was only natural, since they were hungry, and was even permitted in the law. But it was probably interpreted by the Pharisees as working, by "harvesting" on the sabbath.[6] So Jesus pointed to the example of "David and those with him" to verify that "*the sabbath was made for Man, not man for the sabbath*" and accentuated this by adding that he as "the Son of Man" was "*Lord, even of the sabbath.*" By saying these things Jesus is restoring the sabbath to its rightful and life-giving place in relation to human life as subservient to humans, albeit while also making himself deity.

---

4. See Moo, *Romans*, 513–515, who cites Ps 65:12–13; Isa 24:4; Jer 4:28, 12:4 as OT examples.

5. As cited in: Baker, *The Decalogue*, 80.

6. See Alexander, *Mark*, 52.

In Mark's accounts of sabbath controversies, the accusation of the disciples develops into the suspicion that Jesus might heal the man with a "withered hand." So, Jesus went ahead and provoked them, telling the man "stretch out your hand!" Knowing they could justify themselves while ironically being *actively* against doing good and saving life *on the sabbath*, even to the point of plotting "to destroy him," led him to anger and grief "at their hardness of heart." Their hardheartedness was revealed by Jesus' confronting their distorted sabbath, which was tied up with their livelihood, their very view of the "world" (the cosmos). Peter Leithart explains the scope and details of the situation, showing why this was an issue of monumental proportions to them:

> The rich got richer, the poor poorer. And the temple, the house that originally housed the tablets of Torah that revealed Yahweh's justice, was the chief promoter of injustice. The temple leaders turned stoicheic priestly hierarchy into a cover for fleshly lusts. Jesus knew where the pressure points were, and he courageously acted and spoke to provoke repentance, with the full realization that he would in fact provoke nothing but fury. His parables parodied Pharisaical pseudo-righteousness: they were the older brother who complained glumly when his brother returned and brought his father joy; they were the vineyard keepers who plotted to kill the son of the vineyard owner—and they played to type by hatching a plot to kill Jesus (Mt 21:33–46). Jesus ate with sinners, calling the Jews to table fellowship, but his table practice became a point of controversy and one of the main charges against him. . . As Yahweh incarnate, he battered down binary oppositions that constitute the fundamental physics of Israel's world, but he also battered at the extra walls that flesh-dominated Torah had erected. These were not breaches of etiquette. If Jesus' way became the way of Israel, then all the hopes and plans of the Pharisees and scribes were doomed, because their plans and hopes depended on maintaining and tightening the taste-not-touch-nots of stoicheic life. . . If Jesus' program were to catch on, if most Jews began sharing tables with sinners, if they all stopped washing their hands before meals, they would be undermining the divisions that structured the reality of Judaism. The physics of Israel's life would be disrupted; Jewish nature itself would unravel.[7]

The Pharisees and scribes were playing for keeps in a high stakes battle for "Israel" and their privileged place in it, against Jesus who "came forth"

---

7. Leithart, *Delivered from the Elements*, 148–149.

to restore the sabbath to its rightful place in God's intention for Israel as a servant of humanity, and creation itself. And as in many such life-or-death struggles, literal death is often the outcome, such as is portrayed in O'Connor's dizzying story about The Misfit and the grandmother.

"THE DIZZINESS OF FREEDOM"

The Misfit had at some earlier point in life been faced with Jesus and the *possibility of offense* he brings to all and was offended. He seems to be in the thralldom of Kierkegaard's "demonic despair of defiance," and his life apparently consists in variously justifying himself in that defiance. This was demonstrated when, with obvious hostility toward everything and everyone, he explains his "existential predicament" based on the two "ifs" regarding Jesus that apparently *requires* him to follow the second and be a nihilist:

> "Jesus was the only One that ever raised the dead." The Misfit continued, "and He shouldn't have done it. He thrown everything off balance. *If* He did what he said, then it's nothing for you to do but throw away everything and follow Him, and *if* He didn't, then it's nothing for you to do but enjoy the few minutes you got left the best way you can—by killing somebody or burning down his house or doing some other meanness to him. No pleasure but meanness," he said, and his voice had become almost a snarl."[8]

The grandmother, before meeting the Misfit, appears to be a rather "spunky" strong-willed character. But she seems to exhibit what Kierkegaard called "the despair in weakness," wherein persons, out of weakness of human spirit, fail to will to be themselves before God. This is evident in her "Christian" character throughout the story but becomes especially evident in the most telling moment when she replies to the Misfit "*maybe he didn't raise the dead*" for the sake of self-preservation. But O'Connor also shows that this was an especially "weak" moment even for her, in "*not knowing what she was saying and feeling so dizzy that she sank down in the ditch with her legs twisted under her.*" Kierkegaard spoke of "the dizziness of freedom," meaning that the experience of human freedom of choice resulted in an anxiety of dizziness, especially if one is conscious of the gravity of what one's choice signifies regarding one's relation to God and oneself:

> Anxiety may be compared with dizziness. He whose eye happens to look down into the yawning abyss becomes dizzy. But

---

8. O'Connor, *The Complete Stories*, 132, emphasis mine.

> what is the reason for this? It is just as much in his own eyes as in the abyss, for suppose he had not looked down. Hence anxiety is the dizziness of freedom, which emerges when the spirit wants to posit the synthesis and freedom looks down into its own possibility, laying hold of finiteness to support itself. Freedom succumbs in this dizziness. Further than this, psychology cannot and will not go. In that moment everything is changed, and freedom, when it again rises, sees that it is guilty. Between these two moments lies the leap, which no science has explained and which no science can explain.[9]

The grandmother in perhaps her ultimate moment of weakness, becomes dizzy at the possibility of her own nihilistic "leap" into the abyss through denying Christ. She experiences the dizziness and anxiety of her freedom. But in the story O'Connor goes on to show her *upward* leap of faith, "becoming a sinner," but also something more. For she both accepts and exhibits Christ's love when she compassionately "becomes a sinner" in solidarity with the Misfit. She thus receives God's grace and becomes an agent thereof in her final moment of this life.

The grandmother's exhibition of the despair in weakness, when her life was at risk by the Misfit, perhaps parallels the same in the Pharisees' when their life (livelihood) was confronted by Jesus. But the Pharisees increasingly moved into the demonic despair of defiance, as does the Misfit. The Misfit has long been living in a demonic despair of defiance. So, when the grandmother "saw the man's face . . . twisted close to her own as if he were going to cry" she embodies love to him, murmuring "why you're one of my babies . . . one of my own children!" His *demonic defiance* was inflamed. In *her moment of grace,* she reaches out to touch the Misfit. But "the Misfit sprang back as if a snake had bitten him and shot her three times through the chest."[10] J. Ramsay Michaels comments,

> O'Connor explained to Andrew Lytle that "The moment of grace excites the devil to frenzy" (Collected Works, 1121), and although the Misfit is not the devil, he sees the grandmother through the devil's eye . . . It is not a matter of the grandmother confronting the Dragon in the person of The Misfit. On the contrary, he is one of her "own children." Instead, The Misfit confronts a gesture of grace that is to him the Dragon or "snake" he fears most. "Grace is never received warmly,"

---

9. Soren Kierkegaard, CA, 61. Kierkegaard seems to be speaking of the "leap" here as the leap of faith, but he also saw the choice for sin as a leap. His point in both was that nether leap can be accounted for by deterministic reasoning.

10. O'Connor, *The Complete Stories*, 132.

O'Connor wrote to Hawkes. "Always a recoil, or so I think" (*Collected Works,* 1150).[11]

The Misfit exhibits the demonic despair of defiance which in the Pharisees was here also inflamed. Their "hardness of heart" led them to reject the overture of grace in the sabbath and the Lord thereof and "recoil" as if from a snake by plotting his murder. O'Connor's story ends with The Misfit responding to the words of his partner in this crime:

> "Some fun!" Bobby Lee said.
> "Shut up, Bobby Lee," The misfit said. "It's no real pleasure in life."[12]

It seems that The Misfit has certainly, at the least, become even more cognizant of the reality of his life apart from grace. What he subsequently does is left to the reader's imagination. Similarly, as Mark's story of the Pharisees unfolds, he leaves room for varied response in "a story that does not end."[13] Had the grandmother lived would she have lived as a real disciple of Christ? Would the Misfit eventually succumb to grace or continue in ironic nihilistic self-gratification even though— "*it's no real pleasure in life*?" Would *any* of the Pharisees come to repentance for their plotting and carrying out the murder of God's anointed? The answer is that open-ended stories leave room for the mysteries of grace and the dizziness of human freedom to impact the reader as they entertain these questions and formulate *their* answer, in faith or nihilism, for better or for worse.

THE DEVIL MADE THEM DO IT?

One ultimate mystery is that God in his freedom would allow humans in their freedom to murder the Son of God, the Lord of the sabbath, and yet that would be "according to plan" (Acts 2:23). Another closely related mystery is the question of the extent of demonic influence. Alan Lewis sees that a balance is needed, such that human responsibility is not denied.

> It may indeed be legitimate from a biblical perspective to attribute to sin, Satan, the devil, or the law a third-party role between God and humanity, tempting us, indwelling us, holding us in bondage (e.g., Gen. 3; Rom. 7:13–25) . . . The fact remains that without the human will there would be no instrumentality

---

11. Michaels, *Passing by the Dragon,* 91.
12. O'Connor, *The Complete Stories,* 133.
13. See Garland, *Theology of Mark,* 549.

by which the captivating powers of evil could wreak their nihilistic havoc.[14]

As Kierkegaard stated, "What Satan spies with keenness of sight as his prey, what all temptation aims at certain of its prey, is the ambiguous."[15] And demonic agency, though not explicitly disclosed in the Pharisee's plot, is certainly to be biblically understood. John 8:44 makes this explicit: "You are of your father the devil, and your will is to do your father's desires. He was a murderer from the beginning, and does not stand in the truth, because there is no truth in him. When he lies, he speaks out of his own character, for he is a liar and the father of lies" (ESV). Gerald L. Borchert explains that,

> The devil was named as both a murderer and liar and therefore as the source of murder and lying. The reference is obviously to the garden of Eden text where the deceit of the serpent/devil led to the "death" of Adam and Eve (Gen 3:1–4; cf. *Wis* 2:24; Rom 5:12). From that point on lying and murder were a pattern of human life (cf. the Cain story in Gen 4:1–15; also 1 John 3:11–14). As a result of the actions of the Jews in relation to his coming, Jesus judged, they made it self-evident that they were children of a different "father": the liar and the murderer.[16]

MAN (ISRAEL) KILLING THE SON OF MAN (THE SON OF ISRAEL)

Turning back then, to the bigger mystery of the more direct human agency in the murder of Jesus, it will be helpful to begin with an excerpt from one of Kierkegaard's retellings of the Abraham and Isaac story.

> On the morning of the fourth day, Abraham said not a word but raised his eyes and saw Mount Moriah in the distance. He left the young servants behind, and taking Isaac's hand, went up the mountain alone. But Abraham said to himself, "I will not hide from Isaac where this walk is taking him." He stood still, he laid his hand on Isaac's head in blessing, and Isaac knelt to receive it. And Abraham's face epitomized fatherliness, his gaze was gentle, his words admonishing. But Isaac could not understand him, his soul could not be uplifted; he clasped Abraham's knees, he pleaded at his feet, he begged for his young life, for his

---

14. Lewis, *Between Cross & Resurrection*, 275.
15. Kierkegaard, PSW, 11–12.
16. Borchert, *John*, 307.

beautiful hopes; he called to mind the joy in Abraham's house, he called to mind the sorrow and solitude. Then Abraham lifted the boy up and walked on, holding his hand, and his words were full of comfort and admonition. But Isaac could not understand him. Abraham climbed Mount Moriah, but Isaac did not understand him. Then Abraham turned away from him for a moment, but when Isaac saw Abraham's face again, it had changed: his gaze was wild, his whole being was sheer terror. He seized Isaac by the chest, threw him to the ground, and said, "Stupid boy, do you think I am your father? I am an idolater. Do you think it is God's command? No, it is my desire." Then Isaac tumbled and cried out in his anguish: "God in heaven, have mercy on me, God of Abraham, have mercy on me; if I have no father on earth, then you be my father!" But Abraham said softly to himself, "Lord God in heaven, I thank you; it is better that he believes me a monster than that he should lose faith in you."[17]

This creative retelling of Abraham and Isaac at Mount Moriah by Kierkegaard was not meant by him to illustrate the relationship of Jesus to his heavenly Father when he was sacrificed on the cross. But it is useful to illustrate the relationship of *Jesus* to Israel through *Isaac's* words: *"God in heaven, have mercy on me, God of Abraham, have mercy on me; if I have no father on earth, then you be my father!"* John's gospel provides the nuance that clarifies the relationship of Jesus to his "earthly father" when he writes: *"He came to his own, but his own people did not receive him."* (John 1:11, ESV). It is the combination of this broken *familial* relationship of Jesus and Israel with Jesus' favorite self-designation "The Son of Man" that reveal an aspect of Christ's death on the cross that seems overlooked.

Though that phrase has given rise to much speculation and controversy, Paul Minear holds that the original gospel usages *"were naturally more eclectic in their vocabulary than modern theologians can readily tolerate."*[18] With this in mind, it is interesting to consider Mark's juxtaposition of Jesus as the Son of Man with Jesus as the vineyard-owner's son (Mark 12:6–8). Inasmuch as the Son of Man title implies divinity, the son of the vineyard owner also does. But when the vineyard's heir willingly submits to murder, he thereby becomes the "servant" of his own servants. This creates a nuance in the "Son of Man" title so that it might be understood to include the idea of the "Servant of Man." This is obviously biblically appropriate, given Isaiah's "Servant Songs" which for the Apostles and gospel authors found fulfillment in Jesus. Minear brings all this together by summarizing,

17. Kierkegaard, FT, 10–11.
18. See Minear, *Images of the Church*, 116–17.

As pictured in the New Testament, *the Son of Man* not only took the form of a slave, but he *carried the slave's obedience so far as to die for others*. As the Gospels express it, "the Son of Man must suffer." He came "to seek and to save the lost" and he accomplished this mission supremely in his death. His Passion was the climax and fulfillment of his work as the Son of Man. Virtually every image of the church in the New Testament reflects the impact of this event: the death was the hidden locus of the world's regeneration.[19]

If one is familiar with Philippians, Minear's allusion to Paul's famous "Servant Song" may be detected in his statement (See Phil 2:1–10). The passage depicts Jesus as *"taking the form of a servant"* and *"becoming obedient to the point of death."* Jason A. Mahn raises an important question about who Jesus was obedient to. Elaborating on the question and its importance he says,

> While most assume that it is to God the Father that Christ becomes "obedient," even unto death on a cross, neither the original Greek nor the English translation specifies the recipient of Christ's submission. Given the wider context of Philippians, it makes sense to suggest that Christ becomes obedient to humanity—becomes humanity's slave.[20]

And we need to also remember that the Lord of the sabbath was a *descendent* of Adam, Abraham, and David, of Man and Israel, *their* Son, though that par excellence (Luke 3:31–38). "As the Lord of the sabbath is truly God, so he is truly human. As Son of David so he is the Lord of David. Belonging to the children of Abraham, yet before Abraham he was (Novation)."[21]

This is where Kierkegaard's portrayal of Isaac's words *"I have no father on earth"* become especially poignant since Jesus as the *Son of Man* suffers the same fate, with only the *heavenly* Father as father, when in a sense he ought to have been received on *earth* by Israel, as in a sense *their* promised Isaac/Son, their "Son of Man—Son of Israel."

The implications of this reading of Jesus' obedience are many, and Mahn goes on to identify and explain several. In summary, he says that the reading: 1) indicates alternative beneficiaries of Christ's obedience; 2) characterizes the obedience not as exhibiting a heroic resoluteness, bravery, and sense of duty, but rather a radical vulnerability and accessibility to

19. Minear, *Images of the Church*, 117–18.
20. Mahn, *Fortunate Fallibility*, 164.
21. Oden & Hall, *Mark*, 35–36.

humanity; 3) serves as a fitting model for disciples in such vulnerability; 4) reconfigures the resurrection from being a fitting reward for resoluteness to an unexpected reversal that surprisingly follows such vulnerability and the relinquishment of power.[22] Mahn believes that these changes cohere with Kierkegaard's understanding of Christ's death and resurrection, and more importantly serve to emphasize Kierkegaard's emphasis of the ultimate abasement of Christ. In our earlier treatment of Mark 2:1–12, Kierkegaard's view was that Christ "came forth" in such a manner to present the possibility of offense for the purpose of preventing would-be disciples from following him without a sense of God as their criterion—and thus "following" in vain. But Kierkegaard probes the depths of Jesus' passion beneath that desire and explores the depths of his love exemplified in his *obedience* and *service to humanity*, saying,

> "Blessed is he who is not offended at me!" Ah, if only you could hear him say that himself, hear him from the fervor that here, too, he is suffering for you, that is, hear the contradiction that despite his love, he out of love cannot make impossible whether or not you will be offended at him, that he who came from far, far away, from heaven's glory, that he who descended so low until he became the lowly human being and now stands there in order to save you also, that he who all powerfully can do all things and yet in love sacrifices everything—powerlessly, which he himself suffers under because he is more concerned for your welfare than you are yourself—must leave it up to you yourself whether you will be offended or not, whether saved by him, you will inherit eternal happiness or bring about your eternal unhappiness and make him as distressed as love can become! Ah, if only you could have an intimation of what happens within him every time he sadly must repeat these words of concern, "Blessed is he who is not offended at me," that he who comes to the world to save all—but alas, it does not happen very speedily—that he repeatedly must say to each individually: Blessed is he who is not offended at me! Ah, if you could hear him say it and have an intimation of what goes on inside him when he says it, to me it seems that you could not possibly be offended at him.[23]

In summary, much transpired on this sabbath day, culminating in the fact that the sabbath of *well-being* for all became a sabbath of *death* for Jesus the Son of Man. But as the sabbath was given for man, so also the sabbath

---

22. My summation of: Mahn, *Fortunate Fallibility*, 164–65.
23. Soren Kierkegaard, PC, 76–77

death of the Son of Man was also for man, even for those who killed him in the dizziness of their freedom which became offense. This open-ended story of sin and grace was given to be a mirror for us all. It was also given by Mark, for the sake of all other "sons and daughters of man" suffering earthly abandonment and threatened with unjust death for following Christ. They too can cry out with "Isaac's prayer," *God in heaven, have mercy on me, God of Abraham, have mercy on me; if I have no father on earth, then you be my father!*

NOTE ON THE "READING" OF KIERKEGAARD'S ABRAHAM

Our usage of Kierkegaard's "first false Abraham" is not being claimed as the intent of Kierkegaard.[24] We use it to illustrate the sad reality of "the Son of Man" being crucified at the instigation of "father Israel." For the falsehood of Kierkegaard's "Abraham" was a charade to protect Isaac from any thought that God demanded his sacrifice. But in the gospel "father Israel" can rightly be illustrated by Kierkegaard's "false Abraham" who wanted to sacrifice Isaac/Jesus as "his desire!" It is interesting, and probably an accidental correlation, but we can nevertheless summarize that Kierkegaard's Abraham (Israel) was the *false father:* an "idolater" and "monster" who gladly sacrifices Isaac (Jesus) and that Isaac the son (Jesus the Son) faithfully prayed to the *true Father:* "God in heaven, have mercy on me, God of Abraham, have mercy on me; if I have no father on earth (Israel), then you be my father!" Interestingly, this closely represents what transpired on the cross as Jesus prayed "Father, into your hands I commit my spirit" (Luke 23:46).

Another interesting reading that we will only mention in passing is that of the "first false Abraham" seen through the lens of Kierkegaard's broken engagement with Regine Olsen. He withdrew from the engagement but staged a failed attempt to safeguard her reputation in the matter by acting before her and others as "false." In short, he played the "villain" to Regine to safeguard her innocence in the matter, but she saw through his charade. He did this because of his own inability to overcome "the knight of infinite resignation" and become "the knight of faith," which we discussed in chapter 11. He wrote in his journal, "If I had had faith, I would have stayed with Regine."[25] It seems the case that when Kierkegaard's first false Abraham says to the innocent Isaac, who God has commanded him to sacrifice, — "Stupid boy, do you think I am your father? I am an idolater. Do you think it is

---

24. The term is from Hanson, *Kierkegaard and the Life,* 52.
25. Kierkegaard, FT, xix (from the historical introduction).

God's command? No, it is my desire!"— "Abraham" is echoing Kierkegaard's own terrible charade with Regine in which "he acts, in his own words, like a scoundrel . . . an arch-scoundrel."[26] As usual, it seems that Kierkegaard's multi-layered writings contain many levels of meaning and application that apply to the many layers of faith in relation to both human and divine interrelationships.

---

26. Backhouse, *A Single Life*, 99.

14

Truth, Boredom, and Crushing Publicity

Popular, Demonic, and Regarding Kierkegaard's Uneven Trousers

Mark 3:7–12 (ESV)

7 Jesus withdrew with his disciples to the sea, and a great crowd followed, from Galilee and Judea 8 and Jerusalem and Idumea and from beyond the Jordan and from around Tyre and Sidon. When the great crowd heard all that he was doing, they came to him. 9 And he told his disciples to have a boat ready for him because of the crowd, lest they crush him, 10 for he had healed many, so that all who had diseases pressed around him to touch him. 11 And whenever the unclean spirits saw him, they fell down before him and cried out, "You are the Son of God." 12 And he strictly ordered them not to make him known.

My earliest recollection of Kierkegaard is that when, as a child, I failed to pull my trousers down carefully and evenly over my boots, which in those days were serviceably long, the nurse would admonish me, saying: "Soren Kierkegaard!" This was how I first heard spoken the name that also echoed so strongly in the ears of the grownups. The caricature drawings in The Corsair had made Kierkegaard's legs known in circles where his genius had not penetrated. His trousers had achieved a fame with us that paralleled that achieved ten years earlier in France by Theophile Gautier's red vest. —Georg Brandes[1]

Most people are other people. Their thoughts are someone else's opinions, their lives a mimicry, their passions a quotation. —Oscar Wilde[2]

The knavish trick of "Christendom" is to take the gift and say good-day to the obligation. —Soren Kierkegaard[3]

GROWING PUBLICITY AND CRUSHING CROWDS

Mark 3:7–12 serves as another of Mark's setting and narrative interludes which glimpses the increasingly ominous situation that follows when Jesus and the disciples "withdraw" from the synagogue to the sea. But *a multitudinous multitude followed him. . ..*[4] The Pharisees have already become dangerous and now the crowds also, though not yet as their murderous mob. Because of "publicity" regarding the miracle-working Jesus, the crowd has increased in number and fervor and now present a "crushing" capability against which he takes precautions.

The demons continue to announce who Jesus is and he continues to order them to stop publicizing him. It is interesting that "publicity," which from Kierkegaard's day to ours has grown to become a modern Babel of confusion through news and "social media," is introduced by Mark as beginning from the mouths of demons. That Jesus resolved to be "incognito" in messianic secrecy was largely because the coming Kingdom would *not* be what was expected, desired, or publicized.

But Jesus' desire to silence the overt demonic publicity was probably based in additional motives on his part. David Watson theorizes that several things may be going on in this interplay between Jesus and the demons. They may have been attempting to "lure Jesus into the standard conventions of honor and shame" that lay beneath the Greco-Roman societal codes that prescribed obligatory practices.[5] Those conventions were contrary to the freedom Jesus was bringing in God's new Kingdom. Watson explains how these demonic "proclamations" of honor might be in continuity with Satan's prior temptations of Jesus in the wilderness:

1. Kirmmse, *Encounters With Kierkegaard*, 97.
2. As cited in Snodgrass, *Who God Says*, 91.
3. Kierkegaard, AC, 280.
4. Gundry, *Mark*, Loc. 728.
5. Watson, *Honor Among Christians*, 58.

By referring to Jesus as the "Holy One of God" or the "Son of God," they issue positive challenges to Jesus. The attempt by Satan to indebt Jesus to him and Jesus' refusal to become indebted to him are more explicit in the temptation stories in Matthew 4:8–10 and Luke 4:5–8 but the same dynamic may be at work in these passages in Mark."[6]

In other words, through these demons, Satan is still seeking for Jesus to worship him and follow *his* way. But God's Kingdom is to arrive and operate on wholly different footings. Garland summarizes,

> First-century readers would have regarded Jesus' commands to silence as a surprising resistance to honor. He has no interest in achieving wider public acclaim. Watson concludes, "Mark's Jesus is not keeping a secret of his messiahship, but demonstrating the standards for establishing honor within the new family of faith." Mark develops this theme because he is intent on presenting a new context for receiving honor, namely, the surrogate family of those believers who obey the will of God (3:31–35), and new criteria by which honor is established, namely, taking up one's cross and following a crucified Savior (8:34).[7]

While the outward publicity promotes frenetic and superficial outward acclamation that too easily accommodates "normal" human values, the positive responsive "spirit" that brings individuality is still for the most part hidden in the ambiguity of the crowd. Mark's thematic development is also likely hinting that the now seemingly "neutral" crowd will become explicitly dangerous by the possibility it can here "innocently" harm Jesus. But the Crowd is not only dangerous to Jesus but to those who by its pressure remain merely a face in the crowd and fail to come from it as Kierkegaard's "single individual." Regarding this "neutral" ambiguity Kierkegaard said, "*If you want to be loathsome to God, just run with the herd.*"[8]

The ambiguity of the crowd in Mark seems to have two main aspects, namely that the crowd itself cannot in the end, as a crowd, follow Christ; and that the crowd contains individuals, perhaps many, that can and will follow Christ by "leaving" the crowd. The authors of "Mark as Story" summarize these two potentialities saying,

> In Mark's story, the people who flock to Jesus are "like sheep without a shepherd"—signifying that the leaders of the nation

---

6. Watson, *Honor Among Christians*, 58.
7. Garland, *Theology of Mark*, 379.
8. Kierkegaard, PSW, 239.

have not taken care of the sheepfold of Israel. By contrast, Jesus has compassion for the crowds; he teaches them and twice feeds a throng in the desert. In general, the response of the crowd reveals their desire for a leader who will attend to their needs . . . The traits of the crowds are often similar to those of the suppliants (individuals). They come to Jesus wherever he is; they desire to be healed and they press on him to touch him . . . the crowds are amazed by Jesus and praise God for these works of power. Such amazement usually reflects an openness to the transforming power of the rule of God. However, as we have said, amazement by itself is not a sufficient response to the rule of God. As long as Jesus is publicly accessible and the outcome of his activity is undetermined, the crowds follow him, respond to his compassion and power, acclaim him, and are "glad to hear him." However, as Jesus approaches Jerusalem, the crowds see him as one who will bring in "the coming rule of our father David" rather than the "rule of God." When Jesus is arrested, taken from the scene, and rendered powerless, they stop following. The crowd now becomes vulnerable to manipulation by the traditional authorities. The high priests, fearing and envying the support of Jesus by the people, stir up the crowd to ask for Pilate to release Barabbas rather than Jesus. In the end, the crowd even calls for the crucifixion and joins the ridicule of Jesus . . . the crowds too fail in following Jesus.[9]

The crowd's desperation ironically makes them susceptible to manipulation and leads us to a major Kierkegaardian theme: *"the crowd is untruth."* Kierkegaard thought and wrote extensively about the existential reality, or better, the *unreality* of the crowd, and to that subject we now turn.

"THE CROWD IS UNTRUTH"

Kierkegaard thought that the crowd, by its very nature, was "untruth"—a mere conglomerate of individuals lacking subjectivity of spirit. More ominously, and somewhat biblically speaking, when a "house" is swept clean of "spirit" it falls prey to more numbers of invading and occupying demons (Matt 12:43–44).

Kierkegaard's *Attack Upon Christendom* was of course in many ways an attack upon "the crowd." This was because the crowd supposed it was Christian, which in the nature of the case is impossible, at least according to Kierkegaard and probably Mark also. Kierkegaard's comments on the crowd

9. Rhoads et al., *Mark as Story,* 134–35.

as untruth are therefore characteristically witty, ironic, and satirical and find the vacuity of truth to be inherent in the basic fact of the crowd, consisting in sheer quantity rather than quality. Following is a sampling.

> God is as infinitely concerned with one person of intensity, yes, as he is infinitely indifferent to the millions and trillions. We humans believe numbers mean something. For God, it is precisely numbers that mean nothing, nothing at all ... To compensate for the emptiness of nuts, we clever human beings get all the more of them. This is ridiculous compensation and also a curse. If the nuts are hollow, it would be better if there were just three or four of them. What agony to have to crack a million empty nuts in order to be convinced that they are hollow! ... The specimen-man tranquilizes himself with human numbers. If something is true, he needs no higher proof than that such and such a number have regarded it as true ... Animal-man has the courage to do the most frightening things as long as he simply has human numbers with him. Christ points to the very opposite. To suffer courageously means precisely to fear God in contrast to fearing the crowd, in contrast to what we as animal-creatures fear most of all—human numbers. No-one dares to be himself; everyone is hiding in "togetherness" ... The crowd is like an envelope. One receives a large package, thinks it is something important, but look, it is a package of envelopes."[10]

The qualitative lack of truth is seen in the fact that though it contains "multitudinous multitudes" the crowd is essentially a nondescript collection. Thus, he calls the crowd things like "specimen-man" and "animal-man" designating a severe falling short of the development God intends for humans. At this point in Mark's story, it seems that these deformities of the crowd are being hinted at.

The swarming "honoring" demons may represent an advance look at the "spirit" of the untrue crowd, just as the demon-possessed man in the synagogue may have represented that of the temple "crowd" of scribes and Pharisees (Mark 1:23).[11] It seems that Mark reveals an order of offense and rejection of Christ as beginning in the demonic realm that percolates through the human. Part of the apocalyptic gospel seems to be a revelation of the strongholds that clandestinely pre-existed Christ's coming, to show that exorcisms were not only redemptive for those possessed, but also *revelatory* of the anti-kingdom of darkness.

10. As cited in Kierkegaard, PSW, 234–237.
11. See Myers, *Binding the Strong Man*, 142.

PROBLEMS WITH PUBLICITY

Kierkegaard's *Attack on Christendom* demonstrates that the publicity of a "Christian" crowd in untruth would be rejected as no better than the demonic publicity we see in Mark. This is because of at least several reasons whether existing in tandem or separately: the triviality of the crowd; the untruth of the publicity; the inauthenticity of the witness; and the lack of affection in the confessor.

1) *The triviality of the crowd* is revealed in the following excerpt from Kierkegaard. The background is that Kierkegaard had himself become an incessant subject of the satirical newspaper "The Corsair" with a repeated emphasis on the uneven lengths of his trouser legs. Kierkegaard lamented not only for himself, but for what this revealed regarding the level of earnestness of his society.

> I am positive that my whole life will never be as important as my trousers have come to be . . . For someone ardently trying to hold to a concept of the greatness in or potential to every man there is something sad about having an abundance of observations which seem only to bear witness to irresponsibility, silliness, crudity, and the like.[12]

And therefore, the triviality of the crowd regarding the most important thing—the identity of Jesus—is revealed in this additional statement:

> So, he makes his appearance; a predecessor has called attention to him, and he himself decidedly attracts attention to himself by wonders and signs that become the talk of the whole country—and he is the hero of the moment; wherever he goes he is surrounded by a countless throng of people . . . Thus, the crowd is enraptured with him; it follows him enthusiastically, sees signs and wonders . . . happy in the hope that the golden age will commence when he becomes king. But the crowd can rarely account for its judgment, has one opinion today, and another tomorrow.[13]

2) *The untruth of the publicity* was revealed in the demons. That Jesus was "the expected one," according to the popular expectation was simply false. But Christendom fully believed that Jesus was the expected one regarding the present order of Golden-Age Denmark. In a Dostoevsky-like entry, Kierkegaard portrays Christendom as waiting for the return of the

---

12. As cited in Backhouse, *A Single Life*, 142.
13. Kierkegaard, PC, 41-42.

expected one and demonstrates that it would become the "Grand Inquisitor" of Jesus and reject him "again"— playing the part that Israel did at the first advent of Christ. This is because the established order(s) do not want God's apocalyptic "revolution" but only an "evolution" of *their* order(s). Thus, Kierkegaard writes,

> Therefore, the authentic expected one will look entirely different, will come as the most glorious flowering and the highest unfolding of the established order. That is how the authentic expected one will come, and he will conduct himself quite differently; he will recognize the established order as the authority, will summon all the clergy to a convention, present to it his achievements, together with his credentials—and then if in balloting he has the majority he will be accepted and hailed as the extraordinary that he is: the expected one.[14]

3) *The inauthenticity of the witness*, that "Jesus is the Son of God," is revealed when we consider several explicit words Kierkegaard self-published in a journal called "The Moment." In the final issue he coined a parable, somewhat reminiscent of Mark 12:1–12, in which Christendom was akin to the Israelite tenants. Its title was "That the crime of Christendom is comparable to that of wishing to obtain stealthily an inheritance to which one is not entitled." He presents his charge saying,

> A man dies and leaves his whole fortune to an heir—but there is a condition, something that is required of the heir; and this the heir does not like. What then does he do? He takes possession of the property bequeathed to him (for he is indeed the heir, says he) and says good-day to the obligation . . . The knavish trick of "Christendom" is to take the gift and say good-day to the obligation . . . However, hypocritical as everything is with "Christendom," they have made it appear as if Christendom too did maintain that Christianity is an obligation—one has to be baptized. Ah! That is making confoundedly short work of obligation! No, the obligation is: the imitation of Jesus Christ.[15]

4) *The lack of affections in the confessor*, is revealed by comparison with the demon's lack. For their "confession" was void of love and obedience. And if faith "works by love" (Gal 5:6), the lack of love-works lies beneath the lack of faith in the triviality, untruth, and inauthenticity of the confessors of "Christendom." Augustine wrote,

---

14. Kierkegaard, PC, 47.
15. Kierkegaard, AC, 279–280.

Both the devils and the faithful confessed Christ. "Thou are Christ, the Son of the living God," said Peter. "We know who thou art. Thou art the Son of God," said the devils. I hear a similar confession, but I do not find a similar charity. In one there is love, in another fear . . . The "faith that works by love," is not the same faith that demons have. "For the devils also believe and tremble," but do they love? If they had not believed, they would not have said: "You are the holy one of God" or "You are the Son of God." But if they had loved, they would not have said "What have we to do with you." (Letter 194 to Sixtus).[16]

And since James equates the supposed "faith" of some "Christians" with that of demons, so also, Augustine and Kierkegaard were warranted to equate that of the crowds of Christendom to demons (James 2:19). Thus, Kierkegaard collided with his society just as the disciples in Mark's audience would collide with theirs. But these collisions participate in the gospel of the apocalyptic Christ who entered the middle of time to inaugurate God's new creation, rather than "complete" the evolution of the established order through the arrival of its "expected one." And therefore, the publicity provided through false "confessions" of Christ—both "Christian" and demonic—all serve to indict the "confessors" as opposers of the apocalyptic gospel. What must be remembered is that this opposition is based in the triviality of untruth, which is itself largely based in boredom, which we now consider.

THE PERENNIAL BOREDOM OF HUMANKIND

Those delighting in the publicity regarding Kierkegaard's trousers may seem to have had little in common with publicity-sharing desperate crowds in Mark. Nevertheless, there may be similarity between Mark's desperate crowd and Kierkegaard's frivolous herd, in *boredom*. The gossiping desperation of the poor of Mark who know they are in despair—the chattering desperation of the bourgeoise philistines who are in the despair of not knowing they are

---

16. As cited in Oden and Hall, *Mark,* 40. A Kierkegaardian reading of James 2:19 alluded to by Augustine that fully applies to Mark's prohibitions of demonic publicity is "namely, that truth is for the particular individual only as he himself produces it in action. If the truth is for the individual in any other way, or if he prevents the truth from being for him in that way, we have the phenomenon of the demonic. Truth has always had many loud proclaimers, but the question is whether a person (or demon) will in the deepest sense acknowledge the truth, will allow it to permeate his whole being." Kierkegaard, CA, 138 (parenthesis mine).

in despair—both seem to reveal crowds that suffer, whether more physically or spiritually, from boredom.[17]

It seems certain that publicity was a factor at the time of Christ as it was in Kierkegaard's world, although not in the same exact way. It also seems that boredom was a factor in both times although also not in the same exact way. The commonality between publicity and boredom is despair—that produces a form of boredom which employs what Blaise Pascal called *diversion*, the conscious and even unconscious habit of diverting oneself from its essential despair.[18] Kierkegaard, and quite possibly Mark also, saw that a favorite method of diversion from boredom has always been publicity, and the frenzies of the crowds. For Kierkegaard's "history of boredom" satirically but truly reveals it as the prime mover of the cosmos for the human crowd:

> Since boredom advances and boredom is the root of all evil, no wonder then, that the world goes backwards, that the evil spreads. This can be traced back to the very beginning. The gods were bored; therefore they created human beings. Adam was bored because he was alone; therefore Eve was created. Since that moment, boredom entered the world and grew in quantity in exact proportion to the growth of population. Adam was bored alone; then Adam and Eve were bored together; then Adam and Eve and Cain and Abel were bored *en famille*. After that, the population of the world increased and the nations were bored *en masse*. To amuse themselves, they hit upon the notion of building a tower so high that it would reach the sky. This notion was just as boring as the tower was high and is a terrible demonstration of how boredom had gained the upper hand. Then they were dispersed around the world, just as people continue to travel abroad. But they continued to be bored. And what consequences this boredom had: humankind stood tall and fell far, first through Eve, then through the Babylonian tower. On the other hand, what was it that delayed the fall of Rome? It was *panis* [bread] and *circenses* [games.][19]

17. Daniel-Rops presents an interesting picture of the classes of the "Province of the Empire" of Jesus' day, divided into the *honestiores*, privileged "aristocracy"; "the mass of *humiliores*, the free or freed men who . . . were given over to a humdrum life without opportunity . . . many of them . . . condemned to mediocrity, sunk more and more into idleness"; and the "even graver peril" of slavery, "this vast servile element, which certainly amounted to at least a third of the total population." Some domestic slaves were "well treated" but many— "those who toiled in the fields and the shops, worse still in the mines, were condemned to the most atrocious lives." Daniel-Rops, *Jesus and His Times*, 181–182.

18. Pascal, *Pascal's Pensees*, 40–43, #139.

19. Kierkegaard, EO 1, 286.

THE BANALITY OF "BOREDOM TOGETHER"

Kierkegaard lamentingly writes of humanity's "life together" in boredom:

> Surrounded by hordes of men, absorbed in all sorts of secular matters, more and more shrewd about the ways of the world—such a person forgets himself, forgets his name divinely understood, does not dare to believe in himself, finds it too hazardous to be himself and far easier and safer to be like the others, to become a copy, a number, a mass man.[20]

The banality of boredom was quite evident when the unevenness of Kierkegaard's trouser legs excited as much publicity as they did. Unfortunately, the publicity following Jesus, in the end, did not rise much higher, and in fact fell even lower, to the crowd's demand that "his blood be on us and on our children!" (Matt 27:25, ESV). Thus, the superfluous banality of the herd's boredom leads to the capacity for the "monstrous" banality of its evil.[21] Ironically, Jesus' blood was on them in either judgment or atonement (see Matt 23:35–36; Acts 2:22–41).

In this chapter we have not concentrated on the even darker elements of publicity that turn the "mass man" into "the mob." These exceed mere "boredom" by becoming violent "outrage" and sometimes outright violence. The power of social media today is evidenced by the deep Babelic divisions it has wrought in America because the one thing all now have in common is the banality of boredom—which may *again* lead to the monstrous banality of evil. Of course, this darkest aspect of the crowd is further developed in Mark's gospel as it proceeds and will be considered more fully under the appropriate texts. For now, we note that certain ingredients: boredom, triviality, superfluity, publicity, the crowd, untruth, banality, and demonic influence at the beginning and end, when mixed are a recipe for societal disaster.

---

20. Kierkegaard, SUD, 33–34.

21. d'Entreves, *Hannah Arendt*, 107. Arendt's view that the masses' sense of being "superfluous . . . atomized mass men" contributes to the dangers of totalitarianism is quite like Kierkegaard's view of modernism's "leveling" wherein persons are "a copy, a number, a mass man" and part of "the public of the Present Age . . . a demonic abstract power that is bigger than the sum of the particular actions of the concrete individuals who comprise it . . . individual choices idolatrously orientated." Tyson, *Kierkegaard's Theological Sociology*, 29. See Canovan, *Hannah Arendt*, 53–55.

15

Plundering the "Goods" of the Strong Man

Mark and Kierkegaard as Exorcists in "The Present Age" . . . of Anxiety

Mark 3:13–35 (ESV)

13 And he went up on the mountain and called to him those whom he desired, and they came to him. 14 And he appointed twelve (whom he also named apostles) so that they might be with him and he might send them out to preach 15 and have authority to cast out demons. 16 He appointed the twelve: Simon (to whom he gave the name Peter); 17 James the son of Zebedee and John the brother of James (to whom he gave the name Boanerges, that is, Sons of Thunder); 18 Andrew, and Philip, and Bartholomew, and Matthew, and Thomas, and James the son of Alphaeus, and Thaddaeus, and Simon the Zealot, 19 and Judas Iscariot, who betrayed him.

20 Then he went home, and the crowd gathered again, so that they could not even eat. 21 And when his family heard it, they went out to seize him, for they were saying, "He is out of his mind."

22 And the scribes who came down from Jerusalem were saying, "He is

possessed by Beelzebul," and "by the prince of demons he casts out the demons." 23 And he called them to him and said to them in parables, "How can Satan cast out Satan? 24 If a kingdom is divided against itself, that kingdom cannot stand. 25 And if a house is divided against itself, that house will not be able to stand. 26 And if Satan has risen up against himself and is divided, he cannot stand, but is coming to an end. 27 But no one can enter a strong man's house and plunder his goods, unless he first binds the strong man. Then indeed he may plunder his house.

28 "Truly, I say to you, all sins will be forgiven the children of man, and whatever blasphemies they utter, 29 but whoever blasphemes against the Holy Spirit never has forgiveness, but is guilty of an eternal sin"— 30 for they were saying, "He has an unclean spirit."

31 And his mother and his brothers came, and standing outside they sent to him and called him. 32 And a crowd was sitting around him, and they said to him, "Your mother and your brothers are outside, seeking you." 33 And he answered them, "Who are my mother and my brothers?" 34 And looking about at those who sat around him, he said, "Here are my mother and my brothers! 35 For whoever does the will of God, he is my brother and sister and mother."

In community the single individual is a microcosm who qualitatively reproduces the cosmos. —Soren Kierkegaard[1]

In truth, there is no place, not even one most disgustingly dedicated to lust and vice, where a human being is more easily corrupted—than in the crowd.
—Soren Kierkegaard[2]

To us a human is primarily food; our aim is the absorption of its will into ours, the increase of our own area of selfhood at its expense.
—Uncle Screwtape[3]

"Real Life Is Meeting."—C. S. Lewis[4]

Each of the two pairs of epigrams above from Kierkegaard and Lewis exhibit a dialectic. Kierkegaard portrays that between the individual and the community, with the moral quality of the community looming in the background.

1. Kierkegaard, JP: III:217, #2952.
2. Kierkegaard, JP: III:306, #2926.
3. Lewis, *The Screwtape Letters*, 46–47.
4. Lewis, *That Hideous Strength*, 292.

Lewis portrays a dialectic between the spiritual quality of two communities, either hellish or heavenly. This section will consider several factors related to the "invasion" of Satan's "kingdom" by that of God's, enacted through the coming of Jesus. Particular emphasis will be given to the opposite qualities of each kingdom and how this all "plays out" in the challenges and prospects for the individual, and for the entire human "community."

THE CREATION OF THE MICROCOSMIC TWELVE

The first scene in this section of Mark is itself framed by opposite pictures. The first portrays Jesus and the disciples drawing apart from the crowds to ascend a mountain, and there solidify a spiritual fellowship in Kingdom service. The second portrays that "heavenly" nucleus of the kingdom returning to the native "home" amidst the tumultuous crowd that seemingly prevents table fellowship (see 3:13 & 20). Most commentators see several allusions in this mountaintop scene. One is the parallel between Moses and representatives of Israel ascending Mount Sinai in Exodus 24:1–4 and Jesus and three disciples ascending the mount of "transfiguration" in 9:2–13. Another is Mark's underlying use of intervals of silence which may serve to highlight the "hidden power" of the *method of operation* of God's kingdom.[5]

Many commentators also think that Jesus' choice of *twelve* representatives points to a theme that develops substantially in this section of Mark, namely that Jesus is creating a new "Israelite" community—a political "confederacy"—that is contrasted to the "old" Israel and is thus microcosmic of God's "heavenly" kingdom which collides with (and overcomes) the "hellish" kingdoms of the world (2 Cor 10:3–4; Eph 6:12; Rev 11:15).[6] In this section of Mark the purpose and nature of God's new community is shown to be the replacement of the demonized "community" of humankind with the "divinized," truly human community. Of course, this was God's original purpose for choosing Abraham and Israel: "to make of you a great nation, and I will bless you and make your name great, so that you will be a blessing. I will bless those who bless you, and him who dishonors you I will curse, *and in you all the families of the earth shall be blessed.*" (Genesis 12:2–3, ESV.)

The creation and purpose of the "twelve community" is thus paradigmatic of the whole church community which is forming around Jesus. It consists in *"being with"* Jesus and being *"sent out to preach and have authority and cast out demons."* These two aspects of discipleship could be qualified

---

5. See Garland, *Theology of Mark*, 396; Juel, *Mark,* 60; Ross, *Silence,* 149.
6. See Myers, *Binding the Strong Man*, 163.

as passive/active and receptive/reproductive, as the disciples "freely receive" and then "freely give" (Matthew 10:8).

MARK'S MOTIF OF POWER AND THE TWO KINGDOMS

Power (and authority) has been an explicit motif of Mark since 1:27. Now it is further developed in the granting of "authority" to the twelve, namely, the power to "cast out demons." It is interesting to note that Mark recognizes that Judas exercised power when he highlights the fact that it was he who "betrayed him." This introduces a dialectic of two contrasting power structures which serves to reveal the "heavenly" nature of the power of God's kingdom, namely *righteous* authority. But that paradoxically appears to require a complete *vulnerability* to unleashed demonic power, with Judas's demonically inspired betrayal of Jesus as the prime evidence. For from the worldly point of view, to be vulnerable to the point of death is to be overcome *because* of that vulnerability. The paradox is that the vulnerability and actual descent of Jesus to the lowest place was the path that God's power took against ultimate evil. Jesus thus retained his righteous power as the highest—and only—*true* power. Thus, the power of God's kingdom is categorically different than the "power" of the rival kingdom that Jesus "*invaded*" and invalidated. In short, God's kingdom *must* subvert the demonic and human conceptions and practices of power, because of God's inherently righteous power.

The development of Mark's power motif is further seen when the earthly family of Jesus, hearing that he was drawing a dinner-disrupting crowd, "went out to seize him" thinking that "He is out of his mind." The natural family of Jesus did not understand Jesus and his power, or the power of the new family he was creating and resorted to a vain exercise of their brand of power which was a combination of raw physical power and natural familial psychological power. They mistakenly thought their diagnoses of his condition required their "treatment."

It is important to note that Jesus' choice of the twelve was a qualified repudiation of both his immediate family and of the larger family of Israel as "givens" requiring his ultimate allegiance. This presented a "power collision" between the "natural" and "religious" families which is further developed when Jesus declares that his "family"—his "mother and brothers"—are those that follow God's will. In describing his *new family,* Jesus adds "*sisters*" probably highlighting the expansive and inclusive qualities of God's family (3:35). God's kingdom basically subverts the basic power structures which support *fallen* human society, including "family," "tribe," and "sabbath" as seen earlier. But it must also be noted that Jesus does not completely repudiate all hierarchical structure per se. Rather, he re-establishes the *absolute* relation to the *absolute* and the *relative* relation to the *relative*.[7]

That Jesus and his followers are considered mad because of their absolute commitment to the absolute is merely the necessary fallout of the *possibility of offense* at Jesus, as was discussed previously. But the positive point is that the willingness of Jesus to become the possibility of offense is because of his redemptive love for those who may become offended. And that love requires and inhabits a wholly different type of power than Satan's heavy-handed quests to control humans. And so, the collision of the two kingdoms is, considering the reality of the self-giving God who *is* light and love, caused by the clash of divine sanity and demonic/human insanity (1 John 1:5; 3:8). Merold Westphal explains that for Kierkegaard this applied as much to "modern man" as it did to ancient Israel, and thus also to all of humanity:

> When the charge is made that Christianity is sheer madness and utter absurdity, he grants that from a certain point of view it surely is, and then goes on to ask for credentials of that point of view. When it is said that "modern man" finds the incarnation incredible, he acknowledges the sociological fact, but not without pausing to ask who "modern man" may be. He wants to know who is mad after all. Might it possibly be that the madness that is Christian faith is the higher, divine madness that actually possesses the truth that human sanity professes to love?[8]

Kierkegaard grants that "reason" is foundational for life, as expressed in Mark in the immediate family of Jesus and the tribal family of Israel, as micro and macro communities seeking to preserve the "basic order of life." But the human profession of its "love" of reason must be open to the criterion of God's love of true reason, which might appear madness. Therefore, Jesus brings the new apocalyptic wine that challenges and judges the old wineskins of human "reason" that try to *violently* "contain" God's new wine. Kierkegaard based an important discourse, called "Becoming Sober," on the recognition that when the Spirit came on Jesus' new family at Pentecost, they were considered drunk by the onlookers. But in the new reality the essential "work" for Christians vis a vis the world is "becoming sober." Kierkegaard summarizes with the simple observation that "*Here as everywhere it is manifest that the world and Christianity have completely opposite conceptions.*"[9]

---

7. Basically, paraphrasing Kierkegaard. See Kierkegaard, CUP, 407.
8. Westphal, *Kierkegaard's Critique of Reason*, 86.
9. Kierkegaard, FSE/JFY, 96.

And those rival conceptions were nowhere more evident than when the scribes thought it "reasonable" to ascribe Jesus' power to *demonic* agency.

THE ETERNAL SIN

Whereas Jesus' immediate family thought he had become insane, the scribes of Israel put forth a more sinister explanation, "*He is possessed by Beelzebul*," and "*by the prince of demons he casts out demons*." They didn't claim that his exorcisms were inauthentic. The evidence was too great for that tactic. The reply of Jesus to the scribes' approach was twofold. First, he pointed out that Satan's kingdom cannot be divided, because if so, it would destroy itself. Second, if Jesus was casting out demons, it could only be because he had power over the "strong man" which enabled him to plunder his house.

Jesus' answer implies two things, one of which he deals with explicitly and one of which he does not. He explicitly addresses the implication that ascribing the Holy Spirit's activity to Satan brings one dangerously close to an "eternal sin." What Jesus does not explain is his implication that Satan's house, or "kingdom" is united. This raises a complex and difficult question regarding the nature of "unity" in Satan's kingdom, which will be dealt with after considering the question of blasphemy against the Holy Spirit, which is possibly the "confessional" basis for individually "entering" any such "unity" in "eternal sin." Interestingly, even in this unity, an individual's interior state is what enters the doorway to participation in its "community."

In answer to the perplexing question of the nature of an *eternal* sin, it is probable that the danger in the blasphemy of the scribes was due to its being indicative of their precarious spiritual condition. In other words, their "faith confession" battled against the Holy Spirit who works *within*, rather than being an offense at Christ's *external* work. Jesus said that the latter was a forgivable sin. *Interiority* is the "place" where the most important relations between any person and God transpire, whether for *faith* in God or for *hardening* in sin. The scribes hardening against Jesus dangerously evidenced an internal hardening against the Spirit. Sin was close to becoming their "confirmed" position of defiance against God. Sylvia Walsh provides an explanation of how this relates to believers, demoniacs, and those in-between in the ambiguity of not yet explicitly becoming spirit, either for or against God:

> Most people are so caught up in the power of sin that they sin daily almost as a matter of course and are not even conscious of the continuity or consistency of sin that dominates their lives. In fact, they live so haphazardly in the moment that they hardly have any idea of what "consistency" is. According

to Anti-Climacus, only two kinds of persons are conscious of and strive for consistency: *believers,* who have a conception of themselves as spirit and seek to realize and sustain consistency in the eternal or the good; and *demonic individuals,* who also know themselves to be spirit but despairingly maintain the consistency of evil . . . (107–8, SUD) Demonic individuals maintain consistency by hardening themselves in opposition to repentance and grace. They will have nothing to do with these possibilities and thus sink deeper into sin. The demonic person's despair thus represents not only sin but the intensification of sin into *despair over sin* . . . (109–10, SUD) In this condition one cannot accept oneself in one's actuality as a sinner, much less humbly acknowledge and repent that one is less than one should be before God. Thus, Anti-Climacus says of the demonic person: "His sorrow, his cares, his despair are selfish . . . because it is self-love that wants to be proud of itself, to be without sin" . . . (112, SUD) Yet adherence to and persistence in this hidden pride and self-love are exactly what fixes the demonic person in sin . . . The greatest possible intensification or positive assertion of sin occurs when the despairing individual becomes entirely offensive and aggressive, denying everything and declaring it to be a falsehood. Anti-Climacus calls this "sin against the Holy Spirit" because it regards Christ as "an invention of the devil," just as in the Gospel of Matthew (12:24–32) the sin of the Jews who accused Jesus of exorcising demons by the help of Beelzebub, the prince of demons, is called the sin against the Holy Spirit (131, SUD).[10]

Kierkegaard's view of demonic "spirit" is demonstrated in Mark's gospel by the demons who are conscious of who Jesus is, but do not follow him in true faith. Instead, the "faith" that inhabits their confessions of who he was, based in defiance, were possibly methods of attack as seen earlier. Perhaps the best way to conceive of the "eternal sin" is to see it as "evidenced" when a person is resolutely confirmed in their defiance, which would be the obverse of being resolutely confirmed in allegiance to Christ as evidence of the reception of "eternal life."

---

10. Walsh, *Living Christianly,* 27–29. "Anti-Climacus" was one of Kierkegaard's pseudonymous authors, a highly Christian one.

THE MEDIATED COMMUNITY OF GOD AND THE BLASPHEMOUS BUREAUCRACY OF SATAN

At this point we will consider the dynamic of each rival community that "builds" its unity in each individual and the "community" as a whole. Kierkegaard writes,

> Sin is a crucial expression for the religious existence. As long as sin is not posited, the suspension becomes a transient factor that in turn vanishes or remains outside life as the totally irregular. Sin, however, is the crucial point of departure for the religious existence, is not a factor within something else, within another order of things, but is itself the beginning of the religious order of things.[11]

So says Johannes Climacus, another of Kierkegaard's pseudonymous authors, as he presents the case that the consciousness of sin is what informs an individual's silent confessions of faith that position them within the "religious order of things." This applies to what we are calling the rival kingdoms wherein each participant has a particular but opposing consciousness of sin, in relation to God. Those in God's kingdom, believers, express their consciousness of sin through faith in God's forgiveness, while those in Satan's express theirs through defiance against God. Thus, in God's Kingdom, all are related to one another by their relation to God, who as the one establishing this community is what Kierkegaard calls "the middle term."

> *Worldly wisdom thinks that love is a relationship between man and man. Christianity teaches that love is a relationship between: man—God—man, that is, that God is the middle term.*[12]

Kierkegaard correctly understood the basic "fractal" structure of God's new family, wherein God alone was the middle term between all. Thus, in God's Kingdom, human power relations which would ignore God as the middle term, have no proper place as the uniting dynamic. In fact, raw human power, can only be disuniting. Most probably drawing directly from Kierkegaard, Dietrich Bonhoeffer spoke of God as the middle-term as the basis of the rejection of all "immediacy" in the community of God:

> Within the spiritual community there is never, in any way whatsoever, an "immediate" relationship of one to another. However, in the self-centered community there exists a profound, elemental emotional desire for community, for immediate

---

11. Kierkegaard, CUP:1, 267–68.
12. Kierkegaard, WOL, 112–13.

contact with other human souls, just as in the flesh there is a yearning for immediate union with other flesh. This desire of the human soul seeks the complete intimate fusion of I and You, whether this occurs through a union of love or—what from this self-centered perspective is after all the same thing—in forcing the other into one's own sphere of power and influence. Here is where the self-centered, strong person enjoys life to the full, securing for themselves the admiration, the love, or the fear of the weak. Here human bonds, suggestive influences, and dependencies are everything. Moreover, everything that is originally and solely characteristic of the community mediated through Christ reappears in the non-mediated community of souls in a distorted form.[13]

Bonhoeffer's pictorial descriptions help to bring this back to Mark. The "secure and self-centered strong person" illustrates the *strong one* who Jesus bound, before plundering his house—which is a "non-mediated community of souls in a distorted form." For the question still looming in our discussion is whether Satan's kingdom has some form of "unity" and if so, in what form? Perhaps the view of Lewis may be helpful here, which was that hell is basically a bureaucracy as depicted imaginatively, humorously, and satirically in his famous book, "The Screwtape Letters." The bureaucratic "organization" is based in the "unity" of a confessional sinful defiance against God, the "Enemy," and is of course "beneficently" led by "Our Father Below."[14] But Lewis also reveals, in a telling moment of Screwtape's impatience over the fumbles of his apprenticed nephew Wormwood, that just as the demon's ultimate purpose for humans is "absorption" of their will into theirs, so also even devils can become "devils-food cake" for other devils:

> To decide what the best use of it is, you must ask what use the enemy wants to make of it, and then do the opposite. Now it may surprise you to learn that in his efforts to get permanent possession of a soul, he relies on the troughs even more than on the peaks; some of his special favourites have gone through longer and deeper troughs than anyone else. The reason is this. To us a human is primarily food; our aim is the absorption of its will into ours, the increase of our own area of selfhood at its expense. But the obedience which the enemy demands of men is quite a different thing. One must face the fact that all the talk

---

13. Bonhoeffer, *Life Together*, 40–41. For Kierkegaard on "God is the middle-term" see WOL, 112–113; Christman, *Gospel in the Dock*, 201–208; Ferreira, *Love's Grateful Striving*, 71–74.

14. Lewis, *The Screwtape Letters*, 4.

about his love for men, and his service being perfect freedom, is not (as one would gladly believe) mere propaganda, but an appalling truth. He really does want to fill the universe with a lot of loathsome little replicas of himself — creatures whose life, on its miniature scale, will be qualitatively like his own, not because he has absorbed them but because their wills freely conform to his. We want cattle who can finally become food; he wants servants who can finally become sons. We want to suck in, he wants to give out. We are empty and would be filled; he is full and flows over. Our war aim is a world in which Our Father Below has drawn all other beings into himself: the enemy wants a world full of beings united to him but still distinct . . . At any rate, you will soon find that the justice of hell is purely realistic, and concerned only with results. Bring us back food, or be food yourself."[15]

Lewis' christologically-informed theological imagination seems on the right track to "reveal" not only the nature of God's kingdom and Satan's, but how power operates in each, particularly since God's will for humans is based in love that aims at what Kierkegaard called "reduplication" of his life in the free and loving response of his creatures. Lewis' portrayal of God living out of his fullness so that his abundance can fill and unify his creatures provides the "negative" of Satan starkly and chillingly living out of his emptiness as a sort of "black hole" that ultimately draws all into itself. *"Which way I fly is hell, myself am hell"* accurately depicts Satan.[16]

Lewis didn't claim to have "special revelation" of the actual nature of things that are ultimately beyond us, but he nevertheless seemed to faithfully extrapolate from what is revealed of God through Christ and the Bible to what seems a viable working hypothesis regarding how power operates in diametrically different ways in each kingdom. Perhaps the most explicit revelation is in the fact that Jesus bound the strong man by allowing himself to be put to death by demonically inspired "powerful" humans, and in that process subverted all such notions of power.

One wonders if there is a possible parody depicted by Mark, "played out" in the futile efforts of Jesus' family to "seize" and restrain him, and the equally futile efforts of society and/or the family of the crazed Gerasenes demoniac to bind him with chains, but whom Jesus easily *unbinds* (Mark 5:1–20). Jesus alone could bind the strong man, unbind his victims, and was not able to be bound by any, and yet gives his life in complete vulnerability. God's rival kingdom is overcome by the unveiling of its ugly "truth"—its

---

15. Lewis, *The Screwtape Letters*, 46–47, 178.
16. From John Milton's Paradise Lost, as cited in Tanner, *Anxiety in Eden*, 145.

power-dynamic that founds "unity" in a totalitarian consumption of all as *one food*. It is overcome by the righteous power dynamic that founds unity in the mediation of self-giving that results in the true community of *many in fellowship*. Thus, Lewis observed that the fallen dynamic is "hideous strength," but God's righteous dynamic is "real life is meeting."[17]

ON CASTING OUT DEMONS TODAY

Hopefully our consideration of this part of Mark can serve in some way to equip modern-day disciples of Christ as they go forth with "authority" to cast out demons. We thus present four "thoughts" that seem to incrementally contribute to that task regarding this admittedly difficult subject.

First, Mark's first portrayals of the demonic demonstrate that it is a hidden reality which, apart from the arrival of Jesus, would remain largely hidden. This means that the gospel is revelatory of the demonic—which by nature (or super-nature)—is normally a clandestine reality. And that reality is only defined by the fact that it represents the hidden powers which are arrayed against God's gospel for the good of humanity and the world. Thus, the gospel brings to light the hidden demonic realm for "when anything is exposed to the light it becomes visible" (Eph 5:13 ESV). Thus, Mark shows Jesus driven by the Spirit into the wilderness to encounter Satan there (1:12–13). When Jesus begins his ministry in Capernaum "immediately there was in the synagogue a man with an unclean spirit." And the spirit already knew who Jesus was, "the Holy One of God" who has "come to destroy" the demons, first and foremost by simply exposing them. This pattern in Mark seems to be that of the entire NT, wherein the casting out of demons only follows their exposure. Therefore, demonic activity is, apart from gospel exposure, largely clandestine. Certainly, there are gospel accounts where the demonic activity was already manifest and known to be demonic, but those episodes are subservient to the overall gospel story which reveals the pattern of the *true* revelation of the hidden *false* forces in the world, human and demonic, for the sake of the world's deliverance.

Second, that pattern of revelation is made clear in Jesus' *revelation* of the "binding of the strong man" which presents a sort of "order of salvation" regarding deliverance from the demonic. For what is presupposed in the exorcisms is the prior "binding of the strong man." Of course, no-one "saw" the binding that Jesus revealed as already accomplished. Curiously, that binding for Mark seems to have occurred in the wilderness encounter with "the strong man" who was presumably decisively defeated there.

---

17. Lewis, *That Hideous Strength*, 292.

Garland therefore sees all the subsequent exorcisms as a "mopping up action" which in Mark 3:27 is called "plundering."[18] This "order of salvation" is therefore the basis of all deliverance from the demonic. What transpired in the hidden wilderness was a decisive "binding" that enables all subsequent authoritative "plundering" of the demonic kingdom. Walter Brueggemann has demonstrated this "order" as not merely Mark's pattern, but as the entire Bible's "gospel" which consists in a "patterned drama . . . the hidden victory . . . the announcement . . . the lived appropriation."[19] Therefore demonic deliverance is always based on the three steps: 1) the *hidden victory* of Christ; 2) the *announcement* of that victory; and 3) the *lived appropriation* of that victory, which for our purposes here is deliverance from the demonic.

Third, Jesus spoke of "plundering the goods" of the strong man's "house," as an allegorical picture of the real invasion of the demonic realm by Jesus, the agent of God's realm. To move from what we have just seen about the "method" of that ongoing conquest, to how that can apply to today's world, we need to allegorically consider the "goods" of the strong man today: as the supposedly "good" things that humankind was given through modernism's secularist atheism. For it seems that that "good" was a Pandora's Box unleashing demonic legions that have ironically plunged modernism's "inevitable forward march of human progress" into "the age of anxiety." In chapter 10 above we introduced and discussed "the 1840s fork" where the modern world followed the secular atheistic sociology of Freud, Marx, and Nietzsche. There we mostly considered that "fork" in relation to Marx and Nietzsche. But that fork was also the place where Freud and secular atheistic psychology was followed. Modern psychology therefore demythologized the demonic and discounted Christ's deliverance from sin in relation to human existence so that all that remained of humanity was essentially soul-less bodies. Of course, this is an oversimplification, because psychology obviously has to do with human minds which are complexes of the conscious, subconscious, and unconscious. Nevertheless, the pervasive "positive" influence of materialistic atheism has been "aggravated" by severe "bumps in the road" to modernism's inevitable progress. Social revolutions, world wars, and "natural disasters," have left modernistic humanity with increasingly recalcitrant—modernism itself might be tempted to say — "demonic anxieties" that modern psychology, perhaps in the despair of not knowing it is in despair, has yet to "cast out." Thus, the fork in the road modernism chose to follow paved the way for "the age of anxiety." But we need to remember that Kierkegaard also stood at that 1840s fork to represent the

---

18. Garland, *Theology of Mark*, 266, 272.
19. Brueggemann, *Biblical Perspectives*, 38–39.

Christian faith. Of course, we need to also remember that Christendom's gradual bankruptcy provoked and therefore contributed to atheistic secular modernism's presentation of its "goods."[20]

Fourth, therefore, we need to consider what the true Christian faith can provide, so that Christ's modern-day disciples can regain the authority to cast out demons in today's "age of anxiety." Since what they provide *is* the explication of the gospel, their help will follow the same steps we have outlined. First, they would reveal the hidden reality of the demonic in the world today; Second, they would base all deliverance on the "order of salvation," Christ's always-prior binding of Satan; Third, they would "plunder" the atheistic "goods" of our modern and now postmodern age and thereby plunder this stronghold of Satan to release its human captives. Therefore, we will now consider several aspects of Mark and Kierkegaard to demonstrate their ability to provide authority to today's disciples for performing the exorcisms needed today.

MARK AND KIERKEGAARD AS EXORCISTS IN "THE PRESENT AGE" . . . OF ANXIETY

Mark provides a deep revelation of the hidden "principalities and powers" as they relate to the modern secular/materialist/atheistic psyche, because he reveals the basic relations of "the principalities and powers" to "normal" human society—political, economic, and social. Therefore, Mark's revelation relates to the always detrimental effects of demonized power structures which of course have contributed to our present "age of anxiety." This aspect of Mark, more accurately the core-revelation of Mark's account of the invasion and plundering of the demonic realm by the kingdom of God, has been painstakingly detailed in the "political reading" of Mark provided by Ched Myers.[21] His "magnum opus" demonstrates the scope of the demonic realm that the arrival of Jesus exposes. It also demonstrates why some demons are not so easily cast out, so that the exorcisms Jesus performed were in one sense only pictures of the greater exorcisms *through prayer* that would be necessary as the deep demonic strongholds in the fallen world's systems are revealed. Would that it was as easy as casting out personal demons from certain individuals since the real scope of demonization is much deeper and broader. Perhaps this reality underlies Jesus statements in Mark 9:28–29 and John 14:12.

---

20. Dostoevsky wrote that "the image of Christ in the West . . . was dimmed not by science, as the liberals maintain, but by the Western Church itself." As cited in Sandoz, *Political Apocalypse*, 47.

21. Myers, *Binding the Strong Man*.

Mark's revelation of the broad scope of demonization of societies and the world demonstrates that our emphasis on the psychological, Kierkegaard's forte, is only one part of the modern collision of kingdoms, though obviously in itself much needed given the vast numbers suffering today from psychological anxieties. Of course, Kierkegaard's critiques are also far-reaching, touching on many domains of human life, as we have seen and will continue to see.

Kierkegaard provides a deep revelation of the unseen psychological/spiritual/demonic realm that, had the choice at the 1840s fork been different, perhaps the present age of anxiety might have been somewhat alleviated. The substantial factor that Kierkegaard offers is his integration of Socratic and Christian spirituality.[22] This is of paramount importance given that humans are both spirit and body. His holistic approach is amenable to pluralistic cultures where the "anxiety-demons" seek "possession" of all, no matter the "faith" or lack thereof. The Socratic/Christian spirituality Kierkegaard promoted was based in the fact that "natural" and Christian self-hood are not mutually exclusive. The cultivation of the former was conducive to the reception of the latter, even though, strictly speaking, the latter required the "leap of faith" because of the "infinite qualitative distinction" between God and man. Nevertheless, humans becoming more *truly* human is always a good thing, especially in the modern age where self-hood is simply "manufactured" by becoming a number, a mass man, part of the herd. Of course, that *false* reductionism of human flourishing has contributed to the anxieties, identity crises, and obsessions, of the still raging age of anxiety. Thus, history and the biblical stories thereof such as Adam and Eve and Jesus' parable of the prodigal son, attest that humankind "come of age" brings the temptation to human autonomy which is the essence of "modernism" in any day, and thus the vicious cycle of human progress/anxiety.

Mark and Kierkegaard reveal that there are many false "goods" of "the strong man" that need plundering and demonstrate ways to do so. More importantly, they show that the gospel is not merely to cast out and leave a "waterless" void, but to fill the previously possessed house with the presence of *the* Spirit. Otherwise "the unclean spirit" may return with "seven other spirits more evil . . . enter and dwell there" leaving "the last state . . . worse than the first" which may have been the case when modernism cast out the spirit of Christendom (Luke 11:24–26, ESV).

---

22. See Evans, *Kierkegaard and Spirituality*, 63–161. Evans demonstrates the broader applicability of Kierkegaard's psychology in Evans, *Kierkegaard's Christian Psychology*, 95–129. For an introduction to Kierkegaard's Socratic/Christian mission see Christman, "Lewis and Kierkegaard."

16

The Sower of Human Freedom, Responsibility, and Fruitfulness, and "The Parable of the Sower in Christendom"

Mark 4:1–20

The greatest good... that can be done for a being, greater than anything else that one can do for it, is to make it free. —Soren Kierkegaard[1]

In this chapter we divide Mark's text in 4:1–20 into five parts, following its natural outline. That said, we must explain the outline. Dan Via sees the entire parabolic section of Mark 4:1–34 as exhibiting two concentric patterns, each of which contains a center.[2] The first and smaller circle is vv. 2b-20, and we follow Via's five divisions of 4:1–20 in this chapter.[3] Most important is Via's understanding that vv. 11–12 is its center (183):

> And He was saying to them, "To you has been given the mystery of the kingdom of God, but those who are outside get everything in

---

1. As cited in Barnett, *Despair to Faith*, 28.
2. Via, *Mark's Gospel*, 183. Other references to Via in this chapter will be cited in our discussion above.
3. Except that we include v. 1, while Via starts with 2b.

> *parables, so that while seeing, they may see and not perceive, and while hearing, they may hear and not understand, otherwise they might return and be forgiven"* (NASB).

Via summarizes, "In Mark 4:11–12 the very purpose of teaching in parables is to keep the outsiders out, to prevent their seeing and hearing from issuing in understanding" (Via, 183–184). But Via sees the center of the larger circle of 4:1–34, namely vv. 21–25, as importantly and dialectically qualifying the first center:

> *And he said to them, "Is a lamp brought in to be put under a basket, or under a bed, and not on a stand? For nothing is hidden except to be made manifest; nor is anything secret except to come to light. If anyone has ears to hear, let him hear." And he said to them, "Pay attention to what you hear: with the measure you use, it will be measured to you, and still more will be added to you. For to the one who has, more will be given, and from the one who has not, even what he has will be taken away"* (NASB, see Via, 183).

Via notes the glaring contrast of this larger circle's center to 4:11–12 saying, "Over against this stands the center . . . with its affirmation that the intention of the word is revelation, to bring things to light" (Via, 183). Via therefore summarizes both circles and centers to adequately characterize the dialectic between God's sovereignty and human freedom in Mark's parables:

> Mark 4:1–34 deserves special attention because it contains the harshest and most extreme expression of the concealed revelation motif: Jesus teaches in parable-enigmas in order that the outsiders might not understand, repent, and find forgiveness (4:10–12). It also suggests a way out of the impasse: nothing is hidden except in order to be brought to light (4:21–23) (Via, 182–183).

Part 1) Mark 4:1–9 He began to teach again by the sea. And such a very large crowd gathered to Him that He got into a boat in the sea and sat down; and the whole crowd was by the sea on the land. 2 And He was teaching them many things in parables, and was saying to them in His teaching, 3 "Listen to this! Behold, the sower went out to sow; 4 as he was sowing, some seed fell beside the road, and the birds came and ate it up. 5 Other seed fell on the rocky ground where it did not have much soil; and immediately it sprang up because it had no depth of soil. 6 And after the sun had risen, it was scorched; and because it had no root, it withered away. 7 Other seed fell among the thorns, and the thorns came up and choked it, and it yielded no crop. 8 Other seeds fell into the good soil, and as they grew up and increased, they yielded a crop and produced thirty, sixty, and a hundredfold." 9 And He was saying, "He who has ears to hear, let him hear" (NASB).

THE PARABLE, "THE CHANGELESSNESS OF GOD" AND HUMAN FREEDOM

Up to this point, Mark has emphasized external events and observed outward responses to Jesus. Now it is as though a veil is withdrawn to reveal *more* holistic responses through the indirect communication of *imaginative parables* that provide a pictorial "cartography" of the hearts and lives of the hearers.[4]

The crowd is still generally ever-present. That Jesus "retreated" into a boat may again ominously signify its "mob" potential. But the parable of the sower reveals that the sower in one sense determines everything. Kierkegaard would say that the crowd" must have an opinion about it," since all must be offended or find faith. But this "determinism" is odd, as we should expect given the nature of God's self-giving power as was just discussed in the previous chapter. For the determinism of God is importantly qualified by the fact that the sower "knows not how" the seed "sprouts and grows" while "he sleeps and rises night and day," and *observes* (Mark 4:26). Via goes so far as to say "But how, when, or whether the word will evoke faith remains a mystery. Just what the relationship is between seed and fruit, between word and faith-love, the sower does not know" (Via, 186).

It seems that the crop "depends" on the soil and the circumstances. But that does not mean that the parable was meant to provide a map to locate oneself therein as if pre-determined. For the hearers are *meant* to consider *how their "soil" hears*. That presents important qualifications against determinism. It is true that the soil is sterile for germinating and growing the viable "germ" of the seed—the life of God. But the parable depicts the soil as *responsible* for the results. The parable is not meant for fatalistically

---

4. "Often *indirect communication* describes the communicative strategies that are necessary to enable a learner to develop a capacity to act or feel in a new manner. It is differentiated from the transmitting of mere information. Sometimes *indirect communication* more narrowly indicates a way of writing that is typified by multiple voices, thick irony, textual disruptions, and other literary strategies that make the meaning of a text problematic and force the reader to struggle with interpretive decisions." Barrett, *Kierkegaard*, 76.

identifying some "given" type of soil we simply *are*. Rather, it is meant to show the various possibilities following upon the sower sowing his seed upon the soil in its circumstances. The parable strongly implies a call for human responsibility, especially because of what was already noted in 4:24–25, the very center of this parabolic section of Mark. Of course, this call was accentuated for the entire crowd in its closing words which declare the parable's *universal* imperative: "He who has ears to hear, let him hear" (4:9). Other *particular* imperatives are embedded in the various circumstances portrayed and are to be drawn out by each "hearer" with ears, as necessary.

Barnett provides what seems the proper way to view the divine and human dynamics of the sowing and seed, soil and response portrayed in this parable, through his explanation of God's sovereignty and human freedom as framed in one of Kierkegaard's final discourses, "*The Changelessness of God.*" Barnett writes,

> "The greatest good . . . that can be done for a being, greater than anything else that one can do for it, is to make it free." And yet, he adds, only an omnipotent being can make another being free . . . But how is this possible? According to Kierkegaard, it is possible only because God is, as it were, on a different level of being than creatures. God does not compete with human beings, nor does he have need of their cooperation. "Omnipotence is not ensconced in a relationship to another, for there is no other to which it is comparable . . ." In a nutshell, the relationship between God and humanity is *noncompetitive*. From God the human being receives the entire field of being and becoming as a gift. To go forth in the world as a free creature is precisely to realize that gift. Kierkegaard sums it up in this way: "He to whom I owe absolutely everything, although he still absolutely controls everything, has in fact made me independent."[5]

Barnett adequately summarizes what has been considered to this point and sets the proper framework for further detailing this parable in which God is always the sovereign sower of human freedom, responsibility, and fruitfulness.

Part 2) Mark 4:10 As soon as He was alone, His followers, along with the twelve, began asking Him about the parables (NASB).

---

5. Barnett, *Despair to Faith*, 28, 29–30.

THE QUESTIONS OF THE DISCIPLES: "TO NEED GOD IS THE HIGHEST PERFECTION"

The response of the disciples strongly mitigates against the view that the parable was meant to portray that soil productivity is only given to "chosen insiders." For if we are to presume that true disciples will persevere to produce varying degrees of fruitfulness, the reason for that is already beginning to be revealed as the result of their "responsive" questions. If their fruitfulness was determined, then their "perfection" would simply be complicity with God's determinism, which of course would not be compliance but simple mechanics. But their perfection is revealed in their questioning, which displays their *desire—to know*, which itself reveals the awareness of their *need—to know*. Hence, another sermon of Kierkegaard aptly summarizes the real key to "productive soil," which is the truth that "to need God is a human being's highest perfection."[6] What is most important, to do justice to the parable and Kierkegaard, is that the "soils'" need of God is continual, so that "soil" has the gift and task of *becoming* good soil. Simply *being* good soil would be determinism. Therefore, Kierkegaard saw "becoming a Christian" as the gift and task of a lifetime.

Kierkegaard recognized that, "With respect to the earthly, one needs little and to the degree that one needs less, the more perfect one is."[7] But the need of God is the continual neediness, the "before" necessary to the gift and task. Needing God as the "before" necessary for "accomplishments" is not the constant need that is the highest perfection. Therefore, the parable is about "fruitfulness" which can only follow from intimate relation to God based in constant need. Therefore, the need is ultimately to live within the dialectic of need/perfection that coheres within the human/divine relation. Human autonomy is opposite to the relation that bears fruit (John 15:1–8). The seed creates life in the soil through continual faith-relation to continual need. Therefore "good soil" is sterile, and only bears fruit through its continual needful response to the life-giving seed. Kierkegaard writes, "But someone who is conscious that he is capable of nothing at all has every day and every moment the desired and irrefragable opportunity to experience that God lives."[8] This is not determinism, but rather the gospel that "to need God is the "highest perfection." Via's study of Mark recognizes these things, as he views discipleship as an eschatology of "good soil." He writes, "Having it and not having it at the same time is, then, not just the situation of the

---

6. Kierkegaard, EUD, 297–326.
7. Kierkegaard, EUD, 303.
8. Kierkegaard, EUD, 322.

would-be disciple or the natural human, but the condition of the *disciple*. All disciples must say, "I believe; help my unbelief!" (9:24)" (Via, 187). Thus, the parable intends that the good soil will *continually* say "I believe—I am good soil—help my hard, shallow, thorny soil of unbelief."

Part 3) Mark 4:11–12 And He was saying to them, "To you has been given the mystery of the kingdom of God, but those who are outside get everything in parables, 12 so that while seeing, they may see and not perceive, and while hearing, they may hear and not understand, otherwise they might return and be forgiven" (NASB).

THE PARADOX OF THE PARABLE: "THE ROAD IS HOW"

We have already considered Mark 4:11–12 as the center of the smaller, first circle, of Mark 4. It appears wholly deterministic, but we have seen that as only apparent. If it was considered actual it destroys the meaning and the revelatory purpose of the parable. This was shown earlier in the significance of the center of the second, larger circle, Mark 4:21–25, which reveals the parable's purpose in the words "pay attention to what you hear."

Thus, Kierkegaard's statement, "the road is how," aptly summarizes the purpose of the parables which is also implied in 4:9. This Kierkegaardian "road is how" is the main subject of the next chapter, so at this point we will simply present a tangential view that Via presents in his comments on 4:11–12:

> We observed that in the strongest possible way Mark stresses the divine initiative in salvation . . . Salvation is impossible for human beings, but all things are possible with God (10:27). In 4:21–23 the divine initiative comes to expression by means of the image of the lamp whose purpose is to give light. But something *is* also expected of human beings: they are put under the imperative to hear (4:23, 24a), and fruitful hearing clearly involves the pre-understanding with which one hears. The *way* the human being hears has something to do with the effectiveness of the seed (4:15, 16, 18, 20) or light (4:24). The measure one brings to hearing conditions the measure of understanding one gets (4:26b). More understanding will be given to the one who already has understanding (4:25a). Recall that the soil or earth is an image of the hearer in Mark 4. The earth produces "of itself"

(*automate*, 4:28). The "of itself" is the pre-understanding of the hearer; it is the measure that he or she already has and brings to the hearing of the word or seeing the light, the measure that enables the latter to produce an effect (Via, 185).

Part 4) Mark 4:13 And He said to them, "Do you not understand this parable? How will you understand all the parables? (NASB).

THE RESPONSIBILITY OF THE HEARERS: INTRODUCING "THE ANXIETY OF IRRESOLUTION"

Jesus is here reproving the disciples, though perhaps only gently. Nevertheless, this reproof implies their responsibility to "hear" (4:9) as has already been discussed. What is implied in "the way is how" of proper hearing is becoming *resolute*. Resolution versus irresolution is the implied factor of fruitfulness against the obstacles of soil conditions and external circumstances. Via writes, "what prevents fruitfulness is not the intention of the revealer or the nature of the word but concrete external circumstances and lack of resolution on the part of hearers" (Via, 184). He further summarizes:

> In considering 4:11–12 and 4:13–20 together, one ought to say that the destiny which prevents responsiveness to the word is spun from a number of strands: God's mysterious tendency to conceal (4:11–12), the power of Satan (4:15), difficult historical and social circumstances (4:17b, 19), and lack of internal staying power in the faith of individuals (4:16b, 17a, 19) (Via, 184).

The "lack of staying power" is obviously of paramount importance in light of the other "strands" that prevent the growth of the seed. Kierkegaard recognized this problem in Christendom in his sermon series: *The Anxieties of the Heathen—Christian Discourses*. The final sermon, perhaps the capstone of them all, was called "The Anxiety of Irresolution, Fickleness and Disconsolateness."[9] In the next section we will consider how irresolution is always a major factor of the unfruitful soils.

In the final section of this chapter, we will slightly shift gears, or nearly several millennia of years to be precise, to provide a "Kierkegaardian reading" of Christendom in light of this parable. This part presents Jesus' own explanation of the parable, so we will seek to apply that explanation to

---

9. Kierkegaard, CD, 83–93.

modern and postmodern society. For we need to "have ears to hear" by paying attention to what we hear *today* (Mark 4:9; 24).

Part 5) Mark 4:14–20 The sower sows the word. 15 These are the ones who are beside the road where the word is sown; and when they hear, immediately Satan comes and takes away the word which has been sown in them. 16 In a similar way these are the ones on whom seed was sown on the rocky places, who, when they hear the word, immediately receive it with joy; 17 and they have no firm root in themselves, but are only temporary; then, when affliction or persecution arises because of the word, immediately they fall away. 18 And others are the ones on whom seed was sown among the thorns; these are the ones who have heard the word, 19 but the worries of the world, and the deceitfulness of riches, and the desires for other things enter in and choke the word, and it becomes unfruitful. 20 And those are the ones on whom seed was sown on the good soil; and they hear the word and accept it and bear fruit, thirty, sixty, and a hundredfold" (NASB).

"THE PARABLE OF THE SOWER IN CHRISTENDOM"

This last section can be considered as a sort of "Parable of the Sower in Christendom" although the form will not present a story. Nonetheless, its parts together may convey a story, a parable in fact, in which we will "see" the parable of the sower taking place in Christendom. The anachronism that we are now in post-Christendom should not prohibit seeing that Christendom's shortcomings in many ways provided the foundation of post-Christendom. Therefore, a reading of the former will invariably include something of a reading of the latter, which is in many ways the re-incarnation of the former anyway.

The Roadside Soil

Kierkegaard saw tragic irony in the fact that the masses of Christendom exhibited the fruitless fate of the soil whose life-giving seed was sown along the busy road of life. Of course, modern "busyness" has been a problem for as long as boredom has, which we saw in chapter 14. Nonetheless, the seed was "sown in them." This indicates that there was *some* contact with their "soil," because they "hear" and are not without culpability as 4:9 says. The agency of "Satan" does not remove this guilt, although it does reveal the externality of the form of life that "requires" human shallowness.

This reveals that both internal and external factors result in shallow soil. The busy form of life in late Christendom, which could be summarized as pre-occupation, is the "road," the way of life in what Kierkegaard called "the present age." It consists in what the social imaginary dictates as the "telos" of life: power, pleasure, wealth, success, and limitless self-expression.[10] But the sense of a true objective good in relation to God, a telos, has been lost to such an age. Ironically, this age is "reflective." Tyson writes,

> Kierkegaard is sociologically fascinated by the outlook he calls reflection. This is the Present Age's propensity to very carefully examine, judge, know about, and master everything. Yet all the judgments and knowledge of this reflection are measured in terms of externalities and practicalities without any vital inner sense of value or ultimate purpose. Thus the double meaning of reflection here is that this age is very thoughtful, but it is only thoughtful about the surface reflections of things—inner meanings, higher purposes, and intrinsically valuable ends are entirely opaque to the present age.[11]

Thus, Kierkegaard revealed how the external and internal "conspire" together against the "word . . . sown in them." The internal irresolution is shown by Kierkegaard to be based in "doubleness, the two wills, masterlessness, or what is the same thing, thralldom."[12] What this means is that "the road" of "the present age" is entered through the toll of thralldom, a "preoccupation" which provides the Satanic birds their opportunity to snatch away the seed. The ironic inverse truth is that the "resolution" to follow the common road is filled with anxiety, which Jesus reveals as the other soils are analyzed.

The Shallow Soil

Kierkegaard presents a direct reading of this passage in Mark, which consists in *his* reading of Christendom's reading of what it means to suffer "tribulation or persecution . . . on account of the word."[13] He writes,

> It is Christianly preached that a person must enter into the kingdom of heaven through many tribulations, that there must be

---

10. Crouther, "Introduction," xiii.
11. Tyson, *Kierkegaard's Theological Sociology*, 26.
12. Kierkegaard, CD, 89.
13. Kierkegaard, PC, 113. His "reading" on this passage is from 108–115.

tribulation. Splendid! That is indeed Christianity! But if we listen more closely, we discover with amazement that these many tribulations are such as sickness, financial embarrassment, cares about next year, what one is going to eat, or cares about "what one ate last year but still has not paid for," or about not having become what one wanted to become in the world, or other calamities. This is Christianly preached about; one weeps humanly and dementedly brings it into connection with Gethsemane. If it were through these many tribulations that one enters into the kingdom of heaven, then, of course, the pagans would also enter the kingdom of heaven, for they go through the same tribulations. No, in an extremely dangerous way, this mode of preaching is the abolition of Christianity, in part even blasphemous.[14]

Kierkegaard shows that Christendom has replaced the sufferings of the kingdom with "the anxieties of the heathen," which was the series of sermons mentioned above. It is also important to note that Jesus precisely named these "tribulations" as mere anxieties of the heathen in Matthew 6:19–34 and reveals the "double-mindedness" of "irresolution" beneath them.

The Thorny Soil

The thorny soil signifies a patch of ground "pre-occupied," with deep noxious roots which allow the seed to start growing but eventually overcome it with their vigorous growth. Jesus explicitly calls these "thorns" the "worries of the world," the anxieties. Ironically the companion to these anxieties is "riches," which reveals their "deceitfulness." For Jesus probably said "thorny" because they cause acute pain while promising pleasure. Thus "desires for other things" namely, anxiety-causing riches, leaves no room for true human flourishing, which is choked out. For the gospel seed is meant to bring "fruitfulness," even that which to "the philistine-bourgeoise mentality" would look "worldly," as was discussed in chapter 11 above. There is again irony, in that Christendom's conceptions of fruitfulness stumble on either asceticism or hedonism, both of which bring anxiety, as we will see next.

The Good Soil

Kierkegaard presented parabolic characters in his book *Either/Or* that demonstrate the paradox of the good soil, namely that it produces not only

14. Kierkegaard, PC, 113.

fruitfulness, but that which far surpasses anything the other "worldly" soils vainly hope for. The lack of true human flourishing is easily seen in *either* the hedonistic aesthete *or* the ascetic ethicist of *Either/Or*. Kierkegaard demonstrated that their approaches to "the good life" failed to deliver the "goods" and instead reaped the anxieties accompanying the unflourishing life. We can perhaps illustrate this for both Christendom and post-Christendom, by considering how the effects of modern consumerism mirrors the life-failures of Kierkegaard's hedonistic aesthete and ascetic ethicist. Our illustration is from Cavanaugh, who writes,

> Consumerism is a restless spirit that is never content with any particular material thing. In this sense, consumerism has some affinities with Christian asceticism, which counsels a certain detachment from material things. The difference is that, in consumerism, detachment continually moves us from one product to another, whereas in Christian life, asceticism is a means to a greater attachment to God and to other people.[15]

Consumerism's "restless spirit" easily mirrors Kierkegaard's hedonistic aesthetes, such as "Don Juan" who moves from woman to woman in "The Rotation of Crops" and seeks to "consume" them in consumeristic fruitfulness.[16] Cavanaugh notes ironic affinities of such hedonism to Christian asceticism. The fact of affinity between pleasure-seeking and asceticism derives from their "detachment" from God and others. This recognition allows us to extrapolate the same affinity of detachment between Kierkegaard's ascetic ethicist in *Fear and Trembling*, "the knight of infinite resignation," and consumerism. We had seen in chapter 11 above that the asceticism of the knight's resignation fails the true faith that can believe and receive the gospel's promise that gains, *instead of consumes,* other people (Mark 10:29–31). Cavanaugh rightly qualifies this with a true asceticism, based in the basic self-denial the gospel requires of all disciples. But true asceticism "is a means to a greater attachment to . . . other people."

This brief expose of consumerism reveals that the fruitfulness of the good soil is not merely related to Kierkegaard's perfection of "needing God" but to the need of attachment to *others*. The unproductive soils fail through consumerism that cannot be "fulfilled" according to their need of detachment. Fruitfulness is either prevented by pre-occupation with self, thwarted by shallow attachment's tribulations, or is choked out by more compelling

---

15. Cavanaugh, *Being Consumed*, xi.

16. See Kierkegaard, EO:1, "The Rotation of Crops," 281–300; "The Seducer's Diary," 301–445. See Miles, *Kierkegaard and Nietzsche*, 14–57 for a thorough discussion of the aesthetic, ethical, and religious "stages" and these characters in Kierkegaard.

detachment or attachment. The conflict of each soil is of consumeristic detachment or attachment. Interestingly, Cavanaugh concludes with the paradox of true Christian asceticism and "consumerism": "We are consumers in the Eucharist, but in consuming the body of Christ we are transformed into the body of Christ."[17]

"Thirty, Sixty, and Hundredfold" Fruitfulness of the Good Soil.

Following our Kierkegaardian reading in this section leads us to the need to consider these variations in relation to the dehumanizing "leveling" that Kierkegaard saw in "the present age." Cutting explains that,

> The leveling process of the present age introduces the concept of equality, but it is an alienating, abstract, mathematical equality (TA, 84–85). Like all averages, the average norms of the public, which all members of society are expected to strive for, level outstanding individuals to the mediocrity of the average. Thus society "grinds smooth the individual's angularity and essential accidentality" (SUD, 33), so that the present-day member of the public "finds it too hazardous to be himself and far easier to be like others, to become a copy, a number, a mass man" (SUD, 34). Thus, equality, like all values at this stage, is relative to the values and size of a given society at a given time."[18]

It may very well be the case that the varying fruitfulness of the soils signifies that God's kingdom does not operate on what is now called "outcome based" policies which essentially are leveling policies. Furthermore, such leveling can easily work against personal responsibility and preclude the part that free agency plays even in relation to the fruitfulness of the gospel. As the ultimate sower, God sows the word and "grows" freedom, responsibility, and fruitfulness in his gospel "crop." It seems that this parable provides an amazing mirror of the possibilities of the gospel-seed, albeit realistically balanced by the sterility of our soil. But as we should expect with the gospel, the emphasis is on God's sovereign intent. Karl Hefty writes,

> Hearing the word, in the end, means hearing one's very life said in it, so that it is we, in the end, who are the invincible proof of what it tells us.[19]

---

17. Cavanaugh, *Being Consumed*, xi.
18. Cutting, "Levels of Interpersonal," 80.
19. In Henry, *Words of Christ*, xxix.

17

"If Anyone Has Ears to Hear … for Disciples the Road is How"

Mark 4:21–25 (NIV)

21 He said to them, "Do you bring in a lamp to put it under a bowl or a bed? Instead, don't you put it on its stand? 22 For whatever is hidden is meant to be disclosed, and whatever is concealed is meant to be brought out into the open. 23 If anyone has ears to hear, let them hear." 24 "Consider carefully what you hear," he continued. "With the measure you use, it will be measured to you—and even more. 25 Whoever has will be given more; whoever does not have, even what they have will be taken from them."

It is well known that Christ consistently used the expression "follower." He never asks for admirers, worshippers, or adherents. No, he calls disciples. It is not adherents of a teaching but followers of a life Christ is looking for.
—Soren Kierkegaard[1]

We have seen that Jesus' telling of parables was a form of indirect communication. That Mark reproduces Jesus' parables shows that Mark (naturally)

---

1. Kierkegaard, PSW, 83.

endorses and employs the method. In fact, his entire gospel is in a sense an indirect communication, since it is not a mere compendium of doctrines or facts about Jesus' life, but rather the representation of *a life*. In like manner, those called by the gospel to be its witnesses, are also themselves to be vehicles of indirect communication, in that their lives as a whole are meant to speak the gospel more than their periodic words can. Thus, Jesus intended that his gospel would be perpetuated by followers of *his* life, with *their* lives an indirect communication thereof. This section will more fully consider God's intent for indirect communication, which could perhaps also be called "imaginative communication." It contrasts with the "more rational" method of direct communication which has been humanity's infatuation since "The Enlightenment." This is especially important because when it comes to the gospel the manner and effectiveness of communication is of the utmost importance. Furthermore, if evangelism becomes mostly practiced under the auspices of direct communication, it may well fall short of its purpose, not to mention the method of Jesus.

DIRECT AND INDIRECT COMMUNICATION[2]

For Christians, it ought to be a given that Jesus was a highly effective communicator. In fact, the entire biblical tradition exists because meaningful life-changing communication is of the utmost importance. But that blanket statement must be augmented by the fact that the Bible is a patchwork of many genres, authorial voices, and methods of communication. Jesus' own communication exhibits much variety including symbolic actions, proclamations based on OT texts, metaphorical parables, riddle-like statements and proverbs, and apocalyptic prophecies. Most important was his life that fully demonstrated his total message. To see Christ is to see his message.

---

2. Mark Tietjen explains Kierkegaard's idea and method of Christian communication: "Kierkegaard labels Christian communication *direct-indirect*. It is direct insofar as it communicates truth claims—doctrines like the incarnation, for example. Christian witness necessarily includes the communication of these doctrines as knowledge claims the recipient must wrestle with and ultimately should accept should he or she come to faith. But that is not all—the Christian witness is indirect as well, since it does not stop with assent to those beliefs but looks to the implications of those beliefs on one's life. There is a second reason why the Christian witness will make use of indirect methods. If one's audience is overly familiar with Christianity, as was Kierkegaard's, then clearly what is missing is not theoretical knowledge. In that case what is needed is communication that seeks to evoke from cultural Christians actions that are actually Christian. *This* is what Kierkegaard believes to be precisely lacking not just in the Christians of his day but in pastors specifically." Tietjen, *Kierkegaard, Christian Missionary*, 114.

Therefore, it seems that it would also be a given that Christians would understand and recognize the value of indirect communication. But indirect communication has become de-valued, ironically even in much of Christianity that capitulated to modernist values wherein *only* "seeing is believing." The varied means of knowledge have been reduced, devolving as scientific knowledge evolved. Ancient cave paintings reveal that "cave men" were storytellers and artists.[3] But "scientific" and "systematic" man, whether modernist or fundamentalist, has often largely forgotten art and meaningful story for "the facts." Real scientific advance has been tempted to a *scientism* that ignores that "what we cannot speak about we must pass over in silence."[4] But ironically, its presumptive speaking is inadequate to the totality of factors and domains involved in "personal knowledge" and impoverished regarding the *relative* certitude truth is meant to bring.[5] Kierkegaard writes,

> But he who has observed the present generation can hardly deny that the discrepancy in it and the reason for its anxiety and unrest is this, that in one direction truth increases in scope and in quantity, and partly also in abstract clarity, while in the opposite direction certainty constantly declines.[6]

The modern fetishization of "direct communication" reduces the full scope of reality and human knowing and results in diminishment and perversion of the meaning of life, if not its complete annulment. But real communicators such as Jesus, Mark, and Kierkegaard, knew otherwise, because life cannot be so simply communicated. What Mark Tietjen says about Kierkegaard is true of all:

> There is something deeply important about what Kierkegaard is trying to communicate. If his aims are primarily edifying and *not* academic (or entertaining, teasing, deceiving), if

---

3. Chesterton, *The Everlasting Man*, 29–30.

4. Ludwig Wittgenstein, as cited in Thiselton, *Thiselton on Hermeneutics*, 103.

5. This is a direct reference to the magnum opus of Michael Polanyi, "Personal Knowledge," which demonstrates the paucity, hubris, and perversity of the "just the facts" approach of the ironically fiduciary "personal knowledge" of modernism. Citing Polanyi, Brueggemann relates the reception Barth received when he revealed the real nature of modernistic theology: "Since Barth exposed objective scholarship as theory-laden, it does not follow that his theological premise would be granted any privilege. It does, however, make inescapable the recognition that there is no innocent or neutral scholarship, but that all theological and interpretive scholarship is in one way or another fiduciary." Brueggemann, *Theology*, 18. On "relativity" as basic to finite created humans and therefore also "good" see Smith, *Who's Afraid of Relativism*.

6. Kierkegaard, CA, 139.

> Kierkegaard wishes to accomplish something as significant as assisting his reader to grow in faith, or love, or courage, or to question whether one's commitments in life contribute to a whole, flourishing self, then to miss or to dismiss this purpose is detrimental—both to one's interpretation of Kierkegaard and—what is more—existentially to one's life.[7]

Combining Jesus' parable of the sower with Kierkegaard's thought, one might say that the sower's seed is life-giving, providing *existence communication*. That is why *the word* as seed takes various discursive forms, so that together—parable, proclamation, prophecy, and plain-talk can conjure up a life.

This is also why Jesus exhorts disciples against keeping their lives hidden as lamps placed under a bowl or a bed. The life must be communicated to be seed for new life in others. It may be that the parable of the seeds "hidden" in soils might mistakenly be thought to convey the idea that the Christian life ought to remain largely hidden. Especially when it consists in a struggle against worldly "scorching" persecutions and "thorny" entanglements. Jesus intends the seeds to break forth as fruitful plants in the light of day, or as lamps in the darkness of night. The sower didn't sow seeds, or the lamplighter light lamps, to no larger purpose. Though the new life of discipleship begins in the hidden depth of the soil, it is not to remain there, for *"whatever is hidden is meant to be disclosed, and whatever is concealed is meant to be brought out into the open."*

ONLY SUBJECTIVE DOERS, NOT "OBJECTIVE" HEARERS, HAVE GOSPEL KNOWLEDGE

Since the would-be witness of the gospel is to communicate their life, it naturally follows that they must be doers of the word and not just hearers. Jesus said, *"Consider carefully what you hear . . . With the measure you use, it will be measured to you—and even more. Whoever has will be given more; whoever does not have, even what they have will be taken from them."* Hearing the word and acting upon it is the way that a person *increases* "the word" they already *have*. One *has*, initially, the *hearing*. If one *acts* upon that with *doing*, then one *truly has* and that *has* can grow exponentially, *"thirty, sixty, and a hundredfold."* But apart from turning the initial "has" into the *truer* has, the initial "has" will be *"taken from them."* What each would-be disciple

---

7. Tietjen, *Kierkegaard, Communication, and Virtue*, 4.

does in this regard is therefore the *"measure"* they do or don't use, and by which they will or will not receive.

All this describes the process of growth in fruitfulness, in being "lamps," in receiving *existence communication* which is the subjective life the gospel "communicates" rather than the "objective" facts of the gospel. Of course, the shape of that life is Christ's life, the prototype which the disciple follows. Thus, the life to be communicated exhibits some measure of authentic *"reduplication"* of Christ's life and is *therefore* an authentic life-witness to the gospel. Apart from this the life communicated, regardless of words claiming otherwise, will remain largely formed by *"the secular mentality's earthly mother tongue"* and will ironically only witness of that. In his journal Kierkegaard writes,

> The essential sermon is one's own existence. A person preaches with this every hour of the day and with power quite different from that of the most eloquent speaker in his most eloquent moment. To let one's existence express the opposite and then let one's mouth run with eloquent babbling about the opposite is in a deepest sense nonsense and, Christianly, this means to become liable to eternal judgment, even though in the temporal world it is the way to high positions, honor, reputation, popularity, and the like.[8]

In *Practice in Christianity,* he relates the disciple's subjective life to the truth of Christ's life:

> Truth in the sense in which Christ is the truth is not a sum of statements, not a definition etc., but a life . . . the being of truth is the redoubling of truth within yourself, within me, within him, that your life, my life, his life expresses the truth approximately in the striving for it, just as the truth was in Christ a *life,* for he was the truth.[9]

THE PITFALLS OF "WHAT"

A reductive modernistic theory of knowing inhabits much Christianity today and has contributed to faith and discipleship becoming dominated by the realm of the intellect—at least when it is thought about—since our

---

8. Soren Kierkegaard, JP: I:460, #1056.

9. Kierkegaard, PC, 205. Note that Kierkegaard's reference to "him" seems to be referring to "an apostle" whom he had referenced a bit earlier.

age is ironically anti-intellectual.[10] Because of this pseudo-intellectual orientation (and holistic disorientation) much "discipleship" consists in a "pastoral" data-dump which is simply (and uncritically) "received" by the one-sided "disciple." But the "receiving" person, ruled by the habits of fallen affections, remains basically unchanged.[11] I think much of what we are currently seeing with the rise of Evangelical "deconstruction" is fallout from when the "what" of rationalistic/formulaic doctrine, falsely elevated to the place of faith-confessional status, cannot hold that place and upon falling leaves that "faith" empty and without *existential* meaning. Speaking to the preoccupation of "what" that had already become predominant in his day, Kierkegaard says,

> I also find that men everywhere are preoccupied with the WHAT which is to be communicated . . . The modern age has—and I regard this as its basic damage—abolished personality and made everything objective. Therefore men do not come to dwell on the thought of what does it mean to communicate. And since almost every such *what,* even at first glance, reveals itself to be something very prolix, there is in the passage of time even less of an opportunity or place for considering what it means to communicate. A philosopher, a dogmatician, a pastor, etc.—they all begin immediately with the *what* they wish to communicate, with studies and preliminary sketches of it.[12]

The problems of preoccupation with the "what" include these: 1) Looking *at the mirror* of God's word rather than looking *in the mirror*, and turning God and his word into the object for examination when the truth of the matter should be the reverse; 2) Over-excusing a *seemingly necessary* delay of believing the gospel (Mark 1:15) for the sake of "rational" evaluations of "the faith," which is a perilous situation given our susceptibility to the hardening effects of sin, the diversionary effects of the world, and the demonic devouring of gospel seeds; 3) Burying the reality of the "existence communication" of the gospel under "objective reasoning" which is neither the primary part of life nor what constitutes true human personhood;[13]

---

10. Robert W. Jenson wrote "The nation built on Enlightenment has not merely become ignorant and unthinking, or even anti-intellectual . . . but is becoming incapable of thought." Cited in Green, *Gospel And The Mind*, 21.

11. James K. A. Smith has presented the case that humans as primarily "thinking things" is a modernistic fiction. The truth is that we are ruled by our desires, for worse or for better, if they are redeemed. See Smith, *Desiring the Kingdom*.

12. Soren Kierkegaard, JP: I:304, #657.

13. For a sustained treatment of the reductionism of human knowing in objectivity rather than subjectivity see Kierkegaard, PSW, 56–59; Kierkegaard, CUP:1, 192–203.

4) Relegating God and the gospel to stand under fallen human judgment which has been falsely elevated to the place of authority.

KIERKEGAARD'S "READING" OF THE FIVE ROADS FROM JERICHO TO JERUSALEM

In his reading of perhaps the most well-known parable of Jesus, "The Good Samaritan" (Luke 10:25-37), Kierkegaard deconstructs the modernistic idea that there was one objective road, discoverable to any by purely empirical reason, that everyone walked from Jericho to Jerusalem.[14] He shows instead that there were five roads walked in that parable, each of which demonstrates that "the road is how." He writes,

> The story tells of five people who walked "along the same road." The highway, alas, makes no difference; it is the spiritual that makes the difference and distinguishes the road. Let us consider more carefully how this is. The first man was a peaceful traveler who walked along the road from Jericho to Jerusalem, along *a lawful road*. The second man was a robber who "walked along the same road"—and yet on *an unlawful road*. Then a priest came "along the same road"—and we see the poor unfortunate man who has been assaulted by the robber. Perhaps he was momentarily moved but went right on by. He walked on *the road of indifference*. Next a Levite came "along the same road." He saw the poor unfortunate man; he too walked "along the same road" but was walking his way, *the way of selfishness and indifference*. Finally a Samaritan came "along the same road." He found the poor unfortunate man on the road of mercy. He showed the example how to walk *the road of mercy*; he demonstrated that the road, spiritually speaking, is precisely this; *how* one walks. This is why the Gospel says, "Go and do likewise." Yes, there were five travelers who walked "along the same road," and yet each one walked his own road.[15]

Simon Weil has perhaps most movingly portrayed the mercy of *the one* who is ultimately portrayed in the parable "for him who has ears to hear." She writes of:

---

14. I am doubtful that materialistic reason could account for the moral and spiritual reality of the five roads without being reductionistic of the full nature of human existence, though "materialism" would like to reduce it to one road, a nihilistic one.

15. Kierkegaard, PSW, 54, (emphasis mine). Moore has greatly condensed the full reading, for which see: Kierkegaard, UDVS, 290.

> . . . a little piece of flesh, naked, inert, and bleeding beside a ditch; he is nameless; no one knows anything about him. Those who pass by this thing scarcely notice it, and a few minutes afterward do not even know that they saw it. Only one stops and turns his attention toward it.[16]

By stopping, turning, and paying attention to *the other* in dire need, Jesus demonstrated a parable for all would-be disciples: "The road is how."

---

16. Weil, *Waiting for God*, 90.

18

The "Fine Species" of Seed that Sows Purity of Heart

God's Unity and Man's Disunity

Mark 4:26–29 (ESV)

26 And he said, "The kingdom of God is as if a man should scatter seed on the ground. 27 He sleeps and rises night and day, and the seed sprouts and grows; he knows not how. 28 The earth produces by itself, first the blade, then the ear, then the full grain in the ear. 29 But when the grain is ripe, at once he puts in the sickle, because the harvest has come."

The entire grave site is then to be leveled and sown with a fine species of low grass . . . in each corner a little spot of Turkish roses . . . Then I may rest in halls of roses, and unceasingly, and unceasingly speak with my Jesus.
—Soren Kierkegaard[1]

Mark again narrates a parable of Jesus, the second of three concerning seeds and sowers. We noted that the first parable provided a world-picture of the internal and external factors related to the growth-response to the gospel-word of the kingdom. In this parable we see a picture of the micro

---

1. Cited in Garff, Soren Kierkegaard, 811. (Instructions for the family grave site and several of the words on his headstone.)

and macro levels of the growing kingdom of God. The reason these two levels of God's kingdom can be portrayed in the same imaginative parable, is because of the "*fractal*" nature of God's kingdom. At every level the same dynamic workings are at play, which manifest themselves in a harmonious and unified process.

In our reading of the parable, at the micro level we will see how the seed grows individuals as unified within themselves, "the blade . . . the ear . . . the full grain in the ear." At the macro level we will see that these unified individual selves grow collectively into a unified whole, "the ripe grain . . . the harvest. The micro and macro levels of the "world" portrayed in this parable are tied together by an essential unity, a repeated fractal pattern of God, the Christian individual, and the Christian community.

GOD'S UNITY AND THE HUMAN SELF'S DISUNITY

Many Christians view salvation almost solely through the legal categories of sin/debt and faith/justification. This is not categorically wrong, but it can hide the integral connection between justification and sanctification, sometimes to the diminishment of the *transformation* that is *the whole*, the *experience* of salvation. This is why Kierkegaard viewed salvation as an *existence-communication,* and not merely a change in one's outward legal status.

Viewing salvation in this way, Kierkegaard held that the complete "inner" unity of God, and the inner disunity of each human that leaves us in despair, were the contrasting poles that reveal not only the need of salvation, but its unifying *shape* which "follows" in the person-formation of the one "saved." In essence, the shape of salvation is the gift, task, and achievement of *unity* in the human self as that person receives a unified self from the One who is indeed *only* One and is never disunited, albeit in the triune unity. (We won't here discuss the difficult question of unity/separation of the *One* at the cross, depicted in Mark 15:34.) The essential unity of God and sinful disunity of the human self—fallen from the glory of God (Rom 3:23)—reveals part of the qualitative difference between God and man. Kierkegaard writes,

> That you and I are sinners . . . confirms the qualitative difference between God and man . . . As sinner, man is separated from God by the most chasmic qualitative abyss. In turn, of course, God is separated from man by the same chasmic qualitative abyss when he forgives sins. If by some kind of reverse adjustment the divine could be shifted over to the human, there is one way in which man could never in all eternity come to be like God: in forgiving sins.[2]

2. Kierkegaard, SUD, 121, 122.

Kierkegaard thus points to forgiveness as the way to salvation for man at such difference and distance from God. And the key point is that forgiveness brings unity. Because of forgiveness the divine quality of unity can become a human quality, but only because it is, first and foremost, the essential quality of God. And Jesus, *in* God's unity as fully human, overcame the divided self-hood of fallen humanity. This reveals that the gospel "seed" is to "plant" and "grow" human wholeness, thereby fulfilling the basic human "calling" of self-hood through "participation" in God's unity achieved for all humanity in Jesus the God-man. Thus, Jesus was "the firstborn of many" who through the "seed" of the gospel grow in the new family-resemblance of unified selves. (Rom 8:29). Tying together this fractal pattern, pictured at the two opposite poles of the human calling of "willing one thing" and God's eternal "accomplishment" of unity, Sponheim writes, "The human calling is to 'will one thing.' Such willing would image the Creator, who does will one thing. Part of the secret of God's artful power is this unity of willing."[3]

THE SEED THAT PRODUCES UNIFIED SELVES

In Kierkegaard's discourse *Purity of Heart is to Will One Thing*, "willing one thing" is the "spiritual discipline" that unites the divided heart. But what is the one thing that *must* be willed? Kierkegaard rightly saw that that one thing was "the Good" which ultimately both derives from and points to God.[4] In this discipline, Kierkegaard, as is typical, honestly, and exhaustively considers all obstacles and necessities that interrogate any supposed achievement of this willing of the one good, God. Foremost among the obstacles are "the reward disease," willing for the sake of reward, and "the fear of punishment" which does not strictly will relation to God only but to avoid punishment.[5] After encountering these and other humanly insurmountable obstacles one simply falls, exhausted at the impossibility of willing one thing. But as is often the case with Kierkegaard—the one who expressly desired to "deceive people into the truth"—he has set everyone up, including himself.[6] Noting the corner Kierkegaard has painted himself and all into, he reveals the way out:

3. Sponheim, *God's Availing Power*, 17.
4. Kierkegaard, PH, 53–54.
5. Kierkegaard, PH, 68, 79.
6. "One must not let oneself be deceived by the word 'deception' . . . to recall old Socrates, one can deceive a person into the truth. Indeed it is only . . . by deceiving him that it is possible to bring into the truth the one who is in an illusion." As cited in Thiselton, *Thiselton On Hermeneutics*, 516.

But what, then, shall we do, if the questions sound like accusations? Above all else, each one will himself become an individual with his responsibility to God. Each one will himself be subject to the stern judgment of this individuality. Is not this the purpose of the office of confession? Only the individual can truthfully will the Good, and even though the penitent toils heavily not merely in the eleventh hour of confession, with all the questions standing as accusations of himself, but also in their daily use in repentance, yet the way is the right one. For he is in touch with the demand that calls for purity of heart by willing one thing.[7]

For what the individual has found is the juxtaposition of the calling to be a unified self before God with Christ as our only advocate because he "willed one thing"—relation to God—for *each,* and *every,* person. And therefore, our call to will one thing is expressed in the confession and repentance that unites us with the Father who *in eternity* "wills one thing" and with Christ who "willed one thing" *in time* and under the temptation "common to man" to *not* will one thing (1 Cor 10:13). The willing of one thing that was sought as though *outside* us, beyond our possibility, is given *in* us, through "Christ in us, the hope of glory" (Col 1:27). Thus Kierkegaard writes, "What is sought is given," for the one thing to be willed is the repentant confession of sin before the God who is love.[8] This willing of this one thing is apart from the reward disease and the fear of punishment, for *God is the reward* and *the perfect love* who casts out all fear (1 John 4:8, 18). This "willing of one thing" fulfills the fractal pattern's call for the unified self that is "first the blade, then the ear, then the full grain in the ear."

THE SEED THAT PRODUCES A UNIFIED CROP

Following the fractal pattern of unity, the unified selves—the plants—when seen together with other plants germinated from that seed, will be a unified crop. Simply put, sowing a field with wheat will yield individual wheat plants in one wheat field. Unity is the DNA of *one* grain, which yields the internal and external quality of the unity of *the One* (Eph 4:4–6).

Kierkegaard has been seen by some as the arch-individualist, without any vision for the church as the unified community of God. But this was

---

7. Kierkegaard, PH, 214, 217.

8. Kierkegaard, TDIO, 23. "*Confession,* is indeed like changing one's clothes to divest oneself of multiplicity in order to make up one's mind about one thing . . . the prayer does not change God, but changes the one who prays." Kierkegaard, UDVS, 21–22.

only because he saw that apart from the sowing of the unity through the seed of God there was no possibility of a unified field of God's grain. In a sense, he held that the field had been thoroughly sown with "tare" seed, as portrayed in the anti-type of this parable, that of the wheat and the tares (Matt 13:24–30).

We cannot present a reading of that parable but will simply say that the point of Mark's is the purity, viability, and vitality of the one seed of the kingdom that produces "after its kind" in the new creation of the Gospel (Gen 1:11–12). For that seed contains the fractal pattern of the DNA/unity of the triune God, sown upon the earth to grow a new field of humanity in Christ, who only willed one thing, "the Good," for the sake of all creation and the glory of God (John 5:17–19; 17:3–5). And we may participate in that unity through the gospel's "existence communication." It is a mistake to atomistically restrict the gospel's DNA Kierkegaard recognized as essential for becoming "the single individual" to the individual, for it is the DNA of "the fine species of low grass" that *is* God's field of the *one* new family of humanity in Christ.

19

The Lowly Mustard-Plant Growing in "The Present Age" . . . of Loftiness

Mark 4:30–34 (NIV)

30 Again he said, "What shall we say the kingdom of God is like, or what parable shall we use to describe it? 31 It is like a mustard seed, which is the smallest of all seeds on earth. 32 Yet when planted, it grows and becomes the largest of all garden plants, with such big branches that the birds can perch in its shade."

33 With many similar parables Jesus spoke the word to them, as much as they could understand. 34 He did not say anything to them without using a parable. But when he was alone with his own disciples, he explained everything.

This great tree is known by its extension into the whole world and is not adequately embodied by an inwardly turned or detached or separated branch. —Augustine[1]

The church is the church only when it is there for others. —Dietrich Bonhoeffer[2]

---

1. As cited in Oden & Hall, *Mark*, 60.
2. Bonhoeffer, *Letters and Papers*, 503.

So while it would be hard to find many adherents of Hegel's philosophy of world history as such, we nonetheless believe that our form of society—democratic, capitalist, and scientific—is the goal of human history: the last, best hope of the world. —Merold Westphal.[3]

EZEKIEL'S TREE AND CHRIST'S MUSTARD PLANT

Thus says the Lord God: "I myself will take a sprig from the lofty top of the cedar and will set it out. I will break off from the topmost of its young twigs a tender one, and I myself will plant it on a high and lofty mountain. On the mountain height of Israel will I plant it, that it may bear branches and produce fruit and become a noble cedar. And under it will dwell every kind of bird; in the shade of its branches birds of every sort will nest. And all the trees of the field shall know that I am the Lord; I bring low the high tree, and make high the low tree, dry up the green tree, and make the dry tree flourish. I am the Lord; I have spoken, and I will do it." (Ezek 17:22–24; ESV.)

Thus reads the Old Testament text that looms behind this third "seed" parable of Jesus. There are many similarities and some important differences that support Jesus' proclamation of the kingdom that surpasses prior expectations. The similarities include: the small and humble beginnings; the growth to become the greatest of kingdoms; the comparison to other "kingdoms;" the benefits provided to others signified by inviting shade and lodging birds; being planted by the God of Israel, and the glory brought to God by them. The contrasts include: the difference of size between the "twig" and the "mustard seed;" the lack of mention of any sacred geographical place where the seed is planted; the qualitative difference between the "noble cedar" of Israel and the mere "garden plant." It seems that Jesus has purposely chosen the mustard seed to convey beginnings even more humble than the kingdom Ezekiel and Israel expected, and categorically different in its government. One commentator notes the implications of these contrasts, saying,

> The further contrast between cedar and mustard shrub suggests that the hope proclaimed by Jesus is of a different quality than that of Israel's prophets and of the usual human vision of greatness. The parable of the cedar announces the restoration of the Davidic kingdom among the kingdoms of the earth. Other kingdoms will dry up, while that of David will flourish and outlast them. The parable of the mustard seed speaks of a kingdom

3. Westphal, *Kierkegaard's Critique of Reason*, 125.

which, for all its miraculous extension, remains lowly. Mustard is an annual plant; its perpetuation depends on renewed sowing, and its perennial promise depends on the life of the seed. It is an image which corresponds closely to the picture of the Kingdom of God in Mark: a mystery whose realization will come as a surprise; a reality whose weakness is its power . . . The function of the story is encouragement, the issue is hope, and the mode of teaching is metaphor. Interpretation, therefore, should point to meaning but should not pontificate; it should suggest significance but should not define it, to the end that the weary may be sustained by the word.[4]

With the third of three seed parables, Mark develops the theme of the Kingdom of God substantially, in congruence with what has already been intuited of it in Jesus' attitude toward Israelite society and the "old wineskin" expectations of Israel. The ever-growing conflict with established practices, entrenched power, and self-serving expectations is implied and further developed in this parable that depicts the differences between Israel's and Christ's views of the development of the kingdom of God then arriving in the world.

KIERKEGAARD'S *THE PRESENT AGE*, AND CHRISTENDOM

In Kierkegaard's time the parable can be seen as depicting a further episode of the ongoing collision of utterly contrasting kingdoms. In Jesus' time it was the collision of God's kingdom with Israel's religion and Rome's empire. In Kierkegaard's it was of true Christianity with Christendom.

Kierkegaard was therefore concerned with the inner and outer dynamics of modern "Christian" life and its connection or disconnection to true faith, and the subsequent outworking of that in society. One of Kierkegaard's books dealing with these subjects was his book-length 1845 "review" of a popular novel titled "Two Ages." The title of his review was called "*Two Ages: The Age of Revolution and The Present Age, A Literary Review.*"

As mentioned previously, Kierkegaard is often misconstrued as being solely concerned with "the individual," with no concern for the church or society at large. But since his *society* was Danish *Christendom*, integrally supported by the church in both theory and practice, all his efforts at promoting authentic Christianity within such a setting amount to support of the true *Church*. Kierkegaard's "individualism" was a means to restore the

---

4. Williamson, *Mark*, 99.

church, through the means of God's word and the necessity of following the life of Christ. Kierkegaard's intent was mirrored by Dietrich Bonhoeffer's own efforts in relation to the compromised German church, especially as set forth in his book *Discipleship*.[5] Kierkegaard's recognition of the true church and his intents toward it, are shown when he wrote,

> Solomon's judgment may be applied to the Church. It was clear that the *true* mother was the one who would rather give up the child than have half. So it is with the Church, the true mother: it would rather let go of the individual, let him still live, than have half of him—and spiritually it is just as impossible to have half a person as it is physically.[6]

Kierkegaard recognized that the survival of the true church is dependent on its "doctrine" of the individual upon which "the body of many members" is constructed (1 Cor 12:12). And for Christendom, the false "mother," to "sacrifice" the individual for selfish reasons was to preserve the church in untruth as a *crowd* in untruth. Kierkegaard recognized that the church only exists when built upon the foundation of God as *the middle term of each individual* in the church body-relationship.[7] Kierkegaard thought this omission by Christendom was caused by undervaluing the spiritual/existential dynamic of true community in the household of faith:

> The definition of "Church" found in the Augsburg Confession, that it is the communion [*Samfund*] of saints where the word is rightly taught and the sacraments rightly administered, this quite correctly (that is, not correctly) grasped only the two points about doctrine and sacraments and has overlooked the first, the communion of saints (in which there is qualification in the direction of the existential [*Existentielle*]. Thus the Church is made into a communion of indifferent existences [*Existentser*] (or where the existential is a matter of indifference)—but the "doctrine" is correct and the sacraments are rightly administered. This is really paganism.[8]

Thus, what is supposed to be "*the communion of the saints*" is "really paganism." Christendom, which ought to be the lowly "mustard plant," mistakenly conceives itself to be the "lofty Cedar"—but rather than attracting

---

5. See Kirkpatrick, *Attacks on Christendom*, 216–222..
6. Kierkegaard, JP, I:241–42, #596.
7. See under "The Mediated Community of God . . ." in chapter 15 above.
8. Kierkegaard, JP, I:244, #600.

the pagans to its sanctity it captivates its own "saints" to "paganism." The Sower himself laments and asks,

> *I had planted you like a choice vine* of sound and reliable stock.
> How then did you turn against me into a corrupt, wild vine?
> (Jer 2:21, NIV).

Kierkegaard saw this mistake as the temptation for the church to only esteem and emulate the lofty results of Christianity rather than follow the life upon which all was founded: the lowly life of Christ, the prototype for discipleship in the kingdom. Therefore, Kierkegaard boldly asked, "Is the result of Christ's life more important than his life?"[9] Luther considered that temptation the "fall" inherent in a "theology of glory," when true faith is in the "theology of the cross."[10]

"THE PRESENT AGE" OF LOFTINESS

At this point we will consider several reasons why the parable's vision of the kingdom's lowly "mustard plant" collides with the human desire for loftiness. The basic fact is that loftiness is always esteemed greater than lowliness by sinful humanity. So perhaps this is merely a consideration of what sins are involved in that "esteem."

One reason was already noted, simply a faithless and fearful self-preservation. But the church can only provide its beneficent fruitfulness by remaining in the vine of Christ's lowliness (John 15:1–25). And in the first place, remaining in the vine of Christ's lowliness presupposes the fact that the kingdom is only received by the lowly, not the lofty (Luke 1:46–55).

Another reason is that the mustard plant "exists for others" and is not "inwardly turned" as declared in this chapter's epigrams from Augustine and Bonhoeffer. This simply notes the reason that "self" oriented Christianity results in the "self-preservation" mentality discussed above. That the *lowly* mustard plant exists for others raises the issue of *how* the church should relate itself to broader humanity, especially in relation to the "thorns" of "cares," even of "deceitful riches and the desires for other things" that society and state may "provide."

The third of the chapter epigrams above satirically reveals the gravity of the situation when the lowly mustard plant is tempted to become "the lofty cedar" through self-aggrandizement and compromising relations to

---

9. Kierkegaard, PC, 31.

10. Forde, *On Being a Theologian*, 69. Jesus saw what is *naturally* "esteemed" by humanity as "abomination" (Luke 16:15).

the state. Westphal's observation notes the tendency of the church-state toward "self-absolutizing" and recognizes that if the mustard plant is to be truly beneficial, it must not become the "chaplain" for "the secular mentality's earthly mother tongue." In other words, the birds are meant to lodge in the branches of "Christianity" because it provides something of an "outpost" of the kingdom of God, this side of the full realization of the kingdom. It does not build a holy "shrine" for the culture which Westphal notes was the reason "Socrates and the early Christians were accused of atheism" when they didn't do so.[11]

Kierkegaard seemed to believe that the church not only ought to be, but could be, the place where genuine interpersonal relations could exist. That the church ought to be so was simply due to the fact just discussed above, that the church should be a community of individuals who have become so through Christ the mediator of God-given individuality unto sociality. In fact, the symmetry of any "community" to the Kingdom of God is exactly due to how it relates to individuals, and aids, hinders, or prevents their becoming individuals through God. In essence, it seems Kierkegaardian to say that the *criterion* of the community is *the individual*.

Therefore, Kierkegaard saw three stages or "ages" of community, all distinguished by how each related to *the individual*. These three stages are defined and the last two given more detail by Patricia Cutting:

> The ages of interpersonal relationships include an earlier age of provisional immediacy, in which outstanding individuals determine the values and norms for the others; the present age, which levels the outstanding individuals but establishes an abstract public that dictates the norms and values of the society; and the highest stage . . . in which the authentic individual can establish genuine interpersonal relationships . . . In the age of genuine interpersonal relationships, the highest stage in the dialectical movement, there is absolute, essential equality, rather than the relative, accidental equality of the intermediate present age. According to Kierkegaard, true equality can only be achieved at the highest level where there is authentic individuality capable of genuine community with others. Here, each individual, rather than relating himself or herself to the relative norms of the public, relates absolutely to the absolute. And "it is true that before God and the absolute *telos* we human beings are all equal" (CUP:1, 359).[12]

---

11. Westphal, *Kierkegaard's Critique*, 125. Note that their "atheism" was essentially treasonous.

12. Cutting, "Levels of Interpersonal," 75, 80–81.

According to Cutting, Kierkegaard saw the present age as providing a "necessary mediating stage between the earlier age and the age of genuine interpersonal relationships" since in the earlier age "there was no real equality."[13] But the "leveling process" of the present age reduced this to "an alienating, abstract, mathematical equality" which Kierkegaard said "grinds smooth the individual's angularity" resulting in the pressures in which the individual finds it "far easier and safer to be like the others, to become a copy, a number, a mass man" (SUD, 34).[14] Essentially, Kierkegaard saw the "equality" of the present age as an artificial imposition of society rather than an organic outgrowth of the kingdom of God.

It would bring us too far from our purposes here to detail how the shortcomings of the earlier age and the present age transgress God's intentions for human communities, and why the "wild birds" cannot find true lodging among the mustard plant's branches. So, a few brief comments will have to suffice.

First, the most basic transgression, from which all other transgressions flow as from a fountain, is in the dehumanization of the community due to the suppression of true individuality.

Second, the factor of love reveals the ideal from which human and supposedly humane societies fall short in many ways. Cutting relates the ideal community to Kierkegaard's "Works of Love," saying,

> This essential and absolute equality is the basis for one of the main requirements for genuine interpersonal relationships: Thou shalt love thy neighbor with a nonpreferential love (WL, pt. 1. sec.2B). "Love to one's neighbor is therefore eternal equality in loving, but this eternal equality is the opposite of exclusive love or preference . . . Equality is just this, not to make distinctions, and eternal equality is absolutely not to make the slightest distinction" (WL, 70). Thus, authentic nonpreferential love "means, while remaining within the earthly distinctions allowed to one, essentially to will to exist equally for every human being without exception" (WL, 92).[15]

The Kingdom of God, compared to a mustard plant in its inception, development, and maturity, is just as surprising and shocking today as it undoubtedly was when first spoken by Jesus. This is because the Kingdom was at first as a mustard seed, seemingly insignificant and without potential. But the mustard seed germinated a plant that eventually grew to seemingly

---

13. Cutting, "Levels of Interpersonal," 80.
14. Cutting, "Levels of Interpersonal," 80.
15. Cutting, "The Levels of Interpersonal," 81.

fill the world with the branches of flourishing Christendom. We cannot say that there were *no* "lodgings" found in those branches. But Christendom became more like Ezekiel's lofty tree than Jesus' lowly shrub and thereby lost the lowliness that would most authenticate it as a sign and promise of God's kingdom.

Now, following the demise of Christendom, the church must look to the manner of its original "planting" through the *mustard seed* that grows a *mustard plant*. And the church, again existing in a place that automatically renders it inconspicuous and insignificant, must consider God's will for its *essential* lowliness.[16] Its true power lies hidden in the smallest—yet viable seeds it sows. In the early church the martyr's blood watered that seed, such that the blood sowed the seed of the church. G. K. Chesterton noted that the church is most like its Lord in its susceptibility to death, but also to resurrection:

> Christendom has had a series of revolutions and in each one of them Christianity has died. Christianity has died many times and risen again; for it had a God who knew the way out of the grave.[17]

Liability to "death," is part of the "job description," *the middle term of discipleship* as discussed in chapter 6, and especially so for "lofty" trees of centuries meant to be lowly *annual* plants that nevertheless endure through their ever-newness. Thus, Jesus said "indeed, fire will be everyone's seasoning" (Mark 9:49).[18] This is part and parcel of the gift and task implied in the lowly, and for that reason, beneficial mustard plant, planted and growing to protest against the loftiness of the present age with its "mustard-tree" life of God's new creation.

---

16. Jan-Olav Henriksen writes, "We have to live with uncertainty, and with the insight that what we construct may be fragile and subject to criticism. That Lessing, Kierkegaard, and Nietzsche use various positions as points of departure for their thinking shows not only how they are familiar with these effects of historicity and finitude, but also that their understanding of the issues that are central to the understanding of what it means to be human are based on the insight that *closure* and *system* are not viable options if we want to safeguard a true development of humanity, human existence, and human freedom (most profoundly so in Kierkegaard, but also in different other ways in the others). This is the lesson here to be learned as well for those that think that religion is linked to existing as truly human." Henriksen, *The Reconstruction of Religion*, 198–99.

17. Chesterton, *The Everlasting Man*, 250.

18. Cassirer, *God's New Covenant*, 84.

20

The Situation for Coming to Faith

"Out on 70,000 Fathoms of Water"

Mark 4:35–41 (NIV)

35 That day when evening came, he said to his disciples, "Let us go over to the other side." 36 Leaving the crowd behind, they took him along, just as he was, in the boat. There were also other boats with him. 37 A furious squall came up, and the waves broke over the boat, so that it was nearly swamped. 38 Jesus was in the stern, sleeping on a cushion. The disciples woke him and said to him, "Teacher, don't you care if we drown?"

39 He got up, rebuked the wind and said to the waves, "Quiet! Be still!" Then the wind died down and it was completely calm.

40 He said to his disciples, "Why are you so afraid? Do you still have no faith?"

41 They were terrified and asked each other, "Who is this? Even the wind and the waves obey him!"

And whatever a person's fate in the world is to be, however buffeted by the storms of life, blessed is the one who is not offended but believes that he rebuked the waves and it became dead calm. —Anti-Climacus[1]

---

1. Kierkegaard, PC, 75. "Anti-Climacus" was Kierkegaard's pseudonymous author of "Practice in Christianity."

... the mortal danger of lying out on 70,000 fathoms of water, and only there finding God. —Johannes Climacus[2]

Mark's parabolic "behind the scenes" interlude of 4:1–34 is withdrawn only to return to the fast-cutting *chaos cinema* of frenetic activity—ironically featuring Jesus serenely asleep amid an unruly storm at sea while the disciples fear for their lives. In short, the adventure resumes "*out on 70,000 fathoms*" during a dangerous storm where the disciples didn't want to be. But it was the place where Kierkegaard's *Johannes Climacus* not only wanted to be, but apparently wanted to *live*, if he were to truly have faith! Johannes writes,

> Without risk, no faith. Faith is the contradiction between the infinite passion of inwardness and the objective uncertainty. If I am able to apprehend God objectively, I do not have faith; but because I cannot do this, I must have faith. If I want to keep myself in faith, I must continually see to it that I hold fast the objective uncertainty, see to it that in the objective uncertainty I am "out on 70,000 fathoms of water" and still have faith.[3]

JOHANNES CLIMACUS AND THE SITUATION

So, who is Johannes Climacus, and is his view of faith *normal* from a biblical point of view? Johannes Climacus' book, "Philosophical Fragments" which is ironically a 175-page book of "fragments," contains an 8-page biographical sketch of him. Based on this sketch, Robert Roberts summarizes,

> His biographer tells us that he lived, as entirely as a human being can, in a world of thought and imagination. He gets his name, "the climber," because he, like Hegel, climbs up to heaven by syllogisms. His namesake, a Byzantine monk of the seventh and eighth centuries, wrote a treatise entitled *Scala Paradisi* containing advice to monks for attaining spiritual perfection.[4]

But Johannes' "ladder" was a philosophical one. Ironically, he is not a Christian, but he is greatly interested in Christianity because he cares about what it means to exist as a human being. Johannes recognizes that Christianity portends to be a solution to the question and perceives that overfamiliarity with Christianity on the part of his contemporaries seems to

2. Kierkegaard, CUP:1, 232.
3. Kierkegaard, CUP:1, 204.
4. Roberts, *Faith, Reason, and History*, 8.

show that their lives do not actually benefit from it. Therefore, the *humorous* intent of Climacus is "to make it difficult to become a Christian, yet not more difficult than it is."[5]

So, does Johannes belong in the boat with the disciples? Apparently, Kierkegaard thought so, because he placed him in the boat with his Danish contemporaries for whom faith was certainly not thought to involve such constant *risk*. In a journal entry, Kierkegaard, sounding much like Johannes, writes:

> The matter is quite simple. In order to have faith, there must first be existence, an existential-qualification. This is what I am never sufficiently able to emphasize—that to have faith, before there can be any question about having faith, there must be the *situation*. And this situation must be brought about by an existential step on the part of the individual. We have completely done away with the propaedeutic element. We let the individual go on in his customary mediocre rut—and so he gets faith by and by, just about the way one can learn lessons word-perfect without needing the situation. Take an example, the rich young ruler. What did Christ require as the preliminary act? He required action that would shoot the rich young ruler out into the infinite. The requirement is that you must venture out, out into water 70,000 fathoms deep. This is the situation. Now there can be no question of having faith, or of despairing.[6]

We thus learn several things. *First*, "out into water 70,000 fathoms deep" is one of Kierkegaard's own favorite metaphors. *Second*, Kierkegaard would not only put Johannes Climacus in the boat, but also the "rich young ruler" who comes to Jesus in Mark 10:17–22. *Third*, Kierkegaard saw *the situation* as essential to faith or despair, and thus very much like "the halt" that comes through Christ as "the possibility of offense" discussed earlier. *Fourth*, it implies that the worldly context of *the situation* is the place where the human decision of faith or despair is made, rather than some abstract place where humans exercise "pure reason."

Altogether, *the situation* signifies that the existential nature of human life *requires* the decision of faith—or despair. This is why Johannes Climacus finds some humor in the situation in Christendom, which is *no situation*, because faith is *unnecessary* since "Christians" are simply born into the faith

---

5. See Tietjen's discussion where he writes that Johannes Climacus "*embodies* the 'comic,' an umbrella term that includes humor and irony as well as jokes, satire, and wit." Tietjen, *Kierkegaard, Communication and Virtue*, 36. (See CUP:1, 557.)

6. Kierkegaard, JP: II:20, #1142.

by natural birth. Therefore, they need to discover the real situation of being "*out on 70,000 fathoms of water*" where they must come to faith or despair.

LIFE'S PERMANENT SITUATION THAT CALLS FORTH FAITH, OR DESPAIR

In some sense we have so far been living in the land of metaphor in our discussion of this seafaring tale. Not that *these* dangerous types of situations never occur, for which faith would be highly desirable to have. But this *situation* is metaphorical, not of the various *situations* of life, but of the *entirety* of life itself. Thus, *the situation* is always present. Johannes and Kierkegaard both state this, Johannes, when he says that he must "*see to it*" that he always recognizes that "objective uncertainty" *is* the situation, and Kierkegaard, when he says Jesus "*required action that would shoot the rich young ruler out into the infinite.*" Kierkegaard is implying that human life is always already lived in objective uncertainty over 70,000 fathoms of water.

But if we don't know this or have already adopted a "cheap faith" that does not recognize *the situation*, then we have removed ourselves from reality, and therefore have not "realized" real existence. It is this ambiguous state, apart from *the situation* of *real existence*, that God initially seeks to dislodge us from. But we may not at first be dislodged *to* faith, but *to* despair. As Kierkegaard said, "now there can be no question of having faith, or of despairing." Therefore, the confession of C. S. Lewis from his atheist days—that in the trenches of WW1 he "never sunk so low as to pray"—reveals that he was already consciously living in *the situation* even before he went to war.[7] And as an atheist he had already embraced *despair* as the only answer to life always already lived out over 70,000 fathoms. Eventually embracing faith, he illustrates that the ongoing *situation* of life continually calls forth either faith or despair. He also shows that neither the one nor the other is a simple matter of fate or determinism since he knew and embraced *both* in his life-response.

Several of the disciples were seasoned fisherman and would probably have had continual awareness of the dangers inherent in their livelihood. But we again must remember that "over 70,000 fathoms" is a metaphor for the precariousness of life. Therefore, to sharpen the metaphor against an over-literalness that prevents understanding it, we must clarify that "out on 70,000 fathoms of water" signifies *objective uncertainty* and *the infinite*. The rising storm signifies that the reality of the situation must become known. So, when the storm arose, the situation became acute, and fear replaced the

7. Cited in Downing, *Most Reluctant Convert*, 11.

"usual" certainty with uncertainty. But the true reality was that they *always* lived in that *situation* of life-uncertainty. But the ongoing *situation* is the opportunity, the call, for a *perennial* faith.

Of course, we have barely mentioned Jesus, who was *always* present, but sleeping. Perhaps this is meant to show that in the face of uncertainty and the infinite, when fear rises as *the situation* becomes acutely known, God is asleep and seemingly *irrelevant*. And extrapolating outward into all the situations of life, if God seems *absent* in the most acute circumstances, should we presume the divine presence in *any* situations of life? But that is why we must extrapolate in the other direction, from the "normal" to the "acute," so that the lull of "still waters" and its easy to come by fair-weather "faith" won't dull us to the essential uncertainty of life—always "out on 70,000 fathoms of water" and the need for faith *there*. And we of course must remember the two levels depicted in this story under our Kierkegaardian reading, the literal and the metaphorical. Because the literal story is that real life is always lived out on 70,000 fathoms. But the metaphorical story reveals that Jesus entered the depths of the world's uncertainty to reveal the perennial *situation* and provide us faith to overcome its despair (John 16:33).

THE GOD-MAN "OUT ON 70,000 FATHOMS OF WATER"

The reality of God, depicted by the sleeping Jesus, is that he is "ever-present" "out on 70,000 fathoms." The problem of humans is our non-recognition of being "ever-needful." Thus, the challenge of faith is for it to become our "ever-exercised" way of life in conscious relation to life's perennial *situation* and our *Savior*. Recognizing their dire need, the disciples managed to wake Jesus and be saved from the storm by his rebuke of the wind that calmed the sea. Jesus asked them why they had been so afraid and had no faith, as if faith overcoming fear was normal for life that's always lived in uncertainty. But this led them to an even greater fear, of who he might be. Indeed, what can cause more objective uncertainty than the paradox of Jesus, the God-man. To be faced with *Him* is more fearful than being *out on 70,000 fathoms of water*. But the latter is only the context in which we are to realize his ever-present reality. Thus, humans often prefer enacting a charade of fearless faith that denies thought regarding the uncertainties of life and God. And the "boat" of Christendom also prefers the unreal non-situation, with harmless waters and a non-threatening Jesus whose sleeping is more desired than not.

Mark's tumultuous scene advanced for his original readers the theme of the disciple's faith and would have served to illustrate the lives of the followers of Christ, consciously gone "out on 70,000 fathoms of water" *with* the fearsome God-man. But though they might not comprehend him, they knew he would rebuke the waves and calm their sea. For the proper and essential fear is that of God—revealed in Jesus asleep in the faith-ark of humanity out over 70,000 fathoms of the deep. For in this *situation* Jesus always arises and says "peace, be still!" not only to the dangerous storm but to his fearful followers yet struggling for *real* faith.

Epilogue

Jesus and Jonah, and the Ordeal of Sin and Death

Mark 4:37–38a (NIV)

37 A furious squall came up, and the waves broke over the boat, so that it was nearly swamped. 38 Jesus was in the stern, sleeping on a cushion.

. . . in all this raging tumult, Jonah sleeps his hideous sleep. He sees no black sky and raging sea, feels not the reeling timbers, and little hears he or heeds the far rush of the mighty whale, which even now with open mouth is cleaving the seas after him. —Father Mapple[1]

But here it is not a matter of a few paltry premises one wishes to draw a conclusion from but of the most dreadful thing of all, an eternal torment: a personal existence that cannot coalesce in a conclusion . . . When the whale is wounded, it plunges to the bottom of the ocean and spouts great jets of blood; in its dying it is most terrible. —Frater Taciturnus[2]

It is the Spirit who gives life. Yes, the Spirit gives life—through death. —Soren Kierkegaard[3]

---

1. Melville, *Moby-Dick*, 48.
2. Kierkegaard, SLW, 232, 235. "Frater Taciturnus" is the author of Kierkegaard's *"Guilty?" /"Not Guilty?"*
3. Kierkegaard, FSE/JFY 77.

THE ORDEAL OF LACKING "EPILOGUE"

This epilogue further develops the reading of the previous chapter and serves to focus in a very precise way on a major theme and challenge in Mark and the gospel itself, how to "overcome" the ordeal of sin and death. The ordeal is caused by the fact that none of us can "fulfill the universally binding ethical demand" to overcome sin *through* death.[4] I use the title of epilogue as not only a preliminary conclusion to this volume but because of the challenge of finding "conclusion" for what Kierkegaard calls "*the most dreadful thing of all, an eternal torment: a personal existence that cannot coalesce in a conclusion.*" For the ordeal is the seemingly impossible challenge of ending the *living death*. Kierkegaard describes *that* death as akin to a whale's dying, plunged below 70,000 fathoms "to the bottom of the ocean" and spouting "great jets of blood; in its dying it is most terrible." For that terrible description of *the process* of dying is a metaphor of the living death of the *despairing* "inability to die" that is *the sickness unto death*.[5] This problem was briefly touched on when we saw Simon *leprosus* in chapter 9 above, but here we will seek to provide further elucidation.

THE PROBLEM OF DEATH

In the previous chapter we discussed "the situation." Here we need to focus on what was perhaps the unmentioned elephant in the room, *death*. For that is the perennial possibility that always haunts the situation. Death was what was feared by the disciples when the "furious squall" revealed what was *always* possible in life *always* lived "out on 70,000 fathoms of water." But here we wish to point out that this ever-present possibility results in an ever-present dread: despair. Of course, humans are generally able to quarantine that fear to the subconscious realm by what Pascal called *diversion*. Nevertheless, that does not preclude the fact that this amounts to a sort of living death no matter the level of consciousness of that despair. For not we, but God is "the true criterion of our spiritual health."[6] Thus Kierkegaard held that "not being conscious of being in despair, is precisely a form of despair."[7]

---

4. Taylor, "Ordeal and Repetition," 46. It is from this essay that we have borrowed the language of "ordeal."

5. Kierkegaard, SUD, 21. See Connell, "Knights and Knaves," 26–27.

6. Merold Westphal, as cited in Connell, "Knights and Knaves," 32

7. Kierkegaard, SUD, 23.

Of course, the disciples at that moment in the storm were quite despairing over their potentially impending death. And yet, to consider the first epigram above,

> ... in all this raging tumult, Jesus sleeps his hideous sleep. He sees no black sky and raging sea, feels not the reeling timbers, and little hears he or heeds the far rush of the mighty whale, which even now with open mouth is cleaving the seas after him.

But wait, didn't Herman Melville write of the "hideous sleep" of *Jonah*? Yes, but I have substituted Jesus for Jonah to begin to answer our existential questions that depend upon *the gospel's* ability to substitute Jesus for Jonah (or vice-versa). Therefore, we will consider how this switch brings us to the core of the gospel by introducing Jonah as biblically "typological" of Jesus and by also introducing the "god" personified in the sea's murderous storm—namely the waiting "Leviathan" with open mouth "cleaving the seas" after its bounty. This switch also helps us to see that sin is the overlooked factor of "the situation," now become "the ordeal," out on 70,000 fathoms, precisely because we cannot die to our living death.

THE DEATHLY SLEEP OF JESUS

Before we consider how these typologies are related to the *ordeal* of dying to our living death, we will consider an excerpt from Kierkegaard where he describes the difficulty of fulfilling the "universally binding ethical demand" to die to *sin*. He writes,

> To what feeling does a person cling to more firmly than the feeling of being alive; what does one crave more strongly and violently than really to feel life in oneself; from what does one shrink more than to die![8]

Therefore, it is quite natural for us to cling to life, even our living death which whether we know it in despair or not is, after all, the only life we *naturally* know. To give it up would seem to be giving up all. But that call is the gospel's call that Kierkegaard also portrays:

> Jesus Christ is presented; one says, "Hear his voice—how he calls, gently inviting, all to himself, all those who suffer, and promises to give them rest for their souls. And truly this is so; God forbid that I should say anything else, but yet, yet—before this rest for the soul falls to your lot and in order that it can fall to

---

8. Kierkegaard, FSE/JFY, 76.

your lot, it is required that you first of all die, die to (something the inviter also says, something his whole life on earth expressed every single day and every single hour of the day)—is this so inviting? . . . Death goes in between; this is what Christianity teaches, you must die to.[9]

These statements of Kierkegaard reveal the difficulty, or more accurately the impossibility, of man to "die to." But Kierkegaard holds that Jesus did what no man could do, and "expressed" *dying to* "every single day and every single hour of the day" of his "whole life." This would mean that he was expressing this *while he was serenely asleep* on a cushion during the furious storm at sea with ravenous "Leviathan" lurking beneath. But this would also mean that his sleep was not "hideous" as Jonah's was, though it seemed so to the panicking disciples. The truth is that Jesus was *already* enjoying the "rest for the soul" the gospel promises to all. But why? The answer is that he was *already* living the "dying to" that is required to overcome the living death that all humans are constantly living (or dying). Of course, the whole of Jesus' life was not yet lived, and he would have to persevere to express "dying to" on through Gethsemane and the death of the cross. But the truth was that he had already "died to" the self that clings to itself apart from God and amounts to sin. And that was the practice of his entire life through his reliance on his Father. Jesus had no anxieties "about tomorrow" and knew that this storm at sea would not be bring his life to its appointed end nor the lives of his disciples with him (Matt 6:34; 26:2,18). Jesus had already overcome the Devil so that he had no fear of death on account of him or the sting of death that gives him his accusatory power over humans, namely their sin against God's law (Heb 2:14–15; 1 Cor 15:55–56; Rev 12:10–11).

On the other hand, Jonah did "sleep a hideous sleep." His sleep was in indifference to the fate of his shipmates, although when found out by them he was willing to be sacrificed to appease the storm that threatened their lives on his account (Jonah 1:6–12). Jonah slept despairingly because he was fleeing God's call, but Jesus slept peacefully in the rest of perfect obedience. Jonah's sleep was in ignorance of God's storm that fell on all on account of him and of the whale which would swallow him, while Jesus' sleep was seemingly aware that God would at the right time allow "the perfect storm of atonement" in which the "Leviathan" that was after him would think it devoured its bounty.[10] In short, Jonah was in sin; Jesus was in faith. To

9. Kierkegaard, FSE/JFY, 76.

10. See Christman, *Gospel in the Dock*, 73–90 for an extensive development of the typological connections between Jonah and Jesus. Melville certainly intended the whale to signify the biblical "Leviathan" which I intend to signify as the devil by drawing (with some biblical liberty) on the OT Leviathan texts and Rev 12:4 and 13:1.

summarize this point, Jonah was in the despair of his living soul-death to which he could not die, while Jesus was in joy of the soul-rest of living faith because he had already "died to" the living death common to humankind since the fall.

But how does any of this help all those who cannot "die to" their living death, whether wayward Jonah, the disciples in the boat, Mark, Kierkegaard, or all of humanity? The answer is the substitution of Jesus for "Jonah," or more accurately that Jesus *became* what Jonah represented, *sinful humanity clinging to its living death*. As Paul wrote, "For our sake he made him to be sin who knew no sin, so that in him we might become the righteousness of God" (2 Cor 5:21 ESV).

THE RECKONING OF DEATH

In our contemplation of "A Leper's Self-Contemplation" in chapter 9 we saw that Kierkegaard stated that the solution to the living death of despair and sin was in the paradoxical formula "I would have perished had I not perished." That statement, which Kierkegaard borrowed from the philosopher J. G. Hamann, points to the dilemma of a life of living death, a perishing, that can only be overcome by perishing.[11] But we have still not answered exactly how the *saving* perishing takes place. Kierkegaard provides the answer by speaking of the Spirit's coming to the apostles on the day of Pentecost:

> The life-giving Spirit is the very one who slays you; the first thing the life-giving Spirit says is that you must enter into death, that you must die to . . . It is the Spirit who gives life. Yes, the Spirit gives life—through death . . . Then came the Spirit who gives life—the apostles were indeed dead, dead to every merely earthly hope, to every human confidence in their own powers or in human assistance.[12]

Never one to promote systematic doctrinal formulations, due to the already over-objective under-subjectivity of Christendom, Kierkegaard's statements of the "slaying" of humanity in Christ must be contented with the sum of the matter rather than its "mechanics." Here he seems to credit the Spirit with what normal Christian systematic theology would frame as the Father's "plan" of providing new life for humanity through the "substitutionary atonement" of the incarnate Son which is made effectual in human

---

11. Kierkegaard, SLW, 174, 706 n15.
12. Kierkegaard, FSE/JFY, 76–77.

subjectivity by the Spirit. The apostle Paul frames this atonement "complex" in regard to humankind's unsolvable problem of "dying to," as follows:

> 3 Do you not know that all of us who have been baptized into Christ Jesus were baptized into his death? 4 We were buried therefore with him by baptism into death, in order that, just as Christ was raised from the dead by the glory of the Father, we too might walk in newness of life. 5 For if we have been united together in the likeness of His death, certainly we also shall be *in the likeness* of *His* resurrection, 6 knowing this, that our old man was crucified with *Him,* that the body of sin might be done away with, that we should no longer be slaves of sin. 7 For he who has died has been freed from sin. 8 Now if we died with Christ, we believe that we shall also live with Him, 9 knowing that Christ, having been raised from the dead, dies no more. Death no longer has dominion over Him. 10 For *the death* that He died, He died to sin once for all; but *the life* that He lives, He lives to God. 11 Likewise you also, reckon yourselves to be dead indeed to sin, but alive to God in Christ Jesus our Lord (Romans 6:3–11 NKJV).

Kierkegaard seems to only allude to Paul's understanding that humanity "died to" in Christ, in the statement just below where he simply presupposes what Paul wrote: "I have been crucified with Christ. It is no longer I who live, but Christ who lives in me. And the life I now live I live by faith in the Son of God who loved me and gave himself for me (Gal 2:20, ESV). Kierkegaard, regarding the "dying to" already accomplished in Christ's death, less explicitly writes,

> You are really to live in and together with him; he is to be and become your life, so that you do not live to yourself, no longer live yourself, but Christ lives in you."[13]

Without elaboration such as Paul provided, Kierkegaard simply says that we can now "live to" because our "dying to" our living death, which we could not achieve, was accomplished by our union with Christ, including being united with Christ's death by the Spirit. Therefore, Kierkegaard seems to agree with Paul that the call for Christians is not to, in and of themselves, or even by the help of the Spirit, "die to," but to "reckon" themselves *already dead* in Christ, which the Spirit then helps them trust so that all is "from faith for faith" (Rom 1:17 ESV). Thus, God brings to definitive "conclusion"

---

13. Kierkegaard as cited in Hughes, *Kierkegaard and the Staging,* 93.

what our "personal existence" could not "coalesce," namely, the "living death" we could not "die to."

We should also note that this "reckoning of death" is not merely for individuals but for the church which is also "baptized" into the death of Christ. Again, Kierkegaard as the arch-individualist is a caricature because he simply wanted the church to consist of disciples that had "died to" the philistine bourgeoise mentality of Christendom. Peter Leithart seems to aptly frame this in almost Kierkegaardian fashion, for today's situation where "disciples" and the church at large still resists "dying to." He writes,

> Christian faith is not safe if you suffer from vertigo, if you are not willing to have your world upended. It is only in this faith that we can embrace the death that God demands of us. I dearly hope that the Protestant tribalism of American denominationalism dies. I will do all in my power to kill it, not least in myself . . . I hope to see . . . rationalist and nationalist Protestantism slip into the grave . . . But death is never the last word for the church of the living God, the God who is faithful to death, and then again faithful.[14]

In conclusion, the accomplished "dying to" of Jesus enabled him to be fast asleep in "the situation" out on 70,000 fathoms with the Devil's "Leviathan jaws" waiting beneath, hungry for their prey. For when Jesus at the appointed time *became* Jonah in his hideous sinful sleep of living death and was consumed by Leviathan when he died on the cross, the living death of sin that all humanity could not "die to," died. In sum, the ordeal of sin and death was overcome by the one sleeping on a cushion amid the storm, that we might also enter God's rest through faith. For Jesus knew that ultimately the key to "dying to" was "living for," or more accurately, *living with God* through the power of the Spirit who "gives life—through death."[15] And by the same Spirit we may participate in that death and life of Jesus since the God-man "lived for" God and thereby for us. And furthermore, the sacrificed "Isaac" is then always received back as from the dead.

---

14. Leithart, *End of Protestantism*, 191.
15. See Simmons, "Kierkegaard and Pentecostal Philosophy," 393.

Conclusion to Volume 1

John Douglas Mullen asks the only appropriate question of any book related to Kierkegaard, in the conclusion of his own book on the ever perplexing and fascinating writer.

> Do you think that you now "understand Kierkegaard"? If so, this book has failed. It claims only to be a guide, a series of maps, an index of phrases with translations. Its purpose is not to replace the visit but to encourage it and make it more fruitful. Kierkegaard's authorship is as vast and complex as any European city. To be appreciated it must be confronted. To be beneficial it must be experienced.[1]

We might add that the same could be said regarding the mysterious Mark and his intriguing Gospel that has been one of the most influential books in the history of the world.

Kierkegaard and Mark do not so much open windows to let light in as open doorways to be walked through by the single individual, venturing out away from the comforts, or despairs, of "home," and the familiar chatter of the *"secular mentality's earthly mother tongue."* The doorways lead to disorientation, but only to be re-oriented in the new world/creation of Jesus the Son of God and God-man. For Christ *the inviter* provides the "help" of a new family, language, and home, all increased and enduring to the ages—albeit "with persecution" (Mark 10:30). Yes, the call is to live out over 70,000 fathoms, but that is but to recognize our true situation anyway, though the despairing "the herd" would ironically say otherwise. But always, the secret of the kingdom, for each individual and their new-creation community is

---

1. Mullen, *Kierkegaard's Philosophy*, 160.

the confession "I would have perished had I not perished." Thus, we have sought to introduce the doorways of Mark and Kierkegaard, there because of *the door* that *is* Christ, the way, the truth, and the life (John 14:6).

The eclectic nature of our Kierkegaardian reading of Mark, which we did not really attempt to detail beforehand, is now evident, not that the eclectic can or should be systematized. We have probably done little justice to the treatment that Mark deserves. But hopefully, whether presenting Kierkegaardian close readings or rabbit-trail excursions, we eventually circled back to Mark's evocative text of the kingdom's expansive new wine that cannot be contained by our old wineskins. Thus, we have sought to follow where the juxtaposition of Mark's apocalyptic texts and Kierkegaard's explosive writings have led, according to the limited extent of our knowledge and capacity on both counts.

As Mark has presented a new genre worthy of the narrative of Christ, so we hope that this reading may perhaps demonstrate the potential of new genre of Kierkegaardian narratives of entire biblical texts. Of course, Kierkegaard has already given the lead with his readings of scriptural portions. In any case, we hope to have presented some basic launches out over 70,000 fathoms of Kierkegaardian faith, with Mark as our "tour guide" and Jesus as our ever-present helmsman (though sometimes sleeping—and possibly now doing so because of Soren's incessant talking with him). Through Mark's "beginning of the gospel" we may become Christians, beholding, and becoming part of the new family of Jesus.

We will close this first volume with an excerpt from Kierkegaard which he builds on an understanding of the difference between becoming a Christian in Mark's day and in his own, in Christendom. We trust that all that has preceded in this volume will allow Kierkegaard's words to be perspicuous, provocative, and proclamatory regarding becoming a Christian in the remnants of Christendom that linger in today's (Post) Christendom, which carries much of the same baggage. Although we must preface what follows with the qualification that in the wake of Christendom's day, in many places it is again becoming difficult in the right ways, to become a Christian. Kierkegaard writes,

> When Christ came into the world it was difficult to become a Christian, and for this reason one did not become preoccupied with trying to understand it. Now we have almost reached the parody that to become a Christian is nothing at all, but it is a difficult and very involved task to understand it. Everything is reversed. Christianity is transformed into a kind of world-view, a way of thinking about life, and the task of faith consists in understanding and articulating it. But faith essentially relates

itself to existence, and *becoming* a Christian is what is important ... The immediate identifying mark of every misunderstanding of Christianity is that faith is changed into a belief and drawn into the range of intellectuality—a matter of understanding, of knowledge. Infinite interestedness in the actuality and authority of the Teacher, absolute commitment, *becoming* Christian—that is the sole passion and object of faith.[2]

Thus, we conclude this first volume of our Kierkegaardian reading of Mark, in hopes that the reader may better behold Jesus' mother and brothers (and sisters), the beginning of the gospel, and becoming a Christian in (Post) Christendom.

---

2. Kierkegaard, PSW, 64.

Bibliography

Alexander, Joseph Addison. "A Commentary on Mark." In *Geneva Series Commentary*. Edinburgh: Banner of Truth, 1984.

Allen, Diogenes. *Three Outsiders: Soren Kierkegaard, Blaise Pascal, Simone Weil*. Boston: Cowley, 1983.

Andic, Martin. "The Mirror." In *For Self-Examination and Judge for Yourself!: International Kierkegaard Commentary*, Volume 21, edited by Robert L. Perkins, 335–362. Macon: Mercer University Press, 2002.

Backhouse, Stephen. *Kierkegaard: A Single Life*. Grand Rapids: Zondervan, 2016.

———. "Politics as Indirect Communication in *The Moment* and the *Attack upon "Christendom."* In *Kierkegaard and Political Theology*, edited by Roberto Sirvent et al., 43–62. Eugene: Pickwick, 2018.

Baggett, John F. *Seeing Through the Eyes of Jesus: His Revolutionary View of Reality & His Transcendent Significance for Faith*. Grand Rapids: Eerdmans, 2008.

Baker, David L. *The Decalogue: Living as the People of God*. Downers Grove: IVP, 2017.

Barnett, Christopher B. *From Despair to Faith: The Spirituality of Soren Kierkegaard*. Minneapolis: Fortress, 2014.

Barrett, Lee C. III. *Kierkegaard*. Abingdon Pillars of Theology. Nashville: Abingdon, 2010.

Barrett, William, *Death of the Soul: From Descartes to the Computer*, Garden City: Anchor/Doubleday, 1986.

Belmonte, Kevin. *Defiant Joy: The Remarkable Life & Impact of G. K. Chesterton*, Nashville: Thomas Nelson, 2011.

Berger, Peter L. *The Sacred Canopy: Elements of a Sociological Theory of Religion*. Kindle Edition. New York: Open Road Integrated Media, 2011.

Bock, Darrell L. "Luke." In *The IVP New Testament Commentary Series*, edited by Grant R. Osborne. Downers Grove: InterVarsity, 1994.

Bonhoeffer, Dietrich. *The Cost of Discipleship*. Translated by R. H. Fuller. New York: Simon & Schuster, 1959.

———. *Discipleship*, Translated by Barbra Green and Reinhard Krauss. Dietrich Bonhoeffer Works 4. Minneapolis: Fortress, 2001.

———. *Letters and Papers from Prison*, Translated by Isabel Best, Lisa E. Dahill, Reinhard Krauss, and Nancy Lukens. Dietrich Bonhoeffer Works 8. Minneapolis: Fortress, 2010.

———. *Life Together—Prayerbook of the Bible*, Translated by Daniel W. Bloesch and James H. Burtnessaelm. Dietrich Bonhoeffer Works 5. Minneapolis: Fortress, 1996.

Borchert, Gerald L. "John 1–11." In *The New American Commentary*, edited by E. Ray Clendenen. Nashville: Broadman & Holman, 1996,

Bray, Gerald. *God Has Spoken: A History of Christian Theology*. Wheaton: Crossway, 2014.

Bruce, F. F. *New Testament History*. New York: Doubleday, 1969.

Brueggemann, Walter. *Biblical Evangelism—Living in a Three-Storied Universe*. Nashville: Abingdon, 1993.

———. *Theology of the Old Testament: Testimony, Dispute, Advocacy*. Minneapolis: Fortress, 1997.

Bukdahl, Jorgen. *Soren Kierkegaard & The Common Man*. Translated by Bruce H. Kirmmse. Grand Rapids: Eerdmans, 2001.

Canovan, Margaret. *Hannah Arendt: A Reinterpretation of Her Political Thought*, Cambridge: Cambridge University Press, 1992.

Cassirer, Heinz W. *God's New Covenant: A New Testament Translation*. Grand Rapids: Eerdmans, 1989.

Cavanaugh, William T. *Being Consumed: Economics and Christian Desire*. Grand Rapids: Eerdmans, 2008.

Chesterton, G. K. *The Everlasting Man*. San Francisco: Ignatius, 1993.

———. *Heretics/Orthodoxy*. Nelson's Royal Classics. Nashville: Thomas Nelson, 2000.

Christman, Bryan M. *The Gospel in the Dock: Is the Gospel of Jesus Christ Good for the Church, Humanity, and the World*. Eugene: Resource Publications, 2021.

———. "Lewis and Kierkegaard as Missionaries to Post-Christian Pagans." In *Evangelical Review of Theology*, 46:2 (2022) 123–136, Eugene: Wipf and Stock.

Connell, George B. *Kierkegaard and the Paradox of Religious Diversity*. Kierkegaard as a Christian Thinker, edited by C. Stephen Evans et al. Grand Rapids: Eerdmans, 2016.

———. "Knights and Knaves of the Living dead: Kierkegaard's Use of Living Death as a Metaphor for Despair." In *Kierkegaard and Death*, edited by Patrick Stokes et al., 21–43. Indiana Series in the Philosophy of Religion. Bloomington: Indiana University Press, 2011.

Critchley, Simon. *The Faith of the Faithless: Experiments in Political Theology*. London: Verso, 2012.

Crouther, Ian. "Introduction." In *Permanent Things*. Edited by Andrew A. Tadie, Michael H. Macdonald. Grand Rapids: Eerdmans, 1995.

Cutting, Patricia. "The Levels of Interpersonal Relationships in Kierkegaard's Two Ages." In *Two Ages: International Kierkegaard Commentary*, Volume 14, edited by Robert L. Perkins, 73–86. Macon: Mercer University Press, 1984.

Daniel-Rops. *Jesus and His Times: A New Life of Christ*. Translated by Ruby Millar. New York: E. P. Dutton & Co., 1954.

d'Entreves, Maurizio Passerin. *The Political Philosophy of Hannah Arendt*, London: Routledge, 1994.

Downing, David C. *The Most Reluctant Convert: C. S. Lewis's Journey to Faith*. Downers Grove: IVP, 2002.

Driskell, Leon V. and Brittain, Joan T. *The Eternal Crossroads: The Art of Flannery O'Connor*, Lexington: University Press of Kentucky, 1971.

Dru, Alexander. *The Soul of Kierkegaard: Selections from His Journals*, Mineola: Dover, 2003.

Elliott, John H. *A Home for the Homeless: A Social-Scientific Criticism of I Peter, Its Situation and Strategy*. Minneapolis: Fortress, 1990.

Evans, C. Stephen. *Kierkegaard and Spirituality: Accountability as the Meaning of Human Existence*. Kierkegaard as a Christian Thinker, edited by C. Stephen Evans et al. Grand Rapids: Eerdmans, 2019.

———. "Merold Westphal on the Sociopolitical Implications of Kierkegaard's Thought." In *Gazing Through a Prism Darkly: Reflections on Merold Westphal's Hermeneutical Epistemology*, edited by B. Keith Putt, 35–45. Perspectives in Continental Philosophy, edited by John D. Caputo. New York: Fordham University Press, 2009.

———. *Soren Kierkegaard's Christian Psychology—Insight for Counseling and Pastoral Care*. Vancouver: Regent College Publishing, 1990.

Fee, Gordon D. "The First Epistle to the Corinthians." In *The New International Commentary on the New Testament*, edited by F. F. Bruce. Grand Rapids: Eerdmans, 1987.

Ferguson, Harvie. *Melancholy and the Critique of Modernity: Soren Kierkegaard's Religious Psychology*. London: Routledge, 1995.

Ferreira. M. Jamie. *Love's Grateful Striving: A Commentary on Kierkegaard's Works of Love*, New York: Oxford University Press, 2001.

Forde, Gerhard O. *On Being a Theologian of the Cross: Reflections on Luther's Heidelberg Disputation, 1518*. Grand Rapids: Eerdmans, 1997.

Fredrickson, David E. *Eros and the Christ: Longing and Envy in Paul's Christology*. Paul in Critical Contexts. Minneapolis: Fortress, 2013.

Garff, Joakim. "Formation and the Critique of Culture." In *The Oxford Handbook of Kierkegaard*, edited by John Lippitt et al., 252–272. Oxford: Oxford University Press, 2013.

———. *Soren Kierkegaard: A Biography*. Translated by Bruce Kirmmse. Princeton: Princeton University Press, 2000.

Garland, David E. "A Theology of Mark's Gospel." In *The Biblical Theology of the New Testament*, edited by Andreas J. Köstenberger. Grand Rapids: Zondervan, 2015.

———. "Mark." In *The NIV Application Commentary*, edited by Terry Muck. Grand Rapids: Zondervan, 1996.

Green, Bradley C. *The Gospel and the Mind: Recovering and Shaping the Intellectual Life*, Wheaton: Crossway, 2010.

Gundry, Robert H. Commentary on Mark. In *Commentary on the New Testament*. Grand Rapids: Baker Academic, 2011. Ebook edition.

Hanson, Jeffrey. *Kierkegaard and the Life of Faith: The Aesthetic, the Ethical, and the Religious in Fear and Trembling*. Indiana Series in the Philosophy of Religion, edited by Merold Westphal. Bloomington: Indiana University Press, 2017.

Harvey, Barry. *Taking Hold of the Real: Dietrich Bonhoeffer and the Profound Worldliness of Christianity*. Kindle version. Eugene: Cascade Books, 2015.

Hays, Richard B. "First Corinthians." In *Interpretation: A Bible Commentary for Preaching and Teaching*, edited by James L. Mays. Louisville: John Knox, 1997.

Henriksen, Jan-Olav. *The Reconstruction of Religion: Lessing, Kierkegaard, and Nietzsche*. Grand Rapids: Eerdmans, 2001.

Henry, Michel. *Words of Christ*. Translated by Christina M. Gschwandtner, Interventions. Grand Rapids: Eerdmans, 2012.

Horne, Mark. *The Victory According to Mark: An Exposition of the Second Gospel*. Moscow: Canon, 2003.

Hubben, William. *Dostoevsky, Kierkegaard, Nietzsche and Kafka*. New York: Simon & Schuster, 1952.

Hughes, Carl S. *Kierkegaard and the Staging of Desire: Rhetoric and Performance in a Theology of Eros*. New York: Fordham University Press, 2014.

Janz, Denis R. *The Westminster Handbook of Martin Luther*. The Westminster Handbook to Christian Theology. Louisville: Westminster John Knox, 2010.

Joustra, Robert., and Alissa Wilkinson. *How to Survive the Apocalypse—Zombies, Cylons, Faith, and Politics*. Grand Rapids: Eerdmans, 2016.

Juel, Donald H. "Mark." In *Augsburg Commentary on the New Testament*, edited by Roy A. Harrisville, et al. Minneapolis: Augsburg Fortress, 1990.

Keller, Timothy. *King's Cross: The Story of the World in the Life of Jesus*. New York: Dutton, 2011.

Kenny, Anthony. *Philosophy in the Modern World*. A New History of Western Philosophy, Volume 4. Oxford: Clarendon, 2007.

Kessler, Rainer. *The Social History of Ancient Israel: An Introduction*. Translated by Linda M. Maloney. Minneapolis: Fortress, 2008.

Kierkegaard, Soren. *Christian Discourses and The Lilies of the Field and the Birds of the Air and Three discourses at the Communion on Fridays*. Translated by Walter Lowrie, London: Oxford University Press, 1940.

———. *The Concept of Anxiety: A Simple Psychologically Orienting Deliberation on the Dogmatic Issue of Hereditary Sin*. Translated by Reidar Thomte, Kierkegaard's Writings, VIII. Princeton: Princeton University Press, 1980.

———. *Concluding Unscientific Postscript to Philosophical Fragments, Volume I*. Kierkegaard's Writings, XII.1. Translated by Howard V. Hong and Edna H. Hong, Princeton: Princeton University Press, 1992.

———. *Eighteen Upbuilding Discourses*. Kierkegaard's Writings, V. Translated by Howard V. Hong and Edna H. Hong, Princeton: Princeton University Press, 1990.

———. *Either/Or Part I*, Kierkegaard's Writings, III. Translated by Howard V. Hong and Edna H. Hong, Princeton: Princeton University Press, 1987.

———. *Either/Or Volume II*. Translated by Walter Lowrie. Princeton: Princeton University Press, 1972.

———. *Fear and Trembling/Repetition*. Kierkegaard's Writings, VI. Translated by Howard V. Hong and Edna H. Hong, Princeton: Princeton University Press, 1983.

———. *For Self-Examination/Judge for Yourself!* Kierkegaard's Writings, XXI. Translated by Howard V. Hong and Edna H. Hong, Princeton: Princeton University Press, 1990.

———. *Kierkegaard's Attack Upon "Christendom" 1854–1855*. Translated by Walter Lowrie, Princeton: Princeton University Press, 1946.

———. *The Living Thoughts of Kierkegaard*. Presented by W. H. Auden. Bloomington: Indiana University Press, 1971.

———. *Practice in Christianity*. Kierkegaard's Writings, XX. Translated by Howard V. Hong and Edna H. Hong, Princeton: Princeton University Press, 1991.

———. *Provocations: Spiritual Writings of Kierkegaard*. Edited by Charles E. Moore. Walden NY: Plough, 2002.

———. *Purity of Heart is to Will One Thing: Spiritual Preparation for the Office of Confession*. Harper Torchlight. Translated by Douglas V. Steere, New York: Harper & Brothers, 1956.

———. *The Sickness unto Death: A Christian Psychological Exposition for Upbuilding and Awakening*. Kierkegaard's Writings, XIX. Translated by Howard V. Hong and Edna H. Hong, Princeton: Princeton University Press, 1980.

———. *Soren Kierkegaard's Journals and Papers*, 7 Volumes. Translated by Howard V. Hong and Edna H. Hong, Bloomington: Indiana University Press, 1975.

———. *Spiritual Writings—Gift, Creation, Love: Selections from the Upbuilding Discourses*. Translated by George Pattison. Harper Perennial Modern Thought. New York: HarperPerennial, 2010.

———. *Stages on Life's Way*. Kierkegaard's Writings, XI. Translated by Howard V. Hong and Edna H. Hong, Princeton: Princeton University Press, 1988.

———. *Three Discourses on Imagined Occasions*. Kierkegaard's Writings, X. Translated by Howard V. Hong and Edna H. Hong, Princeton: Princeton University Press, 1993.

———. *Upbuilding Discourses in Various Spirits*. Kierkegaard's Writings, XV. Translated by Howard V. Hong and Edna H. Hong, Princeton: Princeton University Press, 1993.

———. *Works of Love*. Translated by Howard V. Hong and Edna H. Hong, Harper Perennial Modern Thought. New York: HarperPerennial, 2009.

———. *Works of Love*. Kierkegaard's Writings, XVI. Translated by Howard V. Hong and Edna H. Hong. Princeton: Princeton University Press, 1995.

Kirkpatrick, Matthew D. *Attacks on Christendom in a World Come of Age—Kierkegaard, Bonhoeffer, and the Question of "Religionless Christianity."* Princeton Theological Monographs Series. Eugene OR: Pickwick, 2011.

Kirmmse, Bruce H. *Encounters with Kierkegaard: A Life as Seen by His Contemporaries*. Princeton: Princeton University Press, 1996.

———. "Kierkegaard and the End of the Danish Golden Age." In *The Oxford Handbook of Kierkegaard*, edited by John Lippitt et al., 28–43. Oxford: Oxford University Press, 2013.

L'Engle, Madeline. *The Irrational Season*. The Crosswicks Journal Book Three. New York: HarperOne, 1977.

Latourette, Kenneth Scott. *A History of Christianity—Volume I: to AD 1500*. Revised Edition Peabody: Prince, 1999.

Leithart, Peter J. *Delivered from the Elements of the World: Atonement, Justification, Mission*. Downers Grove: IVP Academic, 2016.

———. *The End of Protestantism: Pursuing Unity in a Fragmented Church*, Grand Rapids: Brazos, 2016.

Lewis, Alan E. *Between Cross & Resurrection: A Theology of Holy Saturday*. Grand Rapids; Eerdmans, 2001.

Lewis, C. S. *The Abolition of Man: How Education Develops Man's Sense of Morality*. New York: Macmillan, 1943.

———. *Christian Reflections*. Edited by Walter Hooper, Grand Rapids: Eerdmans, 1967.

———. *God in the Dock: Essays on Theology and Ethics*. Grand Rapids: Eerdmans, 1970.

———. *Mere Christianity*. New York: Macmillan. 1978.

———. *Perelandra, A Novel.* New York: Scribner, 1944.

———. *The Screwtape Letters and Screwtape Proposes a Toast.* Annotated Edition by Paul McCusker. New York: HarperOne, 2013.

———. *Surprised by Joy: The Shape of My Early Life.* San Diego: Harcourt Brace, 1955.

———. *That Hideous Strength: A Modern Fairy Tale for Grown-Ups.* New York: Scribner, 1945.

Macquarrie, John. *Two Worlds Are Ours: An Introduction to Christian Mysticism.* Minneapolis: Fortress, 2005.

Marino, Gordon. *The Existentialist's Survival Guide: How to Live Authentically in an Inauthentic Age.* New York: HarperOne, 2018.

Maritain, Jacques. *The Social and Political Philosophy of Jacques Maritain: Selected Readings.* New York: Charles Scribner's Sons, 1955

Martindale, Wayne et al., *The Soul of C. S. Lewis.* Carol Stream: Tyndale, 2010.

Melville, Herman. *Moby Dick.* Dover Thrift Editions, edited by Thomas Crawford. Mineola, New York: Dover, 2003.

Michaels, J. Ramsey. *Passing by the Dragon: The Biblical Tales of Flannery O'Connor.* Eugene: Cascade Books, 2013.

Miles, Thomas P. *Kierkegaard and Nietzsche on the Best Way of Life: A New Method of Ethics.* New York: Palgrave Macmillan, 2013.

Minear. Paul S. *Images of the Church in the New Testament.* Philadelphia: Westminster, 1960.

Mjaaland, Marius Timmann. "Suicide and Despair." In *Kierkegaard and Death,* edited by Patrick Stokes et al., 81–100. Indiana Series in the Philosophy of Religion. Bloomington: Indiana University Press, 2011.

Moo, Douglas. "The Epistle to the Romans." In *The New International Commentary on the New Testament,* edited by Gordon D. Fee. Grand Rapids: Eerdmans, 1996.

Mullen, John Douglas. *Kierkegaard's Philosophy: Self-Deception and Cowardice in the Present Age.* New York: Signet Mentor, 1981.

Myers, Ched. *Binding the Strong Man: A Political Reading of Mark's Story of Jesus,* Maryknoll NY: Orbis, 1988.

Newbigin, Lesslie. *Proper Confidence—Faith, Doubt and Certainty in Christian Discipleship.* Grand Rapids: Eerdmans, 1995.

Nordentoft, Kresten. *Kierkegaard's Psychology.* Translated by Bruce Kirmmse. Volume Seven: Duquesne Studies—Psychological Series, editor Amedeo Giorgi. Pittsburgh: Duquesne University Press, 1978.

O'Connor, Flannery. *Collected Works.* The Library of America. New York: Library of America, 1988.

———. *Complete Stories,* New York: Farrar, Straus and Giroux, 1971.

Oden, Thomas C., and Christopher A. Hall. "Mark." In *Ancient Christian Commentary on Scripture,* New Testament II. Edited by Thomas C. Oden. Downers Grove: IVP, 1998.

Ortlund, Raymond C. Jr. *Whoredom: God's Unfaithful Wife in Biblical Theology,* New Studies in Biblical Theology, D. A., Carson series editor. Grand Rapids: Eerdmans, 1996.

Pascal, Blaise. *Pascal's Pensees,* New York: E. P. Dutton & Co., 1958

Perkins, Roberts L. "Introduction." In International Kierkegaard Commentary, Volume 14, edited by Robert L. Perkins, xiii-xxiv. Macon: Mercer University Press, 1984.

Peterson, Eugene H. *Christ Plays In Ten Thousand Places: A Conversation in Spiritual Theology.* Grand Rapids: Eerdmans, 1999.

———. *Eat This Book: A Conversation on the Art of Spiritual Reading.* Grand Rapids: Eerdmans, 2006.

Podmore, Simon D. "To Die and Yet Not Die: Kierkegaard's Theophany of Death." In *Kierkegaard and Death,* edited by Patrick Stokes et al., 44–64. Indiana Series in the Philosophy of Religion, Bloomington: Indiana University Press, 2011.

Polanyi, Michael. *Personal Knowledge: Towards a Post-Critical Philosophy.* Chicago: University of Chicago Press, 1958.

Polk, Timothy Houston. *The Biblical Kierkegaard: Reading by the Rule of Faith,* Macon GA: Mercer University Press, 1997.

Price, Reynolds. *Three Gospels.* New York: Touchstone, 1996.

Pyper, Hugh S. "Cities of the Dead: the Relation of Person and Polis in Kierkegaard's Works of Love." In *Kierkegaard: The Self in Society,* edited by George Pattison et al., 125–138. New York: St. Martin's, 1998.

———. *The Joy of Kierkegaard: Essays on Kierkegaard as a Biblical Reader.* BibleWorld Series edited by Phillip R. Davies et al. London and New York: Routledge, 2014.

Rae, Murray. *Kierkegaard and Theology.* Philosophy and Theology. New York: T & T. Clark, 2010.

Rhoads, David et al., *Mark as Story: An Introduction to the Narrative of a Gospel.* Third Edition. Minneapolis: Fortress, 2012.

Roberts, Kyle. *Emerging Prophet: Kierkegaard and the Postmodern People of God.* Eugene: Cascade Books, 2013.

Roberts, Robert C. *Faith, Reason, and History: Rethinking Kierkegaard's Philosophical Fragments.* Macon: Mercer University Press, 1986.

———. *Recovering Christian Character: The Psychological Wisdom of Soren Kierkegaard.* Kierkegaard as a Christian Thinker, edited by C. Stephen Evans et al. Grand Rapids: Eerdmans, 2022.

Rosas, L, Joseph III. *Scripture in the Thought of Soren Kierkegaard.* Nashville: Broadman & Holman, 1994.

Ross, Maggie. *Silence: A User's Guide: Volume Two: Application.* iBooks Edition. Eugene: Cascade Books, 2018.

Sacks, Jonathan. *Not in God's Name—Confronting Religious Violence.* New York: Schocken, 2015.

Sandoz, Ellis. *Political Apocalypse: A Study of Dostoevsky's Grand Inquisitor.* Wilmington: ISI, 2000.

Simmons, J. Aaron. "Kierkegaard and Pentecostal Philosophy." In *Kierkegaard's God and the Good Life,* Indiana Series in the Philosophy of Religion, edited by Stephen Minster et al., 374–411, Kindle Version. Bloomington: Indiana University Press, 2017.

Simpson, Christopher Ben. *The Truth is the Way: Kierkegaard's Theologia Viatorum.* Eugene: Cascade Books, 2011.

Sirvent, Roberto, and Duncan Reyburn. "The Spotlight and the 'Courage to be an Absolute Nobody': Toward a Kierkegaardian-Chestertonian Political Theology of Ego." In *Kierkegaard and Political Theology,* edited by Roberto Sirvent et al., 288–303. Eugene: Pickwick, 2018.

Smith, James K. A. *Desiring the Kingdom: Worship, Worldview, and Cultural Formation.* Cultural Liturgies Volume 1. Grand Rapids: Baker Academic, 2009.

———. *How (Not) To Be Secular: Reading Charles Taylor.* Grand Rapids: Eerdmans, 2014.

———. *Who's Afraid of Relativism: Community, Contingency, and Creaturehood.* The Church and Postmodern Culture. Grand Rapids: Baker Academic, 2014.

———. *You Are What You Love: The Spiritual Power of Habit.* Grand Rapids: Brazos, 2016.

Snodgrass, Klyne R. *Who God Says You Are—A Christian Understanding of Identity.* Grand Rapids: Eerdmans, 2018.

Solomon, Robert C. *Continental Philosophy Since 1750: The Rise and Fall of the Self.* A History of Western Philosophy 7. Oxford: Oxford University Press, 1988.

Sponheim, Paul R. *Existing Before God: Soren Kierkegaard and the Human Venture.* Minneapolis: Fortress. 2017.

———. *Love's Availing Power: Imaging God, Imagining the World.* Minneapolis: Fortress, 2011.

Stark, Rodney. *The Triumph of Christianity: How the Jesus Movement Became the World's Largest Religion.* New York: HarperOne, 2011.

Streett, R. Alan. *Subversive Meals: An Analysis of the Lord's Supper under Roman Domination during the First Century.* Eugene: Pickwick, 2013.

Swinburne, Algernon Charles. *Hymn to Proserpine (After the Proclamation in Rome of the Christian Faith).* https://www.public-domain-poetry.com/algernon-charles-swinburne/hymn-to-proserpine-7692

Tanner, John S. *Anxiety in Eden: A Kierkegaardian Reading of Paradise Lost.* New York: Oxford University Press, 1992.

Taylor, Mark Lloyd. "Ordeal and Repetition in Kierkegaard's Treatment of Abraham and Job." In *Foundations of Kierkegaard's Vision of Community: Religion, Ethics, and Politics in Kierkegaard,* edited by George B. Connell et al., 33–53. New Jersey: Humanities, 1992.

Thiselton, Anthony C. *Thiselton on Hermeneutics: Collected Works with New Essays.* Grand Rapids: Eerdmans, 2006.

Tietjen, Mark A. *Kierkegaard—A Christian Missionary to Christians.* Downers Grove: IVP Academic, 2016.

———. *Kierkegaard, Communication, and Virtue: Authorship as Edification.* Indiana Series in the Philosophy of Religion, edited by Merold Westphal. Bloomington: Indiana University Press, 2013.

Torrance, Thomas F. *Atonement: The Person and Work of Christ.* Downers Grove: IVP Academic, 2009.

———. *Incarnation: The Person and Life of Christ.* Downers Grove: IVP Academic, 2008.

Turlington, Henry. "Commentary on Mark." In *The Broadman Bible Commentary,* Volume 8, edited by Clifton J. Allen. Nashville: Broadman, 1969.

Tyson, Paul. *Kierkegaard's Theological Sociology: Prophetic Fire for the Present Age.* Eugene: Cascade Books, 2019.

Van Leeuwen, Arend Theodoor, *Critique of Heaven: The First Series of the Gifford Lectures entitled "Critique of Heaven and Earth."* New York: Charles Scribner's Sons, 1972.

Via, Dan O. Jr. *The Ethics of Mark's Gospel in the Middle of Time.* Philadelphia: Fortress, 1985.

Walsh, Sylvia. *Living Christianly: Kierkegaard's Dialectic of Christian Existence.* University Park: Pennsylvania State University Press, 2005.

———. "Kierkegaard's Theology." In *The Oxford Handbook of Kierkegaard*, edited by John Lippitt et al., 292–308. Oxford: Oxford University Press, 2013.
Watkin, Julia. *Historical Dictionary of Kierkegaard's Philosophy*. Historical Dictionaries of Religions, Philosophies, and Movements, No. 33. Lanham: Scarecrow, 2001.
Watson, David F. *Honor Among Christians: The Cultural Key to the Messianic Secret*. Minneapolis: Fortress, 2010.
Weil, Simone. *The Need for Roots: Prelude to a Declaration of Duties Toward Mankind*, Translated by A. F. Wills, London: Ark, 1987.
———. *Waiting for God*, Translated by Emma Craufield. New York: HarperPerennial, 2009.
Westphal, Merold. *Kierkegaard's Concept of Faith*. Kierkegaard as a Christian Thinker, edited by C. Stephen Evans et al. Grand Rapids: Eerdmans, 2014.
———. *God, Guilt, and Death: An Existential Phenomenology of Religion*. Studies in Phenomenology and Existential Philosophy, James M. Edie, editor. Bloomington: Indiana University Press, 1984.
———. *Kierkegaard's Critique of Reason and Society*. University Park: Pennsylvania State University Press, 1987.
———. *Suspicion & Faith: The Religious Uses of Modern Atheism*. New York: Fordham University Press, 1998.
Williams, Charles. *The Descent of the Dove: A Short History of the Holy Spirit in the Church*. Brooklyn: Angelico, 2021.
Williamson, Lamar, Jr. "Mark." In *Interpretation- A Bible Commentary for Preaching and Teaching*, edited by James Luther Mays. Louisville: John Knox, 1983.
Witherington, Ben III. *The Gospel of Mark: A Socio-Rhetorical Commentary*, Kindle edition. Grand Rapids: Eerdmans, 2001.
Wright, N. T. *The Day the Revolution Began: Reconsidering the Meaning of Jesus's Crucifixion*. New York: HarperOne, 2016.
———. *Matthew for Everyone: Part One, Chapters 1–15*. Louisville: John Knox, 2004.
———. *The New Testament and the People of God: Christian Origins and the Question of God: Volume 1*. Minneapolis: Fortress, 1992.
Ziegler, Philip G. *Militant Grace—The Apocalyptic Turn and the Future of Christian Theology*. Grand Rapids: Baker Academic, 2018.
Zimmermann, Jens. *Incarnational Humanism: A Philosophy of Culture for the Church in the World*. Strategic Initiatives in Evangelical Theology. Downers Grove: IVP Academic, 2012.

Index

Abraham, 83–84, 87–88, 90–91, 94–95, 97, 112, 120–22, 141–43, 145–46, 159
"Abraham's bosom," 87–88, 90–91, 97, 121
Adam/Eve, 30, 41, 83–84, 141, 143, 155, 170
Alanus, 53
apocalyptic, x, 3, 7, 9, 18, 21–25, 39–41, 97, 151, 153–54, 161
apologetics, 2n6, 5, 20, 23–24, 51n22, 182
Arendt, Hannah, 156n21
asceticism, 126–33, 180–82
atheism, 109–10, 168, 201
atonement, 23, 30n8, 156, 213–15
Auden, W.H., xiii
Augsburg Confession, 199
Augustine, Saint, 153–54, 196, 200
authority,
    false, 76, 189
    of the Bible, 1–10
    of the disciples, 160, 167, 169
    of God, 160

baptism, 11–16, 24, 25, 30, 33, 215
Backhouse, Stephen, 12–13, 88n25, 89n28, 146n26,
Baggett, John F., 71–72, 78n11
Barnett, Christopher B., 59n11, 68n8, 174

Barrett, Lee C., 173n4
Barrett, William, 101
blessing, 25, 92, 104, 141, 159
Bock, Darrell L., 81n19
Bonhoeffer, Dietrich, 33, 44–45, 49, 106n16, 164–65, 196, 199–200
Borchert, Gerald R., 141
Bray, Gerald., 58n8
Brueggemann, Walter 168, 185n5
Bukdahl, Jorgen, 20n10, 116

Cailliet, Emile, 5
Cavanaugh, William T., 181–82
Catherine, of Sienna, 64, 71
certainty, 1, 48, 104n11, 185, 203, 205–8
Chesterton, Gilbert Keith. xvii, 72–73, 185, 203
Christian humanism, xvii, 106
church, 19n9, 20n10, 33, 62, 95, 108, 116, 131, 177, 169n20, 194–5, 196–203, 216
community, 79, 81, 90–97, 115, 121–25, 158–59, 162, 164–67, 192–95, 199, 201–2, 217
compassion, 34, 87, 90–97, 125, 139, 150
confession, 15, 54, 82, 93, 153–54, 162–165, 188, 194, 199, 217–18
consumerism, xviii, 181–82
creation, 72, 136
    new, 3, 8, 18–19, 41, 45, 61–62, 115, 154, 159, 195, 203

231

Critchley, Simon, 128n23,
critique, 100, 105n13, 109–110, 125, 170
Critique of Heaven/Critique of Earth, 36–42
crossroad, 98–112, 114
Cutting, Patricia, 182, 201–2

Daniel-Rops, 155n17
death, 8n27, 67, 91–93, 104, 127, 129, 203, 210–16
  "of God," x, 7, 104–5, 110
demons, 8, 59–61, 148–54, 157–70
desire, xvi, 24, 27, 71, 90, 101, 125, 141–2, 144–46, 150, 164–65, 180, 188n11, 200, 208
determinism, 118, 173–75, 207
devil, the, 13, 32, 71, 81–82, 85, 87, 139–41, 213, 216
dialectic, 22n10, 15, 34, 77, 82, 85–86, 100, 119, 126–133, 134–146, 158–60, 172, 175, 201
discipleship, xv–xvi, 33–34, 43–54, 121–25, 126–33, 144, 159–60, 167–69, 175–76, 181, 183–90, 203
diversion, ix, 155, 188, 211
Don't Look Down (The Ozark Mountain Daredevils), 37–38
Dostoyevsky, Fyodor, 152–53, 169n20,
doubt, 1, 50–52, 54, 104n11

"Eden," 26–27, 29, 136, 141
Elliott, John H., 62n16
Enlightenment, the, 51, 101, 106, 184, 188n10
Evangelicalism, ix, 36–38, 188
Evans, C. Stephen, 28, 88–89, 170
existential/existentialism, ix, xviii, 5, 8n27, 9, 14, 38, 42, 138, 150, 185–86, 188, 199, 206
exorcism, 60, 80, 85, 151, 162, 167–70

Fee, Gordon D., 47n10,
fellowship, 80–81, 121–25, 131, 159, 167
  table, 88, 115, 125, 128–29, 137, 159,

Ferguson, Harvie, xviii
Ferreira, M. Jamie, 50
Feuerbach, Ludwig, 110–11
Forde, Gerhard, 3n9
forgiveness, 14, 24, 47n12, 62, 98–112, 115, 162, 164, 172, 192–193
fortunate/unfortunate, 74–97, 104, 115–16, 123, 189
freedom of will, 8n9, 28–29, 40–41, 60, 80, 138–140, 145, 171–182, 203n16
future, the, 7, 58, 67–69, 90, 111–12, 120–22, 133

Garff, Joachim, 7
Garland, David E., 14n11, 20, 30, 149, 168
generation
  of Kierkegaard, 14–15, 104–112, 185
  of Mark, 14–15, 98–104
  of today, 7–8, 16, 161
Gentiles (nations), 70, 79, 94, 155
"Golden-Age Denmark," 19, 22, 110, 152
"Grand Inquisitor," 153
Go to Heaven (The Grateful Dead), 37–38
Gundry, Robert H., 58–59

Hamann, J.G., 75, 214
happiness, 14, 34, 116–17, 144
Hanson, Jeffrey, 145
Harvey, Barry, 106n16
heaven, 21–25, 30, 36–42, 50, 60, 62, 122, 127, 133, 141–45, 159–60, 179–80, 205
Hefty, Karl, 182
Hegel, Georg Wilhelm Friedrich, 111, 197, 205
hell, 85, 106, 159, 165–66
Henriksen, Jan-Olav., 111n25, 203n25
history, 14, 18–19, 42, 46–47, 61, 68, 105n14, 129, 130n7, 155, 170, 197, 235
Holy Spirit, 14–16, 25, 30, 45, 53, 162–63, 167, 214–16

home, xvi, 62, 66, 79, 99, 112, 122–23, 159, 217
honor, 148–49, 151, 187
Horne, Mark, 15, 45
Hubben, William, 24
Hughes, Carl S., 78n14, 125
humanism, 17, 106, 111,
humanity, x–xi, 23–24, 38, 40, 51, 64, 72–73, 106–8, 111, 135–36, 143–44, 156, 168, 174, 184, 193–95, 200, 203n16, 214, 216
Hume, David, 101
"Hymn to Proserpine," 127, 127n3

identity, xviii, 79, 170,
imagination, 45, 67, 75, 102–3, 105, 119, 120n27, 140, 166
inheritance, 120–25, 153
inversion, 74–97, 125
Isaac, 120–24, 141–45, 216
Israel, 14, 20–21, 31, 57–61, 76, 79, 94–95, 103–4, 129, 136–38, 141–43, 159–61, 215–16

James, 4, 8, 154
Jenson, Robert W., 188n10
Jesus
    ascension of, 39, 50–52, 54
    authority of, 55–61, 69, 76, 160, 219
    baptism of, 14–16, 22, 24–25, 30, 49, 59
    cross of, 22, 50, 52, 60, 90, 96, 142–43, 145, 213, 216
    death of, 21, 24–25, 65, 93, 134–46, 160, 166
    desire of, 63–73, 94, 94n35, 144, 148
    leprosus, 94–97, 122–23
    love of, 50
    Gethsemane, in garden of, 32, 62, 65, 67, 180, 213
    Messianic secret of, 94–97, 148–9
    "pale Galilean," 127
    resurrection of, 21, 39, 50, 91, 144, 203, 215
    return of, 152–3
    Servant, the, 59, 61, 142–43
    sleeping, 204, 208, 210, 212–14, 216, 218
    Son of God, the, 24, 59–60, 153–54,
    Son of Man, the, 134–46
    temptation of, 26–35, 59, 71, 148–49
Jewish War, the, 25n23, 103–4, 107
Job, 124
Jonah, 210, 212–14, 216
John the Baptist, xviii, 14–15
judgment, 23, 62, 90, 100, 103–4, 107, 111–12, 152, 156, 179, 187
justice/social justice, 107–9, 111, 137, 166

Keller, Timothy, 5
Kessler, Rainer, 76
Kierkegaard, concepts,
    absurd, the, 121, 161
    admirers of Christ, 48, 131, 183
    anxiety, age of, xvi, 7, 80, 157–70
    becoming a Christian, xv–xviii, 46, 175, 218–19
    becoming a self, xvi, xviii, 6–10, 42, 120
    becoming a sinner, 120, 123, 139
    becoming sober, 70n13, 161
    becoming spirit, 118, 162
    boredom, 17, 154–56, 178
    contemporaneity with Christ, 43–54, 129–33
    contradiction, Jesus as the sign of, 24, 55–62, 144
    criterion, the, 6–8, 12–13, 23, 25, 48, 83–84, 90, 115
    crowd, the, 4, 9, 14–15, 61–62, 71, 105n13, 106, 119, 148–56, 199
    decision, 25, 100, 206
    despair, 11–16, 80–91, 113–25, 133, 138–40, 154–55, 163, 206–8, 211–14
    dizziness of freedom, the, 29, 138–40, 145
    Divine Mr. Goodman, 22–24
    dying to, 48, 79n17, 83, 86, 132, 212–16
    earnestness, 17–25, 32, 39–40, 53, 57, 73
    established order, the, xi, 153–54

Kierkegaard, concepts, (continued)
  existence communication, 1–10, 31, 128, 186–88
  eternal, the, 24–25, 69, 107, 125
  faith, as opposite of sin, 15
  glory of being human, the, 66–73
  God-man, Jesus as the, 56, 101
  happy passion, the, 8, 10, 98–112
  highest perfection, the, 175–76
  honesty, Kierkegaard as, 33–35,
  humans, as a synthesis, 28, 40–41, 53, 77
  impossibility/possibility, 8, 15, 23, 28, 33, 101–103, 112, 118, 139, 161, 193–95, 211, 213
  incognito, Jesus as, 94–96, 101, 132
  indirect communication, 89n28, 173, 183–86
  infinite qualitative distinction, the, 40, 170
  inviter, Jesus as the, 104, 123, 125, 213, 217
  irresolution, 177–80
  Knight of faith/Knight of infinite resignation, the, 120–21, 124, 145, 181
  leap of faith, the, 5, 139, 170
  leveling, societal, 156n21, 182, 202
  loftiness, 130–31, 196–203
  middle term of death, the, 43–54, 93, 129–32
  mirror, God's word as a, 1–10, 188
  moment, the, 25, 36–42, 44, 57, 68–69, 103, 139
  movements of faith, 117, 119–25
  objectivity/subjectivity, 186–90
  offense, 17, 20, 22–24, 101–04, 112, 123–25
  opinion, 4, 17–25, 57, 102, 152, 173
  out on 70,000 fathoms, 204–9, 211–12, 216, 217–18
  paganism (Christian), xi, 22, 47, 118n19, 199
  philistine bourgeoise mentality, 117–25
  power that established the self, God as the, xviii, 86, 88
  present age, the, 12, 106–7, 198, 201–2
  prototype, Jesus as the, 31, 34–35, 48, 131
  purity of heart, 193–95
  reflection, 179
  road is how, the, 188–89
  sacred history, the, 46–47
  sickness unto death, the, 12, 16, 77, 79, 83–88, 107, 109, 117–21
  silence, 67–69
  single individual, the, 23, 106, 151, 158
  situation, the, 46, 131, 206–9
  spirit/spiritlessness, 14, 52–54, 83–84, 118–19, 162–63
  stages of existence, the, 78
  without authority, 59n11, 67–69
Kierkegaard, life, x-xi, xvii-xviii, 19–20, 77–78, 80, 85–86, 89, 104–5, 116–17, 127–28, 145–46, 147–48, 152, 191
Kierkegaard, pseudonyms, 28–29, 78, 181
  Anti-Climacus, 12, 12n3, 17, 29, 88n25, 114, 163, 204
  Frater Taciturnus, 77, 210
  Johannes Climacus, xi, 36, 132, 164, 205–7, 206n5
  Johannes de Silentio, 120, 120n27, 125n36, 135
  Vigilius Haufniensis, 29
Kierkegaard, writings,
  Attack on Christendom, x, 19–20, 150–54
  "A Leper's Self Contemplation," 74–97
  "The Changelessness of God," 173–74
  Christian Discourses, 89, 92n32, 177–79
  The Concept of Anxiety, 29, 118
  Either/Or, 155, 181
  "Guilty?/Not Guilty?," 76–77, 83, 91, 117n17, 210–11
  Fear and Trembling, 120–21, 141–46

For Self-Examination/Judge For Yourself, 1–5, 48–54, 212–15
Journals and Papers, 2, 2n6, 75n2, 106–8, 187–88, 199–200, 206–9
Philosophical Fragments, 205
Practice in Christianity, 123–25, 130–31, 152–53, 179n13, 180, 187, 200–3
Purity of Heart is to Will One Thing, 193–95
"Rotation of Crops," 181, 181n16
"The Seducer's Diary," 181n16
The Sickness Unto Death, 12, 77, 84–88, 117–21
Stages on Life's Way, 76, 77n10, 78
Two Ages, 198–203
Works of Love, 50, 65, 77n10, 164–65, 202
Kingdom of God, x, 18–19, 21–22, 41–42, 58–60, 115, 148–49, 164, 191–95, 196–203
Kirkpatrick, Matthew D., 108
Kirmmse, Bruce H., 19n7, 19n9, 104n12

law, Mosaic, 40, 76, 134–38, 213
Leithart, Peter J., 60n14, 137, 216
L'Engle, Madeline, 79
Lenin, Vladimir, 112
leprosy, 74–97, 122
Lewis, Alan E., 140–41
Lewis, C. S., 29, 51n22, 57n5, 70, 158–59, 167, 207
  The Abolition of Man, 53–54
  That Hideous Strength, 158–59, 167
  Mere Christianity, 24
  Perelandra, 26–29, 63–64, 66–67
  The Screwtape Letters, 28, 165–66
Luther, Martin, 3n9, 51, 218
love, 50, 64–65, 69–73, 87–88, 92, 94n35, 125, 144, 153–54, 161, 164–166, 220
longing, xviii, 97, 125, 132

Mahn, Jason A., 102n5, 118–19, 124, 143–44
Marino, Gordon, 9n29

Maritain, Jacques, xvii
Martindale, Wayne, 27

Mark
  audience, 5, 9, 25, 39, 48, 61–62, 114–15, 154, 173
  family motif, xv–xvi, 61–62, 88, 99, 115, 122, 149, 160–61, 164, 166, 193, 217–18
  foreshadowing/motifs, 3, 44–46, 48, 55–62, 67, 75–77, 99
  genre, x, 18–19, 218
  purpose, x–xi, 3–4, 18–22, 56–57, 61–62, 160–61, 169–70
  style, 3, 9, 18–19, 36–37, 39
Mark as Story (Rhoads/Dewey/Michie), 5n18, 44n4, 124n35, 149–50
Marx, Karl, 37–38, 104–11, 115, 115n7, 122–23, 168
Mediation, 164–67, 199n7
Melville, Herman, 212, 213n10
Michaels, J. Ramsay, 139
Milton, John, 166n16
Minear, Paul, 142–43
Mjaaland, Marius Timmann, 86
Moby Dick (Melville), 210, 212, 213n10
Modernism, 54, 156n21, 168–70, 185n5
Moo, Douglas, 136n4
Moore, Charles E., xiv, 75n5, 189n15
Mullen, John Douglas, 217
Myers, Ched, 18n3, 76n7, 169

name, 79, 122, 190,
nature, 63–73
Nazi Germany, 108, 199
New Testament, 2, 143
new creation, 3, 8, 18–19, 41, 45, 61, 62, 154, 159, 195, 217
Newbigin, Lesslie, 51n21, 104n11
Nietzsche, Friedrich, xi, 7, 45n7, 105n13, 111, 111n15, 168, 203n16
Nordentoft, Kresten, 95

O'Connor, Flannery, 114,
  A Good Man is Hard to Find, 135, 138–40,

Old Testament, 31, 58n8, 197
Olsen, Regine, 75n2, 80, 145–46

parables, 107, 137, 158, 172–82, 183–90, 191–95, 196–203
paradox, 8, 19–24, 49–54, 60, 91, 93, 97, 99, 101–3, 117, 121–25, 132–33, 160, 176, 180–81, 208, 214
Pascal, Blaise, ix, 54, 155, 211
Pattison, George, xiv, 66n5
Paul, 12, 39–40, 47, 50, 60n14, 107, 125, 143, 215
Pentecost, 70, 161, 214
Perkins, Robert L., 128
persecution, x, 22, 124, 179, 186, 217
Peterson, Eugene H., 6, 56
Pharisees/Scribes, 116, 119, 122, 128, 136–140, 148, 151
philosophy, 8, 19n7, 23, 40, 57, 205
Podmore, Simon D., 86–87
Polanyi, Michael, 185n5
politics, xi, 20, 24, 38, 106–8, 111–12, 123, 159, 169
Polk, Timothy Houston, 2n3
Post-Christendom/Post-Christian, xv, xvii-xviii, 9, 12–14, 19–20, 22–23, 47, 104–112, 118, 136, 150–56, 168–69, 178–181, 198–203, 206, 208, 218–19
power, in relation to,
  Christ, 58–60, 144, 162, 213
  Christendom, x, 109
  Christian life, the, 187
  Christianity, (the church), xvii, 203, 216
  crowd, the, (the mob) 71, 148, 156, 173
  demons, 140–41, 166–68
  God, 150, 173, 193
  humans, 29, 111, 132, 164–65, 177, 179, 214
  ideology, 95, 108, 112, 136
  kingdom of God, the, 3–4, 160, 198
  Spirit, Holy, 72, 216
  nature, 64
  powers that be, the 3, 22–23, 39, 169
  struggles with, 31, 34
prayer, 32, 69–70, 92–93, 104, 145, 169, 194n8
Price, Reynolds, 18
"Prodigal Son," 106, 122, 170
promises, of God, 14, 16, 25, 34, 69, 90, 92, 120–25, 143, 181, 203, 212–13
prophecy/prophet/prophetic, x, 16, 20–21, 57, 103–4, 110, 184, 186, 197
psychology/psychological, x, xviii, 27, 29, 51n22, 77, 80, 95n36, 124n35, 139, 160, 168–70
publicity, 147–56
Pyper, Hugh S. 79n17, 93

Rae, Murray, xvi
rationalism/reason, xvi, 22–23, 29, 51–52, 56, 61, 99–104, 107, 112, 139n9, 161–62, 188, 189n14, 206, 218–19
reality, 6–7, 21, 28, 38, 51n22, 68, 72, 110, 137, 167, 185, 187–89, 207–8
redemption, 3, 40–41, 55–62, 82–88
Reformation, the, 108
religion, as an opiate, 38, 112, 122–23
repentance, 14–15, 82–88, 91, 137, 139–40, 163, 194
resurrection, 16, 41, 125, 203, 215
revelation, 2, 4n10, 6, 58n9, 72, 166, 167, 169, 172
revolution, x-xi, 98–112, 153, 167, 198, 203
Rhoads, David, 5n18, 44n4, 124n35, 149–150
Roberts, Robert C., 205
Roman Empire, x, 56, 70, 96, 103, 114, 148

Sabbath, 61, 134–40, 144
salvation, 41, 59, 60, 62, 76, 89, 91–95, 102n5, 117, 123, 168, 176, 192–93
Samson's riddle, 51–52
science, 19n7, 139, 169n20, 185, 197
scientism, 27, 185

secular/secularism, x, xvii-xviii, 9, 31, 70n13, 102n6, 105, 107, 156, 168–69, 187, 201, 217
security/insecurity, 27, 29, 45, 66, 71, 120n27
Simpson, Christopher Ben, 31
sin, 12–16, 28–30, 47n12, 83–85, 87, 89, 96, 105–7, 109, 162–63, 164, 192, 211–16
sinner(s), 76, 95, 115–22, 125, 137, 139
solitude, 63–73
social media, 148, 156
sociology, 104–7, 110, 168
"Social Imaginary," 102–3, 110, 179
socialism, 104, 106–7, 112
Socrates/Socratic method, 4n10, 9, 58n9, 89n28, 170, 193n6, 201
spiritual trial, (anfechtung), 82, 88–89, 121n29
Sponheim, Paul R., 9n29, 193
Stark, Rodney, 124n35
Streett, R. Alan, 115n6
stewardship, 24, 136
subversion, 76, 97
suffering, 21–22, 31, 76–77, 95, 122–25, 127, 132–33, 144–45, 180
suicide, 86, 105

Taylor, Charles, 102n6
Taylor, Mark, 127–28
telos, 111, 179, 209
Temple, the, 20–21, 25, 57–58, 117, 136–37, 151

temptation, 26–35, 82–87, 89, 120–21, 141, 170, 194, 200
The Thin Red Line (Malick), 66–67
Tietjen, Mark A., 184n2, 185, 206n5
Torrance, Thomas F., 30n8
Turlington, Henry, 30
Tyson, Paul, 105, 156n21, 179

unity, xvii, 56, 162, 164–67, 191–95,

Via, Dan O., 3, 171–73, 175–77
Victory, 60, 168
Voltaire, 136

Walsh, Sylvia, 132, 162–63
Watson, David F., 148–49
Weil, Simone, 189–90
Westphal, Merold, 8n27, 105n13, 109, 111, 120n25, 121n28, 161, 197, 201
Wilde, Oscar, 110n23, 148
wilderness, 11–16, 20, 25–26, 29–33, 39, 45, 59–60, 71, 79–80, 149, 167–68
Williams, Charles, xviii
Wittgenstein, Ludwig, 185
"World Come of Age," 106, 106n16, 170
works, 15, 34, 153–54
Wright, N. T., 1n2, 18, 21, 45, 58n8

Zimmermann, Jens, xvii, 106n16, 111

www.ingramcontent.com/pod-product-compliance
Lightning Source LLC
Chambersburg PA
CBHW070246230426
43664CB00014B/2421